Edexcel
GCSE Mathematics
foundation

book 1

Keith Pledger

Gareth Cole

Peter Jolly

Graham Newman

Joe Petran

Sue Bright

www.heinemann.co.uk
✓ Free online support
✓ Useful weblinks
✓ 24 hour online ordering

01865 888058

Heinemann
Inspiring generations

Heinemann Educational Publishers
Halley Court, Jordan Hill, Oxford OX2 8EJ
Part of Harcourt Education Limited

Heinemann is the registered trademark of
Harcourt Education Limited

© Harcourt Education Ltd, 2006

First published 2006

10 09 08 07 06
10 9 8 7 6 5 4 3 2 1

British Library Cataloguing in Publication Data is available from the British Library on request.

10-digit ISBN: 0 435 53618 4
13-digit ISBN: 978 0 435536 18 3

Typeset by Tech-Set Ltd, Gateshead, Tyne and Wear
Original illustrations © Harcourt Education Limited, 2006
Illustrated by Adrian Barclay, Mark Ruffle and HL Studios
Cover design by mccdesign
Printed by CPI Bath Press
Cover photo: Photolibrary.com ©

Acknowledgements
Harcourt Education Ltd would like to thank those schools who helped in the development and trialling of this course.

This high quality material is endorsed by Edexcel and has been through a rigorous quality assurance programme to ensure that it is a suitable companion to the specification for both learners and teachers. This does not mean that its contents will be used verbatim when setting examinations nor is it to be read as being the official specification – a copy of which is available at www.edexcel.org.uk

The publisher's and authors' thanks are due to Edexcel Limited for permission to reproduce questions from past examination papers. These are marked with an [E]. The answers have been provided by the authors and are not the responsibility of Edexcel Limited.

The authors and publisher would like to thank the following individuals and organisations for permission to reproduce photographs: NASA p1; iStockPhoto.com/Nicolas Skaanlid p2 left; Alamy Images; p2 right; iStockPhoto.com/Lidian Neeleman p6; Getty Images/PhotoDisc pp22 top, 53, 97, 145, 156, 185, 186, 242; iStockPhoto.com/Matjaz Slanic p22 bottom; Action +/Neil Tingle p24; Digital Vision p28 left; iStockPhoto.com/Ryan Fuller p28 right; Photos.Com pp29, 172; Corbis pp46 left, 127, 146, 223, 238; ESA p46 right; Richard Smith p72; Empics pp81, 82, 164, 206; Harcourt Education Ltd/Debbie Rowe p96; Alamy Images/Elmtree Images p109; Getty Images/Stone p173; Alamy Images/Transtock Inc. p204; PhotoLibrary.com p211; Harcourt Education Ltd/Martin Sookias p266

Every effort has been made to contact copyright holders of material reproduced in this book. Any omissions will be rectified in subsequent printings if notice is given to the publishers.

Publishing team
Editorial	James Orr, Lindsey Besley, Evan Curnow, Nick Sample, Jim Newall, Alex Sharpe, Laurice Suess, Katherine Pate, Elizabeth Bowden, Ian Crane
Design	Phil Leafe
Production	Siobhan Snowden
Picture research	Chrissie Martin

Websites
There are links to relevant websites in this book. In order to ensure that the links are up-to-date, that the links work, and that the sites aren't inadvertently linked to sites that could be considered offensive, we have made the links available on the Heinemann website at www.heinemann.co.uk/hotlinks. When you access the site, the express code is **4084P**.

Tel: 01865 888058   www.heinemann.co.uk

Quick reference to chapters

Introduction

Introduction

These revised and updated editions have been carefully matched to the new two-tier specification for GCSE Maths. Books 1 and 2 cover everything you need to know to achieve success in your exam, up to and including Grade C. The author team is made up of Senior Examiners, a Chair of Examiners and Senior Moderators, all experienced teachers with an excellent understanding of the requirements of the Edexcel specification.

Key features

- **Chapters** are divided into **sections**, each with a simple explanation followed by clear examples or a worked exam question. These show you how to tackle questions. Each section also contains practice exercises to develop your understanding and help you consolidate your learning.

- **Key points** are highlighted throughout, like this:

  To find the **square** of any number, multiply the number by itself.

  Each chapter ends with a summary of key points you need to remember.

- **Hint boxes** are used to make explanations clearer. They may also remind you of previously learned facts or tell you where in the book to find more information.

  a means $1a$
  so $1a + 1a = 2a$

- **Mixed exercises** are designed to test your understanding across each chapter. They include past exam questions which are marked with an [E]. You will find a mixed exercise at the end of every chapter.

- **Examination practice papers** are included in Book 2 to help you prepare for the exam at the end of your course.

- **Answers** are provided at the back of the book to use as your teacher directs.

Quick reference and detailed Contents pages

- Use the thumb spots on the edge of the **Quick reference** page to help you turn to the right chapter quickly. Note that Book 1 contains Chapters 1–14 and Book 2 contains Chapters 15–28.

- Use the detailed **Contents** to help you find a section on a particular topic. The summary and reference codes on the right show your teacher the part(s) of the specification covered by each section in the book. (For example, NA3h refers to Number and Algebra, section 3 Calculations, subsection h.)

Use of a calculator or a computer

These symbols show you where you must, or must not, use a calculator. Sometimes you will need to use a spreadsheet package on a computer. There are also links to websites and suggested activities that require an internet search.

Coursework

A Coursework Guide is available online at www.zebramaths.co.uk

Contents

4 Patterns and sequences

5 Decimals

6 Angles and turning

7 2-D shapes

8 Fractions

9 Estimating and using measures

10 Collecting and recording data

11 Linear equations

12 Sorting and presenting data

13 3-D shapes

⑭ Units of measure

1 Understanding whole numbers

1.1 Digits and place value

Onboard computers will have taken control of launch systems 30 seconds before lift–off.

Each digit has a value that depends on its position in a number. This is its **place value**.

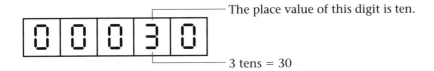

The place value of this digit is ten.

3 tens = 30

Look at this place value diagram:

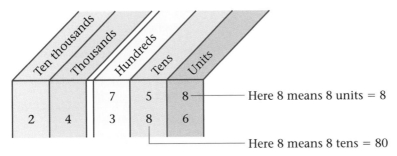

Here 8 means 8 units = 8

Here 8 means 8 tens = 80

758 has three digits. It is also called a three figure number.

Exercise 1A

1 Draw a place value diagram and write in
   (a) a four figure number with a 4 in the thousands column
   (b) a two figure number with a 3 in the tens column
   (c) a five figure number with a 1 in the hundreds column
   (d) a three figure number with a 9 in the units column
   (e) a four figure number with a 0 in the tens column
   (f) a five figure number with a 4 in the hundreds column
   (g) a three figure number with a 7 in every column
   (h) a four figure number with a 6 in the first and last columns.

2 For each teacher, write down five different numbers that they could be thinking about.

3 Write down the value of the 6 in each of these numbers:
(a) 63 (b) 3642 (c) 63 214 (d) 2546 (e) 56 345 [E]

1.2 Reading, writing and ordering numbers

Sometimes you will need to write in words a number that has been written in figures.

Ten thousands	Thousands	Hundreds	Tens	Units	
		9	8	7	— Nine hundred and eighty-seven
1	6	4	1	2	— Sixteen thousand four hundred and twelve

16 412

The thin space separates thousands from hundreds and makes it easier to read the number.

Sometimes you will need to write in figures a number that has been written in words.

Two thousand eight hundred and twenty-two walkers took part in Saturday's charity event.

Some of the thirty-one thousand two hundred and fifty-eight people at an outdoor rock concert

The word numbers from the newspaper examples can be written in figures, like this:

	Ten thousands	Thousands	Hundreds	Tens	Units	
Two thousand eight hundred and twenty-two		2	8	2	2	or 2822
Thirty-one thousand two hundred and fifty-eight	3	1	2	5	8	or 31 258

Zeros are used to show that a column is empty.
This shows that 5004 and 504 are different numbers:

Thousands	Hundreds	Tens	Units	
5	0	0	4	Five thousand and four
	5	0	4	Five hundred and four

Sometimes you will need to rewrite a set of numbers in order of size. Suppose you need to order this set of numbers:

15   8400   6991   2406   2410   84 000

The size of a number depends on how many digits it has. The more digits, the bigger the number.
So 84 000 is bigger than 8400 because it has more digits.

> This is only true for whole numbers.

When two numbers have an equal number of digits, the value of the digit in the highest place value column tells you which is the bigger number.
So 8400 is bigger than 6991 because 8 is bigger than 6.

> 8⟩400   8 is bigger than 6.
> 6⟩991

When two numbers have an equal number of digits and the values of the digits in the highest place value column are the same, then the value of the digit in the next place value column tells you which is the bigger, and so on.
So 2410 is bigger than 2406, because 1 is bigger than 0.

> 24⟩1⟩0   1 is bigger than 0.
> 24⟩0⟩6

Starting with the biggest number, the list above written in order of size is:

84 000   8400   6991   2410   2406   15

You will also have to deal with very big numbers such as hundreds of thousands, and millions:

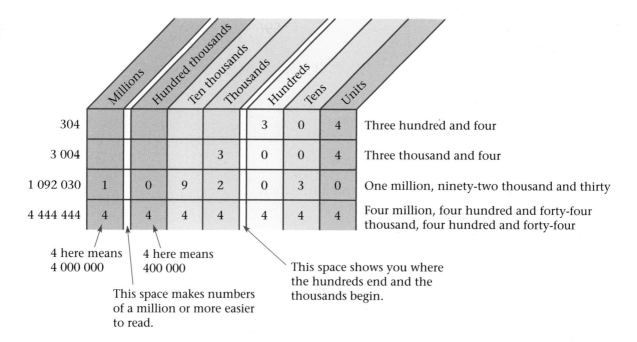

	Millions	Hundred thousands	Ten thousands	Thousands	Hundreds	Tens	Units	
304					3	0	4	Three hundred and four
3 004				3	0	0	4	Three thousand and four
1 092 030	1	0	9	2	0	3	0	One million, ninety-two thousand and thirty
4 444 444	4	4	4	4	4	4	4	Four million, four hundred and forty-four thousand, four hundred and forty-four

4 here means 4 000 000

4 here means 400 000

This space makes numbers of a million or more easier to read.

This space shows you where the hundreds end and the thousands begin.

Example 1

Write the number 1 804 603 in words.

To help you read a very large number, the digits are grouped in threes:

1 804 603 is	Millions	Thousands	Hundreds/Tens/Units		
	1	804	6	0	3

One *million*, eight hundred and four *thousand*, six *hundred* and three.

Example 2

Write these numbers using digits.
(a) six thousand and twenty
(b) two million, fifty-eight thousand, three hundred and six
(c) half a million

(a) 6020
(b) 2 058 306
(c) 1 000 000 ÷ 2 = 500 000

Exercise 1B

1 Write these numbers in words.
  (a) 36   (b) 95   (c) 598
  (d) 246   (e) 5623
  (f) There are 1251 students at James Street School.

2 Write these numbers in words.
  (a) 709   (b) 890   (c) 6054
  (d) 9201   (e) 26 007   (f) 40 200
  (g) 32 000   (h) 70 090
  (i) The number of school leavers in Axeshire last year
      was 13 406.

3 Write these numbers in figures.
  (a) sixty-three
  (b) seven hundred and eight
  (c) seven thousand
  (d) eighteen thousand six hundred
  (e) seventy-five thousand
  (f) eight hundred and nine thousand
  (g) four million
  (h) one million one thousand
  (i) nine thousand and twenty
  (j) forty thousand six hundred

4 This table gives the populations of five member states of
   the European Union in 2004. Write the numbers in words.

	Country	Population
(a)	Belgium	10 348 276
(b)	Luxembourg	462 690
(c)	Spain	40 280 780
(d)	Portugal	10 524 145
(e)	France	60 424 213

5 Write the following numbers in figures.
  (a) The numbers of people employed by a local police
      force are:
      • Traffic wardens: sixty-nine
      • Civilian support staff: one thousand and ten
      • Police officers: two thousand three hundred and six.

(b) The tonnages of three cruise liners are:
- Aurora: seventy-six thousand one hundred and fifty-two
- QE2: seventy thousand three hundred and sixty-three
- Queen Mary 2: one hundred and fifty-one thousand four hundred.

(c) The average daily readerships of four newspapers were:
- *Financial Times*: two hundred and ninety-four thousand
- *The Times*: six hundred and eighty-two thousand
- *Daily Mirror*: two million six hundred thousand
- *The Sun*: three million nine hundred and ninety thousand.

6 Rearrange these lists of numbers into order of size, starting with the largest number.
(a) 86   104   79   88   114   200
(b) 3000   3003   30 300   330 000   3033
(c) 6 000 006   660 000   600 006   990 000   6 102 000

7 Put the numbers in the cloud in order. Start with the *smallest* number.

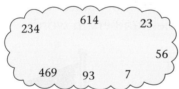

[E]

8 This table gives the prices of some secondhand cars:

Car	Price
Vauxhall Nova	£6755
Volkswagen Polo	£5423
Ford Focus	£7670
Toyota MR2	£3650
Jaguar XK8	£19 650
Land Rover Discovery	£15 560
Volvo V70	£12 375
Mercedes 500SL	£21 200

Rewrite the list in price order, starting with the least expensive.

9   This table shows the numbers of people who were
    seriously injured in road accidents in a part of Britain:

Year	2001	2002	2003	2004	2005
Number	37 346	33 645	31 456	29 788	26 466

In which year were:
(a) the smallest number of people seriously injured
(b) more than 35 000 seriously injured
(c) between 30 000 and 32 000 seriously injured
(d) fewer than 28 000 seriously injured?

10 The table below gives the areas, in km², of five member
    states of the European Union.

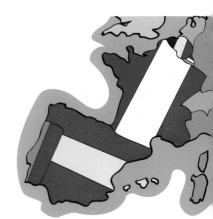

County	Area
Belgium	30 513
Luxembourg	2576
Spain	504 782
Portugal	92 082
France	547 026

(a) Write the area of the countries in words.
(b) List the countries in order of size, largest first.

1.3 Combining numbers

Using a number line

Here is a number line. It goes from 0 to 10.

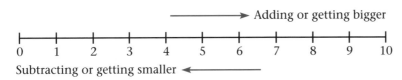

To add, move to the right.
To subtract, move to the left.

On the right is another number line. It goes up from 0 to 20.
It goes down from 20 to 0.

You can use the number line to increase or decrease numbers.

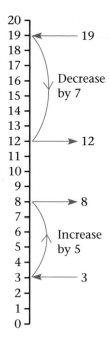

Example 3

(a) Increase 3 by 5.   (b) Decrease 19 by 7.

(a) Start at 3 on the line.
    From 3 count 5 upwards.
    The answer is 8.
(b) Start at 19 on the line.
    From 19 count 7 downwards.
    The answer is 12.

Exercise 1C

You can use a number line to help you with these questions.

1 Increase
   (a) 1 by 6   (b) 5 by 4   (c) 9 by 10
   (d) 8 by 5   (e) 12 by 3

2 Decrease
   (a) 13 by 4   (b) 7 by 6   (c) 18 by 7
   (d) 9 by 6   (e) 15 by 8

3 What increase moves
   (a) 6 to 10   (b) 3 to 11   (c) 12 to 14
   (d) 18 to 20   (e) 16 to 19?

4 What decrease moves
   (a) 7 to 4   (b) 8 to 1   (c) 12 to 3
   (d) 16 to 1   (e) 19 to 8?

5 What change moves
   (a) 6 to 11   (b) 10 to 16   (c) 19 to 14
   (d) 13 to 4   (e) 20 to 0?

> Remember to state whether the change is an increase or a decrease.

Adding

Here are some of the different ways of writing '6 add 9':
- Find the **sum** of 6 and 9.
- Work out 6 **plus** 9.
- Find the **total** of 6 and 9.
- **Add 6 and** 9.
- Work out $6 + 9$.

Example 4

Work out 23 + 693 + 8

$$
\begin{array}{r}
2\,3 \\
6\,9\,3 \\
8\,+ \\
\hline
7\,2\,4 \\
{\scriptstyle 1\ 1}
\end{array}
$$

Step 1 Put the digits in their correct columns.
Step 2 Add the units column: 3 + 3 + 8 = 14
Write 4 in the units column and carry the 1 ten into the tens column.
Step 3 Repeat for the tens column: 2 + 9 = 11 plus the 1 that was carried across = 12.
Write 2 in the tens column and carry the 1 into the hundreds column.
Step 4 Add the 6 and the 1 that was carried across: 7.

Exercise 1D

1 Find the total of 26 and 17.

2 Work out 58 plus 22.

3 Work out 236 + 95

4 In four maths tests, Anna scored 61 marks, 46 marks, 87 marks and 76 marks.
How many marks did she score altogether?

5 Find the sum of all the single digit numbers.

6 In a fishing competition, five competitors caught 16 fish, 31 fish, 8 fish, 19 fish and 22 fish.
Find the total number of fish caught.

7 The number of passengers on a bus was 36 downstairs and 48 upstairs.
How many passengers were on the bus altogether?

8 On her MP3 player Lena had 86 pop songs, 58 rock songs and 72 dance songs.
How many songs did she have in total?

9 Work out 38 + 96 + 127 + 92 + 48

10 On six days in June, 86, 43, 75, 104, 38 and 70 people went bungee jumping over a gorge.
How many people jumped in total?

Subtracting

Here are some different ways of writing '38 subtract 16':

- 38 **minus** 16.
- **Take** 16 **from** 38.
- $38 - 16$
- Find the **difference** between 38 and 16.
- How many **less** is 16 than 38?
- 38 **take away** 16.

Example 5

Take away 84 from 376.

```
  2 1
  ⸝376
    84 −
  ─────
  2 9 2
```

Step 1 Put the digits in their correct columns.
Step 2 In the units column take 4 away from 6, giving 2.
Step 3 In the tens column try taking 8 from 7 (not possible).
            So exchange 1 hundred for 10 tens.
            This gives 17 take 8, which leaves 9.
Step 4 In the hundreds column you are left with the 2 hundreds.

Example 6

Work out $400 - 274$

Method 1

```
     9
  3⸝10 1
  4 ⸝0 0
  2 7 4 −
  ───────
  1 2 6
```

Step 1 Put the digits in their correct columns.
Step 2 In the units column try taking 4 from 0 (not possible).
            So exchange 1 hundred for 10 tens and then exchange 1 ten
            for 10 units. 400 is now written as $300 + 90 + 10$.
Step 3 Now, $10 - 4 = 6$, $9 - 7 = 2$ and $3 - 2 = 1$.

Method 2

Step 1 Count on from 274 to 280 $\rightarrow$ 6
Step 2 Count on from 280 to 300 $\rightarrow$ 20
Step 3 Count on from 300 to 400 $\rightarrow \underline{100}$ +
$$126$$

Exercise 1E

1 Work out $611 - 306$

2 How much is 7260 minus 4094?

3 Take 1007 from 2010

4 In a car boot sale Alistair sells 17 of his 29 CDs.
   How many does he have left?

5 When playing darts, James scored 111 with his first three
darts, Sunita scored 94 with her first three darts and
Nadine scored 75 with her first three darts.

(a) How many more than Nadine did Sunita score?

(b) What is the difference between James's and Sunita's scores?

(c) How many less than James did Nadine score?

6 The winner of the darts match is the first
one to reach 501.
James has now scored 413, Sunita 442
and Nadine 368.

(a) How many is James short of 501?

(b) How many more does Sunita need to
score to reach 501?

(c) How many less than 501 is Nadine's total?

7 The 'thermometer' shows the money raised each
year in a charity appeal. At the start of 2000, the
total raised was £27 854.

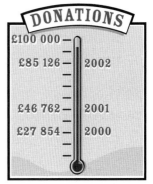

(a) How much was raised between 2001 and 2002?

(b) How much was raised altogether between 2000
and 2002?

(c) How much had to be raised in 2002 to reach the
target of £100 000 before the end of the year?

Multiplying and dividing by 10, 100 and 1000

The easiest numbers to multiply and divide by are 10, 100
and 1000. This is because they are all powers of ten and
our number system is based upon the number 10:

$$10 \times 10 = 100 \quad 100 \div 10 = 10 \quad 10 \times 100 = 1000 \quad 1000 \div 10 = 100$$

Example 7

Work out   (a) 23×10 (b) $3200 \div 100$

(a) 23×10

H	T	U
	2	3
2	3	0	= 230

The 3 moves from the units into the tens column
because $3 \times 10 = 30$

The 2 moves from the tens into the hundreds
column because $20 \times 10 = 200$

(b) $3200 \div 100$

Th	H	T	U
3	2	0	0
		3	2	= 32

The 3 moves from the thousands into the tens
column because $3000 \div 100 = 30$

The 2 moves from the hundreds into the units
column because $200 \div 100 = 2$

Example 8

Work out   (a) 23×400 (b) $3600 \div 30$

(a) 23×400

First multiply 23 by 4, and then multiply by 100, because 23×400 is the same as $23 \times 4 \times 100$:

$23 \times 4 = 92$ $92 \times 100 = 9200$

(b) $3600 \div 30$

First divide 3600 by 3, and then divide by 10, because $3600 \div 30$ is the same as $3600 \div 3 \div 10$:

$3600 \div 3 = 1200$ $1200 \div 10 = 120$

Exercise 1F

1 Multiply each of these numbers by
   (i) 10   (ii) 100   and   (iii) 1000.

   (a) 5   (b) 43   (c) 357   (d) 85   (e) 3000

2 Divide each of these numbers by
   (i) 10   (ii) 100   and   (iii) 1000.

   (a) 5000   (b) 74 000   (c) 865 000   (d) 4 000 000

3 Work out
   (a) 35×20 (b) 26×200 (c) 122×30
   (d) 213×300 (e) 47×40 (f) 36×4000
   (g) 215×500 (h) 365×6000

4 Work out
   (a) $600 \div 20$ (b) $8000 \div 200$ (c) $9000 \div 30$
   (d) $27\,000 \div 900$ (e) $800 \div 400$ (f) $12\,000 \div 60$
   (g) $30\,000 \div 150$ (h) $400\,000 \div 800$

Multiplying

Here are some different ways of writing '80 multiplied by 16':
- Find the **product** of 80 and 16.
- 16 **times** 80.
- **Multiply** 80 by 16.
- **Work out** 80×16.

There are many methods for multiplying two numbers together.

Example 9

Work out 43×6

Traditional method

$$
\begin{array}{r}
4\,3 \\
6\,\times \\
\hline
2\,5\,8 \\
1
\end{array}
$$

$3 \times 6 = 18$

$4 \times 6 = 24$ plus the 1 carried $= 25$

Doubling method

$43 \times 2 = 86$

$43 \times 2 = 86$

$43 \times 2 = 86\ +$

$\overline{43 \times 6 = 258}$

> 3 lots of 43×2 are needed.

Napier's Bones

Step 1 Make a grid:

Step 2 Put in the values of 6×3 and 6×4:

Step 3 Working from right to left, add along the diagonals:

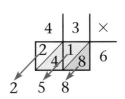

One topic which is almost always tested on the non-calculator paper is long multiplication, or multiplying numbers by a 2 digit number. You should practise doing calculations like these **without** a calculator.

Example 10

Work out 256×37

Traditional method

$$
\begin{array}{r}
2\,5\,6 \\
3\,7\,\times \\
\hline
1\,7\,9\,2 \\
7\,6\,8\,0\,+ \\
\hline
9\,4\,7\,2
\end{array}
$$

Step 1 Multiply 256 by 7.

Step 2 Multiply 256 by 30 (don't forget the 0).

Step 3 Add.

Grid method

200	50	6	$\times$
6000	1500	180	30
1400	350	42	7

$7400 + 1850 + 222 = 9472$

Step 1 Write each digit with its place value.

Step 2 Multiply out and put the answers in the boxes.

Step 3 Add all the numbers in the boxes together.

Napier's Bones

Step 1 Make a grid:

Step 2 Put in the values of 3×2, 3×5, 3×6, 7×2, 7×5 and 7×6:

Step 3 Working from right to left, add along the diagonals:

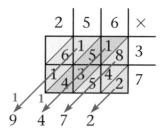

Exercise 1G

1 Work out

(a) 34×20 (b) 65×7 (c) 53×3

(d) 314×6 (e) 523×7 (f) 221×4

(g) 146×5 (h) 132×2

2 Work out

(a) 34×12 (b) 65×15 (c) 53×33

(d) 314×16 (e) 523×47 (f) 221×64

(g) 146×53 (h) 132×25

3 Find the product of 36 and 30.

4 How many is 321 multiplied by 14?

5 In a climbing competition 19 competitors scale a 24 metre high cliff. What is the total distance climbed?

6 What is the product of 63 and 36?

7 Wasim and Jan are training for a charity run.
During each session Wasim runs 50 metres 30 times and Jan runs 7 times round the 400 metre track.
(a) How far does Wasim run each session?
(b) How far does Jan run each session?

By the day of the run, Wasim has trained for 12 sessions and Jan for 20 sessions.
(c) How far has each run in training by run day?

8 Packets of Cheese Flips come in three sizes.
There are 36 Cheese Flips in the economy size, 3 times as many in the large size and 6 times as many in the family size.
How many Cheese Flips are in each size packet?

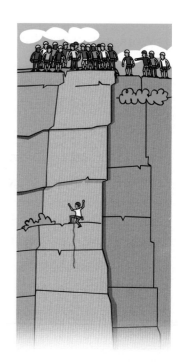

9 The distance from Mr Singh's home to work is 17 miles.
He makes the journey 12 times a week.
How far does he travel
  (a) in one week
  (b) in ten weeks
  (c) in a year?

Remember: 52 weeks make 1 year.

10 Do questions **1–9** again using a different method.

Dividing

Here are some of the different ways of writing '140 divided by 20':

- **Divide** 140 by 20.
- **Share** 140 **between** 20.
- How many times does 20 **go into** 140?
- Work out $140 \div 20$
- Work out $\frac{140}{20}$
- **How many** 20s are there **in** 140?

Remember to write $140 \div 20$, **not** $20 \div 140$

Here are some different methods for carrying out a division:

Example 11

Work out $256 \div 8$

Traditional short division

$$8\overline{)2\,5^{1}6}$$ = 3 2

Step 1 8 into 2 does not go so try
Step 2 8 into 25 goes 3 times remainder 1
Step 3 8 into 16 goes 2 times.

Chunking method

```
  ¹2̸¹5 6
   8 0 −   10
  ⁰1̸¹7 6
   8 0 −   10
   9 6
   8 0 −   10
   1 6
     8 −    1
     8
     8 −    1
     0
```

Step 1 Subtract 10 lots of 8 (that is $10 \times 8 = 80$).

Step 2 Keep subtracting 80 until you cannot do it any more.

Step 3 Now keep subtracting 8 until you cannot do it any more.

Step 4 Add up the parts of your answer:

$10 + 10 + 10 + 1 + 1 = 32$

Example 12

Work out $8704 \div 17$

Traditional long division

Follow these steps:

$$17\overline{)8704}$$

Step 1
17 divides into 87 5 times remainder 2

$$\begin{array}{r} 5 \\ 17\overline{)8704} \\ -\ 85 \\ \hline 2 \end{array}$$

Step 2
17 divides into 20 1 time remainder 3

$$\begin{array}{r} 51 \\ 17\overline{)8704} \\ -\ 85\downarrow \\ \hline 20 \\ -\ 17 \\ \hline 3 \end{array}$$

Step 3
17 divides into 34 2 times exactly

$$\begin{array}{r} 512 \\ 17\overline{)8704} \\ -\ 85 \\ \hline 20 \\ -\ 17\downarrow \\ \hline 34 \\ 34 \\ \hline 0 \end{array}$$

So 17 divides into 8704 512 times.

Short division method

$$\begin{array}{r} 5\ 1\ 2 \\ 17\overline{)87^20^34} \end{array}$$

This is a shorter way of setting out the steps than in the long division method.

Chunking method

$$\begin{array}{rl}
8\ 7\ 0\ 4 & \\
1\ 7\ 0\ 0- & 100 \\
\hline
^6\!\!\not7^10\ 0\ 4 & \\
1\ 7\ 0\ 0- & 100 \\
\hline
^4\!\not5^13\ 0\ 4 & \\
1\ 7\ 0\ 0- & 100 \\
\hline
^2\!\not3^16\ 0\ 4 & \\
1\ 7\ 0\ 0- & 100 \\
\hline
1\ 9\ 0\ 4 & \\
1\ 7\ 0\ 0- & 100 \\
\hline
^1\!\not2^10\ 4 & \\
1\ 7\ 0- & 10 \\
\hline
^2\!\not3^14 & \\
1\ 7- & 1 \\
\hline
1\ 7 & \\
1\ 7- & 1 \\
\hline
0 & \\
\end{array}$$

Step 1
You could take 17 away.
A better way is to take 17×10 or 170 away.
But even better is to take 17×100 or 1700 away.

Step 2
When you can't take 1700 away any more you try 170.

Step 3
When you can't take 170 away any more you try 17.

Step 4
Add up the parts of your answer:
$100 + 100 + 100 + 100 + 100 + 10 + 1 + 1 = 512$

Exercise 1H

1 Work out
   (a) 48 ÷ 2   (b) 69 ÷ 3   (c) 56 ÷ 4   (d) 96 ÷ 6
   (e) 640 ÷ 4   (f) 565 ÷ 5   (g) 72 ÷ 4   (h) 712 ÷ 8
   (i) 828 ÷ 9   (j) 637 ÷ 7   (k) 408 ÷ 2   (l) 1020 ÷ 3

2 Work out
   (a) 256 ÷ 16   (b) 660 ÷ 15
   (c) 512 ÷ 32   (d) 861 ÷ 21
   (e) 756 ÷ 36   (f) 1020 ÷ 30
   (g) 1440 ÷ 36   (h) 7500 ÷ 25

3 (a) Work out 315 ÷ 15
   (b) How many 50s make 750?
   (c) Work out $\dfrac{680}{17}$
   (d) Work out 600 divided by 30.
   (e) Divide 8 into 112.

4 Five people shared a prize draw win of £2400 equally.
   How much did each person receive?

5 In an online computer game tournament players are put
   into groups of 24, with the group winners going through
   to the final.
   How many finalists will there be if there are
   (a) 240 players   (b) 720 players   (c) 864 players?

6 An aeroplane can hold 18 parachute jumpers at a time.
   How many trips does the plane have to make for
   (a) 126 jumps   (b) 234 jumps   (c) 648 jumps?

7 A packing case will hold 72 economy size boxes,
   24 large size boxes or 12 family size boxes.
   How many packing cases would be needed to pack
   (a) 864 economy size boxes
   (b) 984 large size boxes
   (c) 960 family size boxes?

Exercise 1I

Work out these multiplications and divisions.

1 194 × 15   2 3178 ÷ 14   3 306 × 32

4 186 × 36   5 7421 ÷ 41   6 612 × 81

7 12 285 ÷ 91   8 547 × 51   9 32 630 ÷ 65

10 785 × 89   11 20 608 ÷ 28   12 35 342 ÷ 82

You can check your
answers using a
calculator.

13 A lorry delivers 226 boxes of crisps. There are 48 packets in each box.
How many packets are there altogether?

14 A recycling box can hold 24 mobile phones.
How many complete boxes can be filled with 8000 mobiles?

> Hint: there will be some mobile phones left over.

15 There are 12 items in one dozen.
How many items are there in 888 dozen?

1.4 Solving number problems

When you are solving number problems, you need to choose whether to add, subtract, divide or multiply.

Example 13

Find the cost of 7 bath pearls at 50p each.

You could find the cost by adding:

50p + 50p + 50p + 50p + 50p + 50p + 50p = £3.50

or by multiplying:

50p × 7 = £3.50

Here multiplying is quicker than adding.

Example 14

The key words here are **equal shares**. They tell you to **divide**:

£2000 ÷ 5 = £400

Exercise 1J

In this exercise you will need to choose whether to add, subtract, multiply or divide.

> Look at the size of each answer when you have worked it out. This may help you check whether you have chosen + − × or ÷ correctly.

1   Between them, Owen and his friends keep 12 pet hamsters and 21 pet rabbits.
    How many pets do they have altogether?

2   Ranjit and Jane both collect stamps.
    Ranjit has 1310 stamps and Jane has 942 stamps.
    How many more stamps has Ranjit than Jane?

3   42 packing cases of tins of beans are delivered to Simpson's Superstore. The packing cases each hold 48 tins of beans.
    How many tins of beans are delivered altogether?

4   A librarian has 343 DVDs to display in the music library.
    They fill exactly 7 shelves.
    How many DVDs are on each shelf?

5   Robina was given 20 face paints for her birthday.
    4 of the paints were blue, 6 were green and 7 were red.
    The others were brown.

    (a) How many of Robina's paints were brown?

    (b) How many more green paints than blue paints did she have?

    Robina gave 2 paints of each colour to her sister Amanda.

    (c) How many paints did Robina give to Amanda altogether?

    (d) How many paints did Robina have left?

6   Jason bought three boxes of toffees. There were 30 toffees in each box. Jason ate 14 toffees himself then shared all the rest equally between himself and his three sisters.

    (a) How many toffees did Jason have to start with?

    (b) When they were shared out, how many toffees did each person get?

7 This table shows the numbers of students in each year group at Gordon School:

Year 7	Year 8	Year 9	Year 10	Year 11
112	121	104	98	126

    (a) How many students are at the school altogether?

    (b) How many fewer students are in Year 10 than in Year 8?

    (c) Each class in Year 11 has 21 students.
         How many classes are there in Year 11?

    (d) There are 3 times as many students in Bennett School as in Gordon School.
         How many students are in Bennett School?

8 A bus company owns twelve 48-seater coaches.
    Every Saturday all the coaches are used for trips.

    (a) How many people can be carried at the same time in the twelve coaches?

    One Saturday, seven of the coaches each carried 39 people.
    The other coaches each had 11 empty seats.

    (b) How many people went on trips altogether that Saturday?

1.5 Rounding numbers

Sometimes an exact answer is not needed because:

- an approximate answer is good enough
- *or* an approximate answer is easier to understand than an exact answer
- *or* there is no exact answer.

To give an approximate answer you can **round** to the nearest ten, hundred, thousand and so on.

To round to the nearest ten,
look at the digit in the units column.

- If it is less than 5 round down.
- If it is 5 or more round up.

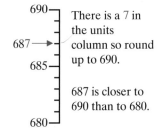

There is a 7 in the units column so round up to 690.

687 is closer to 690 than to 680.

Example 15

Round 687 to the nearest ten.

687 to the nearest ten is 690.

To round to the nearest hundred,
look at the digit in the tens column.

- If it is less than 5 round down.
- If it is 5 or more round up.

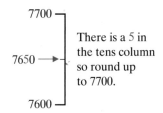

There is a 5 in the tens column so round up to 7700.

Example 16

Round 7650 to the nearest hundred.

7650 to the nearest hundred is 7700.

To round to the nearest thousand,
look at the digit in the hundreds column.

- If it is less than 5 round down.
- If it is 5 or more round up.

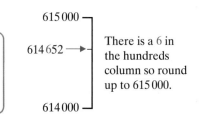

There is a 6 in the hundreds column so round up to 615 000.

Example 17

Round 614 652 to the nearest thousand.

614 652 to the nearest thousand is 615 000.

Exercise 1K

1 Round to the nearest ten
  (a) 57   (b) 63   (c) 185
  (d) 194   (e) 991   (f) 2407

2 Round to the nearest hundred
- (a) 314
- (b) 691
- (c) 2406
- (d) 3094
- (e) 8777
- (f) 29 456

3 Round to the nearest thousand
- (a) 2116
- (b) 36 161
- (c) 28 505
- (d) 321 604
- (e) 717 171
- (f) 2 246 810

4

	Length (ft)	Cruising speed (mph)	Takeoff weight (lbs)
Airbus A310	153	557	36 095
Boeing 737	94	577	130 000
Saab 2000	89	403	50 265
Dornier 228	54	266	12 566
Lockheed L1011	177	615	496 000

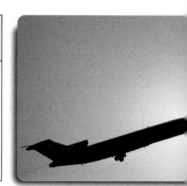

For each of these aircraft, round
- (a) the length to the nearest ten feet
- (b) the takeoff weight to the nearest hundred pounds
- (c) the cruising speed to the nearest ten mph.

5 The table gives the areas of five European Union states and their populations in 2004.

Country	Area (km²)	Population
Greece	131 944	10 645 343
Italy	301 225	57 436 280
Netherlands	33 812	16 318 199
Germany	356 733	83 251 851
Ireland	70 283	3 883 159

Round
- (a) the areas to the nearest thousand km²
- (b) the populations to the nearest hundred thousand.

6 Round each number to the nearest 100, 1000, 10 000, 100 000 or million, as appropriate. Explain your rounding.
- (a) James has a flock of 142 chickens.
- (b) Mrs Wilson sold 306 portions of fish and chips.
- (c) Asif needed 6318 bricks to build his new bungalow.
- (d) A crowd of 40 157 spectators watched Chelsea last night.
- (e) A pop group earned £45 376 290 in a year.
- (f) Newhouse General Hospital treated 13 296 patients last year.

Rounding to 1 significant figure

Sometimes you will be asked to round a number to
1 significant figure (1 s.f.).

To write a number to 1 significant figure, look at the place value
of the first digit and round the number to this place value.

Example 18

Write these numbers to 1 significant figure.
(a) 32   (b) 452   (c) 8780

(a) 32

  The first digit is in the tens column. So you need to round to
  the nearest ten.

  32 to the nearest ten is 30.
  32 to 1 significant figure is 30.

(b) 452

  The first digit is in the hundreds column, so round to the
  nearest hundred.

  452 to 1 significant figure is 500.

(c) 8780

  The first digit is in the thousands column, so round to the
  nearest thousand.

  8780 to 1 significant figure is 9000.

Is your answer reasonable?

When you do a calculation it helps to have a rough estimate
of what answer to expect.

Rounding is used to help you estimate an answer.
To estimate an answer round each number in the calculation
to 1 significant figure.

Example 19

Estimate the answer to $\dfrac{289 \times 96}{184}$

Rounding each of the numbers to 1 significant figure gives

$$\frac{300 \times 100}{200}$$

Working out the simplified calculation gives 150.

Example 20

Work out the exact value of $\dfrac{18 \times 104}{48}$ by calculator.

Check your answer by estimating.

By calculator: $\dfrac{18 \times 104}{48} = \dfrac{1872}{48} = 39$

By estimating: $\dfrac{18 \times 104}{48}$ is about $\dfrac{20 \times 100}{50} = 40$

Exercise 1L

1 Write down these numbers to 1 significant figure.
   (a) 12   (b) 49   (c) 4
   (d) 203   (e) 4960   (f) 501
   (g) 3497   (h) 65   (i) 6034
   (j) 8921   (k) 78 321   (l) 81 476

2 England won 165 medals at the 2002 Commonwealth Games. Write this number to 1 s.f.

3 The population of Clifton is 2437. What is the population of Clifton to 1 s.f.?

4 Showing all your rounding, make an estimate of the answer to

   (a) $\dfrac{63 \times 57}{31}$ (b) $\dfrac{206 \times 311}{154}$

   (c) $\dfrac{9 \times 31 \times 97}{304}$ (d) $\dfrac{2006}{12 \times 99}$

   (e) $\dfrac{498}{11 \times 51}$ (f) $\dfrac{103 \times 87}{21 \times 32}$

Check your answers with a calculator.

5 For each of the following calculations
   (i) work out the exact value by calculator
   (ii) check your answer by estimating.

   (a) $\dfrac{201 \times 96}{51}$ (b) $\dfrac{11 \times 999}{496}$

   (c) $\dfrac{146 \times 51}{69}$ (d) $\dfrac{1000}{9 \times 12}$

   (e) $\dfrac{5206}{131 \times 7}$ (f) $\dfrac{913 \times 81}{39 \times 298}$

If you use your calculator to find an answer, you can check it by estimating.

6 A football grandstand has 49 rows of seats. Each row seats 98 people.
  (a) Estimate the capacity of the grandstand.
  (b) Is your estimate bigger or smaller than the actual number?
      Explain your answer.

7 1335 rugby fans went to an away match by coach.
Each coach carried 47 people.
Estimate the number of coaches needed.

8 Thelma worked out the answer to $916 \times 402 \div 1010$ on her calculator. Her answer was 36.458
By estimating, show whether her answer could be correct.

9 The headteacher lives 16 miles from Inglefield School.
He went to school on 195 days last year.
Estimate how many miles he travelled to and from school.

10 A machine operator produces 121 microchips every hour.
He works 39 hours each week for 47 weeks in the year.
Estimate the operator's annual chip production.

Mixed exercise 1

1
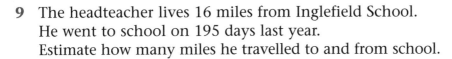

  (a) Write down the number marked with an arrow.

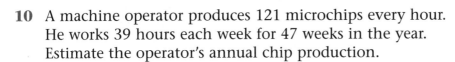

  (b) Write down the number marked with an arrow.   [E]

2 Write these numbers in order of size.

        75 56 37 9 59

Start with the smallest number.   [E]

3 Fatima sold 24 teddy bears for a total of £696.
She sold each teddy bear for the same price.
Work out the price at which Fatima sold each teddy bear. [E]

4 54 327 people watched a concert.
  (a) Write 54 327 to the nearest thousand.
  (b) Write down the value of the 5 in the number
      54 327.   [E]

5   Every day a quarter of a million babies are born in the world.
    (a) Write a quarter of a million using figures.
    (b) Work out the number of babies born in 28 days.
         Give your answer in millions.   [E]

6   Nick fills his van with large wooden crates.
    The weight of each crate is 69 kg.
    The greatest weight the van can hold is 990 kg.
    Work out the greatest number of crates that the van can hold.   [E]

7   800 people took part in a wilderness trek, with 144 failing to finish.
    Work out how many people completed the trek.

8   Sammy does 24 sit-ups every day.
    How many sit-ups will he complete in a year of 365 days?

9   For each of these calculations round each number to 1 significant figure and give an estimate for your answer.
    (a) $\dfrac{205 \times 49}{499}$ (b) $\dfrac{689 + 304}{290 - 98}$ (c) $\dfrac{590}{187 + 103}$

10 Round the following numbers to the nearest ten.
    (a) 77   (b) 643   (c) 18
    (d) 4555   (e) 109   (f) 7001

11 Fiona has four cards.
    Each card has a number written on it.

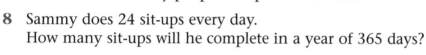

    Fiona puts all four cards on the table to make a number.
    (a) Write the smallest number Fiona can make using all four cards.
    (b) Write the largest number Fiona can make using all four cards.

    Fiona uses the cards to make a true statement.

    (c) Write this calculation.
         Use each of the numbers on Fiona's cards **once**.

    Fiona needs a fifth card to show the result of the multiplication 4915×10.

    (d) Write down the number for the fifth card she needs.   [E]

12 Karen needs to check her electricity bill.

(a) Subtract the 1st reading from the 2nd reading to find the units used.

(b) Multiply the units used by 25 to find the cost in pence of all the units used.

(c) Divide the number of pence by 100 to find the cost in pounds.

(d) Add the standing charge to find the total amount Karen owes.

1st reading	3707
2nd reading	3939
Cost of each unit	25p
Standing charge	£12

Summary of key points

1 Each digit has a value that depends on its position in a number. This is its **place value**. For example:

325

The place value of this digit is hundred. 3 hundreds = 300

2 **To round to the nearest ten,**
look at the digit in the units column.
- If it is less than 5 round down.
- If it is 5 or more round up.

3 **To round to the nearest hundred,**
look at the digit in the tens column.
- If it is less than 5 round down.
- If it is 5 or more round up.

4 **To round to the nearest thousand,**
look at the digit in the hundreds column.
- If it is less than 5 round down.
- If it is 5 or more round up.

5 To write a number to 1 significant figure (1 s.f.), look at the place value of the first digit and round the number to this place value.

6 Rounding is used to help you estimate an answer. To estimate an answer round each number in the calculation to 1 significant figure.

7 There is often more than one method for a calculation.
Make sure you can:
- add
- subtract
- multiply (see pages 12–14 for different methods)
- divide (see pages 15–16 for different methods).

2 Number facts

2.1 Negative numbers

The temperature here is 31 degrees below zero Celsius.

The Dead Sea is the lowest place on the surface of the Earth. It is 396 m below sea level.

You use negative numbers to represent quantities that are less than zero.

−31 °C is 31 degrees below zero.   −396 m is 396 m below sea level.

Exercise 2A

1 Write down the highest and the lowest number in each list.
   (a) 5, −10, −3, 0, 4
   (b) −7, −2, −9, −13, 0
   (c) −3, 6, 13, −15, −6
   (d) −13, −2, −20, −21, −5

2 Write the two missing numbers in each sequence.
   (a) 4, 3, 2, 1, —, —, −2
   (b) 10, 7, 4, 1, —, —, −8
   (c) −13, −9, −5, −1, —, —, 11
   (d) 13, 8, 3, −2, —, —, −17
   (e) 21, 12, 3, −6, —, —, −33
   (f) −13, −10, −7, −4, —, —, 5

```
9
8
7
6
5
4
3
2
1
0
−1
−2
−3
−4
−5
−6
−7
```

3 Use the number line to find the number that is
   (a) 5 more than 2   (b) 4 more than −7
   (c) 7 less than 6   (d) 2 less than −3
   (e) 6 less than 0   (f) 10 more than −7
   (g) 6 more than −6   (h) 4 less than −3
   (i) 10 less than 5   (j) 1 more than −1

4 What number is
(a) 30 more than −70   (b) 50 less than −20
(c) 80 greater than −50   (d) 90 smaller than 60
(e) 130 smaller than −30   (f) 70 bigger than 200
(g) 170 bigger than −200   (h) 100 bigger than −100
(i) 140 more than −20   (j) 200 less than −200?

5 The table gives the highest and lowest temperatures recorded in several cities during one year.

	New York	Brussels	Tripoli	Minsk	Canberra
Highest temperature	27 °C	32 °C	34 °C	28 °C	34 °C
Lowest temperature	−9 °C	−6 °C	8 °C	−21 °C	7 °C

(a) Which city recorded the lowest temperature?
(b) Which city recorded the biggest difference between its highest and lowest temperatures?
(c) Which city recorded the smallest difference between its highest and lowest temperatures?

6 The temperature of the fridge compartment of a fridge–freezer is set at 4 °C. The freezer compartment is set at −18 °C.
What is the difference between these temperature settings?

7 The temperature of a shop freezer should be set at −18 °C. It is set to −12 °C by mistake.
What is the difference between these temperature settings?

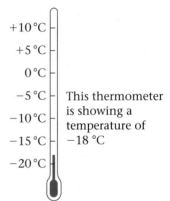

This thermometer is showing a temperature of −18 °C

2.2 Using negative numbers

You can use **negative numbers** to describe quantities such as temperatures less than 0 °C.

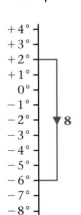

You can use a number line to help you answer questions.

For example:

The temperature at the top of a mountain was 2 °C at 12 noon. By 6 pm it had fallen by 8 °C. So the new temperature at 6 pm was −6 °C.

Temperatures below 0 °C (the freezing point of water) are negative.

Example 1

(a) The temperature was 5 °C. It fell by 8 degrees.
    What is the new temperature?
(b) What is the difference in temperature between 4 °C and
    −4 °C?

(a) From 5 °C count 8 degrees down to −3 °C.
(b) From 4 °C count to −4 °C. There is a difference of
    8 degrees between the two temperatures.

Temperature falls by 8°

Worked examination question

The temperature during an autumn morning went up
from −3 °C to 6 °C.
(a) By how many degrees did the temperature rise?

During the afternoon the temperature then fell by
8 degrees from 6 °C.
(b) What was the temperature at the end of the afternoon?

(a) Counting from −3 °C to 6 °C gives 9 degrees.
(b) Counting down 8 degrees from 6 °C gives −2 °C.   [E]

Exercise 2B

Use this number line going from −10 °C to +10 °C to help
you with these questions.

1 Rearrange each list of temperatures in numerical order,
   lowest temperature first
   (a) 4 °C, −5 °C, 2 °C, −12 °C, 7 °C, 0 °C, −7 °C, −1 °C, 9 °C
   (b) 5 °C, −3 °C, 2 °C, 10 °C, −8 °C, −2 °C, 8 °C, 0 °C, −9 °C
   (c) 7 °C, 3 °C, −7 °C, −4 °C, −1 °C, 8 °C, −6 °C, 5 °C, −3 °C
   (d) −4 °C, 9 °C, 4 °C, −2 °C, 7 °C, −8 °C, 1 °C, −3 °C, 6 °C
   (e) 5 °C, −5 °C, 7 °C, −7 °C, 4 °C, −9 °C, −3 °C, −1 °C,
        8 °C, 0 °C

2 Find the number of degrees between each pair of
   temperatures.
   (a) −3 °C, 2 °C   (b) −4 °C, −1 °C   (c) 2 °C, 8 °C
   (d) −6 °C, 4 °C   (e) 7 °C, −3 °C   (f) 1 °C, 9 °C
   (g) −3 °C, −8 °C   (h) −7 °C, 6 °C

3 Find the new temperature after
   (a) a 2° rises from −4 °C   (b) a 7° fall from 4 °C
   (c) 8 °C falls by 15°   (d) −4 °C rises by 7°
   (e) −5 °C rises by 8°   (f) 4 °C falls by 10°
   (g) −3 °C falls by 6°

+10°
+9°
+8°
+7°
+6°
+5°
+4°
+3°
+2°
+1°
0°
−1°
−2°
−3°
−4°
−5°
−6°
−7°
−8°
−9°
−10°

Adding and subtracting negative numbers

You can also use negative numbers in calculations.

You need to be able to add and subtract negative numbers. To help you get used to working with subtraction signs and negative numbers they are written like this when they appear together in this section:

$^-5$ means negative 5, or 5 below zero

$7 - 4$ means 7 subtract 4

$7 - {}^-5$ means 7 subtract negative 5

Sometimes 3 is written $^+3$.

This table shows lunchtime and evening temperatures in different parts of the world:

Place	Temperature at lunchtime in °C	Temperature in the evening in °C
Bahrain	20	15
London	5	−2
Alaska	−8	−14

- The difference between the lunchtime temperature and the evening temperature in Bahrain can be written:

  lunchtime temperature − evening temperature
  $= {}^+20 - {}^+15 = {}^+5$ or $20 - 15 = 5$
  (Note that $\qquad {}^+20 + {}^-15 = {}^+5$)

- The difference in London is $\quad 5 - {}^-2 \;= {}^+7$
  (Note that $\qquad\qquad\; 5 + {}^+2 \;= 7$)

- The difference in Alaska is $\quad {}^-8 - {}^-14 = 6$
  (Note that $\qquad\qquad\;\; {}^-8 + {}^+14 = 6$)

  Subtracting a positive number has the same effect as adding the negative number: $- {}^+4 = + {}^-4$

  Subtracting a negative number has the same effect as adding the positive number: $- {}^-3 = + {}^+3$

A good way of remembering how to deal with adding and subtracting positive and negative numbers is:

- When you have **two signs that are the same** next to each other, you replace them with a **+**
- When you have **two signs that are different** next to each other, you replace them with a **−**

This means that:

$+ + = +$ so $2 + {}^+5 = 7$ and ${}^-2 + {}^+5 = 3$

$- - = +$ $\qquad 2 - {}^-5 = 7$ $\qquad {}^-2 - {}^-5 = 3$

$+ - = -$ $\qquad 2 + {}^-5 = {}^-3$ $\qquad {}^-2 + {}^-5 = {}^-7$

$- + = -$ $\qquad 2 - {}^+5 = {}^-3$ $\qquad {}^-2 - {}^+5 = {}^-7$

Exercise 2C

Work out these additions and subtractions.

1 (a) $^+3 + ^-3$　　　　(b) $^-4 + 0$
　 (c) $^-9 - ^+5$　　　　(d) $^-9 + ^+5$

2 (a) $^-5 - ^-6$　　　　(b) $^+12 - ^-5$
　 (c) $^-10 + ^+8$　　　　(d) $^+6 - ^-4$

3 (a) $^+8 + ^-13$　　　(b) $^+5 - 0$
　 (c) $^+13 - ^+15$　　　(d) $^-2 + ^-4$

4 (a) $^-3 - ^+8$　　　　(b) $^-3 + ^+6$
　 (c) $^+11 - ^-6$　　　　(d) $^-12 + ^+7$

5 (a) $^-7 + ^-7$　　　　(b) $^+4 - ^+1$
　 (c) $^+3 + ^-8$　　　　(d) $^-3 - ^+6$

Remember:
$+ \; + = +$
$- \; - = +$
$+ \; - = -$
$- \; + = -$

Multiplying and dividing negative numbers

The next exercise uses patterns to investigate how to multiply and divide with negative numbers.

Exercise 2D

First number

-5	-4	-3	-2	-1	0	1	2	3	4	5	×
										25	5
											4
							6				3
											2
								4			1
											0
											-1
											-2
											-3
											-4
											-5

Second number

First number × second number
$= 2 \times 3 = 6$

1 Copy the multiplication grid above.

2 Complete the yellow square for numbers 1 to 5 on your grid.

3   Look at the patterns in the yellow square. Continue these patterns to complete all the horizontal and vertical rows in the table.

4   From your grid write down the values of
(a) $+5 \times +2$ (b) $+4 \times -3$
(c) $-2 \times +4$ (d) -3×-5
(e) $+3 \times +1$ (f) $+2 \times -3$
(g) $-5 \times +4$ (h) -4×-1

This table shows the signs you get when you multiply two numbers together:

+	×	+	=	+
+	×	−	=	−
−	×	+	=	−
−	×	−	=	+

This table shows the signs you get when you divide one number by another:

+	÷	+	=	+
+	÷	−	=	−
−	÷	+	=	−
−	÷	−	=	+

If you know that $-3 \times +4 = -12$ then you also know that $-12 \div +4 = -3$ and $-12 \div -3 = +4$.

Remember: when multiplying or dividing, two like signs give a +, two unlike signs give a −

Exercise 2E

1   Copy and complete this multiplication grid for first number × second number.

First number

×	+5	+3	−6	−2
+2				
+8				
−3				
−4				

Second number

2   Copy and complete this division grid for first number ÷ second number.

First number

÷	+6	−12	−18	+24
+3				
−2				
−6				
+1				

Second number

Example 2

Work out   (a) $+5 \times -2$ (b) $+16 \div +2$
              (c) $-1 \times +3$ (d) $-20 \div -5$

(a) $+5 \times -2 = -10$ (b) $+16 \div +2 = +8$
(c) $-1 \times +3 = -3$ (d) $-20 \div -5 = +4$

Exercise 2F

Work out these multiplications and divisions.

1 (a) $+3 \times -1$ (b) $+24 \div -8$ (c) $+4 \div +1$
   (d) $+2 \times +6$ (e) $-12 \div +3$ (f) $-3 \times +4$

2 (a) $-9 \times +10$ (b) $-32 \div -8$ (c) $-20 \div -4$
   (d) $-2 \times +7$ (e) $+10 \div -5$ (f) -3×-4

3 (a) $-5 \times +4$ (b) $-16 \div -8$ (c) $-4 \times +5$
   (d) $-18 \div -3$ (e) $+18 \div +2$ (f) $-6 \times +7$

4 (a) -8×-3 (b) $-30 \div +2$ (c) $-16 \div +4$
   (d) -3×-9 (e) $+5 \times -8$ (f) $+24 \div +8$

5 (a) $-50 \div -5$ (b) $-7 \times +8$ (c) $+6 \times +6$
   (d) -3×-7 (e) $-9 \div +3$ (f) $-7 \times +6$

2.3 Factors, multiples and primes

You need to be able to recognise the following types of numbers by knowing some of their properties.

- **Even** numbers are whole numbers which divide exactly by 2.
  2, 4, 6, 18, 24 are even numbers.

- Odd numbers are whole numbers which do not divide exactly by 2.
  1, 9, 15, 23, 27 are odd numbers.

- The **factors** of a number are whole numbers that divide exactly into the number. The factors include 1 and the number itself.
  For example, the factors of 12 are 1, 2, 3, 4, 6 and 12.

- **Multiples** of a number are the results of multiplying the number by a positive whole number. For example, some multiples of 3 are 3, 6, 9, 12, 15, 18, 21, 24.

- A **prime** number is a whole number greater than 1 which has only two factors: itself and 1. The first ten prime numbers are 2, 3, 5, 7, 11, 13, 17, 19, 23, 29.
  1 is not a prime number as it can only be divided by **one** number (itself).

- A **prime factor** is a factor that is a prime number.
  For example, the prime factors of 18 are 2 and 3.

Exercise 2G

1 Write down all the even numbers in this list:
   2, 18, 37, 955, 1110, 73 536, 500 000

2 Write down all the odd numbers in this list:
   108, 537, 9216, 811, 36 225, 300 000

3 The first six prime numbers are 2, 3, 5, 7, 11 and 13.
Write down the next seven prime numbers.

4 Here is a list of numbers:
15, 20, 25, 30, 37, 39, 49, 69, 70, 71, 400, 450
Write down
(a) the largest even number
(b) the largest odd number
(c) the largest prime number.

5 Find one factor, other than 1 and the number itself, of
(a) 9   (b) 24   (c) 32
(d) 55   (e) 108   (f) 625

6 Find all six factors of 12.

7 Find all the factors of
(a) 32   (b) 200
(c) 340   (d) 1000

8 Find all the common factors of
(a) 4 and 6   (b) 9 and 12   (c) 15 and 25
(d) 6 and 14   (e) 14 and 35

> A common factor of 4 and 6 is a number that is a factor of *both* 4 *and* 6, e.g. 2.

9 Find all the common factors of
(a) 20 and 30   (b) 90 and 100   (c) 12 and 28
(d) 6 and 18   (e) 18 and 45

10 Find two common factors of
(a) 20 and 50   (b) 12 and 40   (c) 70 and 105
(d) 30 and 42   (e) 18 and 42

11 Find three multiples of 9.

12 Find the nearest number to 100 that is a multiple of 9.

13 Find
(a) three multiples of 6 that are bigger than 50
(b) three multiples of 20 that are between 1000 and 2000
(c) three multiples of 15 that are bigger than 100.

14 Write down
(a) three numbers that have a factor of 8
(b) three numbers that have a factor of 150
(c) three numbers that only have odd-number factors.

15 (a) Copy this set of numbers:
  (b) Draw a line — through numbers with factor 3.
  (c) Draw a line | through numbers with factor 20.
  (d) Draw a line \ through any multiples of 30.
  (e) Draw a line / through any multiples of 90.
  (f) Which number has all four lines through it?

10	20	30	40	50
60	70	80	90	100
110	120	130	140	150
160	170	180	190	200
210	220	230	240	250

2.4 Square numbers and cube numbers

These numbers sometimes occur in number patterns in investigations.

> A **square number** is the result of multiplying a whole number by itself.

Square numbers:

$1 \times 1 = 1$ 1st square number
$2 \times 2 = 4$ 2nd square number
$3 \times 3 = 9$ 3rd square number
$4 \times 4 = 16$ 4th square number

4×4 can also be written as:
- the square of 4
- 4 squared
- 4^2

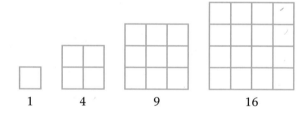

1   4   9   16

A square number can be shown as a pattern of squares.

> A **cube number** is the result of multiplying a whole number by itself, then multiplying by the number again.

Cube numbers:

$1 \times 1 \times 1 = 1$ 1st cube number
$2 \times 2 \times 2 = 8$ 2nd cube number
$3 \times 3 \times 3 = 27$ 3rd cube number
$4 \times 4 \times 4 = 64$ 4th cube number

$4 \times 4 \times 4$ can also be written as:
- the cube of 4
- 4 cubed
- 4^3

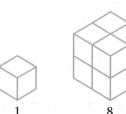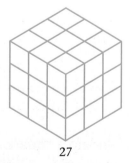

1   8   27

A cube number can be shown as a pattern of cubes.

Example 3

1, 3, 4, 6, 8, 13, 16, 18, 24, 27, 30

From the list write down
(a) the square numbers   (b) the cube numbers.

(a) 1, 4, 16   (b) 1, 8, 27

Exercise 2H

1 Find
(a) the 8th square number   (b) the 7th cube number
(c) the 12th square number   (d) the 10th cube number
(e) the first 12 square numbers (f) the first 8 cube numbers.

2 From each list write down all the numbers which are
(i) square numbers   (ii) cube numbers.

(a) 50, 20, 64, 30, 1, 80, 8, 49, 9
(b) 10, 21, 57, 4, 60, 125, 7, 27, 48, 16, 90, 35
(c) 137, 150, 75, 110, 50, 125, 64, 81, 144
(d) 90, 180, 216, 100, 81, 75, 140, 169, 125

2.5 Finding squares and square roots of numbers

You will need to find squares of numbers and square roots of numbers when you use Pythagoras' theorem (Chapter 25, in Book 2).

Squares

To find the **square** of any number, multiply the number by itself.
The square of $3.7 = 3.7^2 = 3.7 \times 3.7 = 13.69$
The square of $-6.2 = -6.2^2 = -6.2 \times -6.2 = 38.44$

Square roots

$4 \times 4 = 16$ so we say that 4 is a **square root** of 16; it is a number which multiplied by itself gives 16.

You can write the square root of 16 as $\sqrt{16}$.

$1.5 \times 1.5 = 2.25$

So 1.5 is a square root of 2.25, written $\sqrt{2.25}$.

Finding a **square root** of a number is the opposite (inverse) of squaring. A square root of 64 (written $\sqrt{64}$) is 8, since $8^2 = 64$.

> Notice that
> $-4 \times -4 = 16$
> so -4 is also a square root of 16.
> You can write $\sqrt{16} = \pm 4$

Square roots are often not whole numbers. You can find the square root of any positive number. Most calculators have a function key that finds the square root of a number. You often need to round the answer on the calculator display.

> Your calculator may have a key with this symbol:
>
> $\sqrt{}$ square root

Example 4

Use a calculator to find $\sqrt{18}$.

$\sqrt{18} = 4.242\,640\,6 \ldots = 4.24$ (to 2 d.p.)

Using the square root key on your calculator:

> Remember:
> $\sqrt{18}$ can also be -4.24, if it is a sensible answer to the problem you are solving.

2.6 Finding cubes and cube roots of numbers

Cubes

To find the **cube** of any number, multiply the number by itself then multiply by the number again.

The cube of $5.3 = 5.3^3 = 5.3 \times 5.3 \times 5.3 = 148.877$

The cube of $-2.1 = (-2.1)^3 = -2.1 \times -2.1 \times -2.1 = -9.261$

Cube roots

$2 \times 2 \times 2 = 8$ so we say that 2 is the **cube root** of 8: it is a number which multiplied by itself, then multiplied by itself again, gives 8.

You can write the cube root of 8 as $\sqrt[3]{8}$.

$\qquad 3.4 \times 3.4 \times 3.4 = 39.304$

So 3.4 is the cube root of 39.304, written $\sqrt[3]{39.304}$.

> Finding the **cube root** is the opposite (or inverse) of finding the cube.

Cube roots are often not whole numbers. You can find the cube root of any positive or negative number. Some calculators have a cube root function key to find the cube root of numbers. As with square roots, you often have to round the answer.

> Your calculator may have a key with this symbol:
>
>   cube root

Example 5

Use a calculator to find $\sqrt[3]{18}$.

Using the cube root key on your calculator:

$\sqrt[3]{18} = 2.620\,741\,3 \ldots = 2.62$ (to 2 d.p.)

> Notice that $\sqrt[3]{-64} = -4$ because
> $-4 \times -4 \times -4 = -64$

Exercise 2I

Use your calculator to work out:

1 (a) 13^2 (b) 3.5^2 (c) 40^2

   (d) 8.7^2 (e) $(-19.6)^2$ (f) $(-57.4)^2$

2 (a) 6^3 (b) 2.4^3 (c) 20^3

   (d) $(-1.3)^3$ (e) $(-13.4)^3$ (f) 36.2^3

3 (a) $\sqrt{121}$ (b) $\sqrt{225}$ (c) $\sqrt{16\,900}$

   (d) $\sqrt{2.89}$ (e) $\sqrt{0.49}$ (f) $\sqrt{33.64}$

> Sometimes you are asked to leave your answer as a square root or cube root.
> e.g. $x^2 = 5$
> $x = \sqrt{5}$
> This is called writing your answer in **surd form**.

4 In this question give your answers correct to 2 d.p.

   (a) $\sqrt{253}$ (b) $\sqrt{18.4}$ (c) $\sqrt{29.44}$

5 In this question give your answers correct to 3 s.f.

   (a) $\sqrt[3]{68}$ (b) $\sqrt[3]{26.5}$ (c) $\sqrt[3]{882.5}$

> To round to 3 s.f. look at the place value of the 3rd digit from the left, and round the number to this place value.

2.7 Finding square roots and cube roots by trial and improvement

You can also find square roots and cube roots by **trial and improvement**.

Example 6

Use a trial and improvement method to find $\sqrt[3]{20}$ (the cube root of 20), correct to 2 decimal places.

	Try this number	Cube of the number		Bigger or smaller than 20?
Start by trying whole numbers of about the right size.	2	$2 \times 2 \times 2$	$= 8$	smaller
	3	$3 \times 3 \times 3$	$= 27$	bigger
Next try a value between 2 and 3: try 2.5.	2.5	$2.5 \times 2.5 \times 2.5$	$= 15.625$	smaller
Next try 2.8, bigger than 2.5.	2.8	$2.8 \times 2.8 \times 2.8$	$= 21.952$	bigger
Next try 2.7, smaller than 2.8.	2.7	$2.7 \times 2.7 \times 2.7$	$= 19.683$	smaller
Next try a value between 2.7 and 2.8: try 2.75.	2.75	2.75^3	$= 20.797$	bigger
The solution is between 2.71 and 2.72, so try the value halfway between 2.71 and 2.72: try 2.715.	2.71	2.71^3	$= 19.903$	smaller
	2.72	2.72^3	$= 20.124$	bigger
	2.715	2.715^3	$= 20.012876$	bigger

The solution is between 2.71 and 2.715. Any number in this range rounds to 2.71 (to 2 d.p.), so an approximate value for $\sqrt[3]{20}$ is 2.71 (correct to 2 d.p.).

Exercise 2J

Use a trial and improvement method to find these roots correct to 2 decimal places. Use a calculator to check your answers.

> Remember: show all your attempts and working when you have used a trial and improvement method; it gives evidence of the methods you have used.

1 $\sqrt{7}$ **2** $\sqrt[3]{15}$ **3** $\sqrt[3]{12}$ **4** $\sqrt{10}$

5 $\sqrt{20}$ **6** $\sqrt{32}$ **7** $\sqrt[3]{30}$ **8** $\sqrt[3]{42}$

9 $\sqrt{13}$ **10** $\sqrt[3]{50}$ **11** $\sqrt{28}$ **12** $\sqrt[3]{33}$

2.8 Writing numbers as a product of their prime factors

Sometimes you will be asked to write a number as a **product of its prime factors**. This involves splitting the number into all its prime factors. When you multiply the prime factors together you get the number again. Here are two ways of doing this.

> A product results from multiplying two or more numbers together. A number which is itself prime cannot be written as a product of primes.

Method 1: Dividing by prime numbers in order

Example 7

Write 60 as a product of its prime factors.

Step 1   Divide by 2:

$$\begin{array}{r} 30 \\ 2\overline{)60} \end{array}$$

Step 2   Divide the answer 30 by 2:

$$\begin{array}{r} 15 \\ 2\overline{)30} \\ 2\overline{)60} \end{array}$$

Step 3   15 is not divisible by 2, so try the next prime, 3:

$$\begin{array}{r} 5 \\ 3\overline{)15} \\ 2\overline{)30} \\ 2\overline{)60} \end{array}$$

5 is prime.

Answer $60 = 2 \times 2 \times 3 \times 5$ ——— as a product of prime factors

$ = 2^2 \times 3 \times 5$ ——— as a product of powers of its prime factors

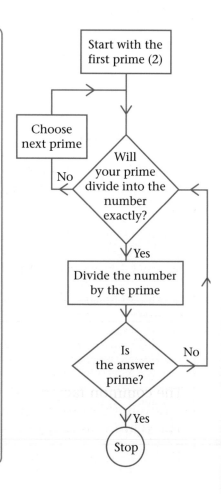

Method 2: Factor trees

Start with the number and keep splitting into pairs of factors until all the factors are prime numbers.

Example 8

Write 48 as a product of its prime factors.

$48 = 6 \times 8$

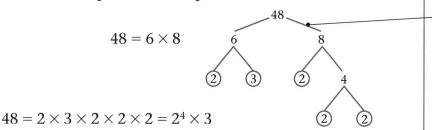

There is often more than one way of splitting a number in a factor tree (e.g. 48 could have been split into 2×24), but all ways give the same answer.

$48 = 2 \times 3 \times 2 \times 2 \times 2 = 2^4 \times 3$

Writing a number as the product of its prime factors is called writing it in **prime factor form**.

Exercise 2K

1 Write these numbers as products of their prime factors.
  (a) 45   (b) 36   (c) 29   (d) 100

2 Write these numbers in prime factor form.
  (a) 24   (b) 32   (c) 18   (d) 13

A number which is itself prime cannot be written as a product of primes.

Finding the highest common factor (HCF)

The **highest common factor** or HCF is exactly what it says.

The **HCF** of two numbers is the highest factor that is common to both of them (or the highest number that divides into both exactly).

Example 9

Find the highest common factor of 60 and 48.

Write each number in prime factor form and pick out the common factors:

$60 = 2 \times 2 \times 3 \times 5$
$48 = 2 \times 2 \times 2 \times 2 \times 3$

The common factors are 2, 2 and 3. To find the HCF we multiply these together: $2 \times 2 \times 3 = 12$.

The HCF of 48 and 60 is 12.

12 is the highest number that divides into 48 and 60 exactly.

Finding the lowest common multiple (LCM)

The **lowest common multiple** or LCM is also exactly what it says.

> The **LCM** of two numbers is the lowest multiple that is common to both of them (or the lowest number that is a multiple of them both).

___Example 10___

Find the lowest common multiple of 4 and 5.

The multiples of 4 are:　　4　8　12　16　20　24　28 …
The multiples of 5 are:　　5　10　15　20　25　30 …

The lowest number that is in both lists is 20.
The LCM of 4 and 5 is 20.
20 is the lowest number that 4 and 5 both divide into.

Exercise 2L

1 Find the highest common factor of
    (a)　4 and 8　　　　(b)　9 and 12　　　(c)　18 and 24
    (d)　18 and 30　　　(e)　21 and 35

2 Find the lowest common multiple of
    (a)　3 and 4　　　　(b)　4 and 6
    (c)　7 and 14　　　(d)　6 and 15

3 Find the lowest common multiple of
    (a)　12 and 15　　　(b)　36 and 16　　　(c)　50 and 85

4 Find the HCF and LCM of
    (a)　12 and 18　　　(b)　120 and 180　　(c)　24 and 84
    (d)　91 and 130　　　(e)　72 and 96　　　(f)　40 and 60

Mixed exercise 2

1 Write these numbers in order of size.

    5　−6　−10　2　−4

Start with the smallest number.　　　　　　　　　　　　　　　[E]

2 Using only the numbers in the cloud, write down
    (a)　all the multiples of 6
    (b)　all the square numbers
    (c)　all the factors of 12
    (d)　all the cube numbers.　　　　　　　　　　　　　　[E]

3 Here is a map of the British Isles. The temperatures in some places, one night last winter are shown on the map.

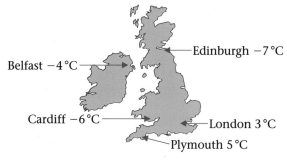

Belfast −4°C
Edinburgh −7°C
Cardiff −6°C
London 3°C
Plymouth 5°C

(a) Write down the names of the two places that had the biggest difference in temperature.

(b) Two pairs of places have a difference in temperature of 2°C
Write down the names of these places.   [E]

4 Sally wrote down the temperature at different times on 1st January 2003.

(a) Write down
  (i) the **highest** temperature
  (ii) the **lowest** temperature.

(b) Work out the difference in the temperature between
  (i) 4 am and 8 am   (ii) 3 pm and 7 pm

At 11 pm that day the temperature had fallen 5°C from its value at 7 pm.

(c) Work out the temperature at 11 pm.   [E]

Time	Temperature
Midnight	−6°C
4 am	−10°C
8 am	−4°C
Noon	7°C
3 pm	6°C
7 pm	−2°C

5 (a) Express 108 as the product of powers of its prime factors.

(b) Find the highest common factor (HCF) of 108 and 24.   [E]

6 (a) Express the following numbers as products of their prime factors.
  (i) 60   (ii) 96

(b) Find the highest common factor of 60 and 96.

(c) Work out the lowest common multiple of 60 and 96.   [E]

7 4, 5, 8, 9, 12, 14, 16, 20, 27, 35, 36, 37
From the numbers in the list write down
(a) the odd numbers   (b) the multiples of 3
(c) the factors of 48   (d) the prime numbers
(e) the square numbers   (f) the cube numbers.

8 Work out
(a) $4 + {}^-2$ (b) $3 + {}^-5$ (c) $3 + {}^-3$ (d) ${}^-2 + 3$
(e) ${}^-2 + {}^-3$ (f) ${}^-6 + 4$ (g) ${}^-6 + {}^-4$ (h) ${}^-5 + 5$
(i) $3 - 4$ (j) $3 - {}^-4$ (k) $5 - 2$ (l) $5 - {}^-2$
(m) ${}^-4 - 5$ (n) ${}^-3 - {}^-5$ (o) ${}^-7 - 6$ (p) ${}^-8 - {}^-4$

9   Calculate

(a) 4×-2 (b) -3×-2 (c) -5×6

(d) -6×-2 (e) $12 \div -3$ (f) $-18 \div -3$

(g) $-24 \div 6$ (h) $-45 \div -9$ (i) $\dfrac{6}{-2}$

(j) $\dfrac{-6}{-2}$ (k) $\dfrac{-16}{2}$ (l) $\dfrac{-14}{-2}$

Summary of key points

1   You can use **negative numbers** to describe quantities such as temperatures less than $0\,°\text{C}$. You can also use negative numbers in calculations: $2 + 4 = 6$

2   Rules for negative numbers.

Adding/Subtracting   Multiplying/dividing

  $+ + = +$ $+ + = +$

  $- - = +$ $- - = +$

  $+ - = -$ $+ - = -$

  $- + = -$ $- + = -$

3   **Even** numbers are whole numbers which divide exactly by 2.
2, 4, 6, 18, 24 are even numbers.

4   Odd numbers are whole numbers which do not divide exactly by 2.
1, 9, 15, 23, 27 are odd numbers.

5   The **factors** of a number are whole numbers that divide exactly into the number. The factors include 1 and the number itself.
For example, the factors of 12 are 1, 2, 3, 4, 6 and 12.

6   **Multiples** of a number are the results of multiplying the number by a positive whole number. For example, some multiples of 3 are 3, 6, 9, 12, 15, 18, 21, 24.

7   A **prime** number is a whole number greater than 1 which has only two factors: itself and 1. The first ten prime numbers are 2, 3, 5, 7, 11, 13, 17, 19, 23, 29.
1 is not a prime number as it can only be divided by **one** number (itself).

8   A **prime factor** is a factor that is a prime number.
For example, the prime factors of 18 are 2 and 3.

9   A **square number** is the result of multiplying a whole number by itself.
The first six square numbers are 1, 4, 9, 16, 25, 36.

10 A **cube number** is the result of multiplying a whole number by itself then multiplying by the number again.
The first six cube numbers are 1, 8, 27, 64, 125, 216.

11 To find the **square** of any number, multiply the number by itself.

12 Finding a **square root** of a number is the opposite (inverse) of squaring:

$$\sqrt{64} = \pm 8$$

13 To find the **cube** of any number, multiply the number by itself then multiply by the number again.

14 Finding the **cube root** is the opposite (inverse) of finding the cube:

$$\sqrt[3]{125} = 5$$

15 Writing a number as the product of its prime factors is called writing it in **prime factor form**. For example, $60 = 2^2 \times 3 \times 5$

16 The **highest common factor** (HCF) of two numbers is the highest factor that is common to both of them.

17 The **lowest common multiple** (LCM) of two numbers is the lowest multiple that is common to both of them (or the lowest number that is a multiple of them both).

③ Essential algebra

3.1 Using letters to represent numbers

Algebra is the branch of mathematics in which letters are used to represent numbers.

This can help solve some mathematical problems.

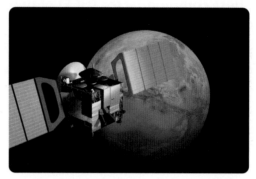

If you know how fast a cyclist is travelling you can use algebra to work out how far he will get in a given time:

$$d = v \times t$$

(distance = velocity × time)

Very complicated algebra is used to calculate the right orbit for spacecraft.

You can use letters even when you do not know the number itself.

Example 1

Jas has some CDs. If he buys 3 more CDs, how many will he have altogether?

You do not know how many CDs Jas starts with, but you can use algebra to say:

    Jas starts with x CDs
    x CDs and 3 CDs is $x + 3$ CDs

Example 2

Ann wins some cinema tickets. She gives 6 to friends. How many tickets has she got left?

You do not know how many tickets she had to start with, but you can say she had y. After giving away 6 tickets she has $y - 6$ tickets left.

Example 3

Yasmin has some sweets. So has Ali.
How many sweets do they have altogether?

Use two different letters: x for Yasmin's sweets and y for Ali's.

Altogether they have $x + y$ sweets.

y sweets

x sweets

Exercise 3A

Use algebra to write:

1 3 more than a

2 x with 4 added

3 x more than 7

4 2 less than b

5 c with 3 taken away

6 p less than q

7 x more than y

8 4 together with a

9 $3b$ with 6 subtracted

10 Paul has d DVDs. He buys 3 more.
How many DVDs has Paul got now?

11 Rob has a apples. He eats 2 apples.
How many apples has Rob got now?

12 Tom has £x. He spends £5.
How much money has Tom got now?

3.2 Adding with letters

In algebra you can add letters that are the same. For example:

$a + a$ can be written as $2a$
$a + a + a$ can be written as $3a$

> a means $1a$
> so $1a + 1a = 2a$

Exercise 3B

Write these in a shorter form. The first one is done for you.

1 $a + a + a + a + a + a = 6a$

2 $p + p + p + p$

3 $b + b + b + b + b$

4 $q + q + q + q + q + q$

5 $c + c$

6 $n + n + n$

7 $w + w + w + w + w$

8 $y + y + y + y + y$

9 $z + z + z + z + z + z + z$

10 $a + a + a + a + a + a + a$

11 $b + b + b + b + b$

12 $p + p + p + p + p + p + p + p$

Write these out in a longer form. The first one is done for you.

13 $4a = a + a + a + a$ **14** $2p$

15 $5p$ **16** $7a$ **17** $2y$ **18** $4q$ **19** $3c$

20 $5d$ **21** $10a$ **22** $5h$ **23** $6g$ **24** $4z$

3.3 Expressions and terms

An **algebraic expression** is a collection of letters, symbols and numbers:

$a + 3b - 2c$ is an algebraic expression

These are each called **terms**.

Terms which use the same letter or arrangement of letters are called **like terms**:

a and $3a$ are like terms

$2g$ and $8g$ are like terms

Sometimes you can make algebraic expressions simpler by adding or subtracting like terms:

You can combine **like terms** by adding them:

$2a + 3a = 5a$

$3b + 4b + b = 8b$

You can combine **like terms** by subtracting them:

$5a - 3a = 2a$

$7a - a = 6a$ •

> Remember:
> this is $7a - 1a$

Exercise 3C

Make these expressions simpler by adding or subtracting like terms.

1 $2a + 4a$ **2** $3b + 4b$ **3** $5c + 2c$

4 $5d - 3d$ **5** $7e - 3e$ **6** $5f - f$

7 $3a + 2a + 2a$ **8** $2a + 5a + a$ **9** $5c + 3c + 4c$

10 $6g + 7g + g$ **11** $7g - 3g$ **12** $9s - 6s$

13 $15q - q$ **14** $3p + 7p + 8p$ **15** $12p - 6p$

3.4 Collecting like terms

Sometimes algebraic expressions have more than one term and you can simplify them by collecting like terms together.

Example 4

Simplify $2a - 4b + 3a + 5b$

Collect the a terms and the b terms:

$2a - 4b + 3a + 5b$

$2a + 3a - 4b + 5b$

Combine the a terms and the b terms:

$5a + b$

> Remember:
> The + or − sign is part of each term.
> The minus sign is part of the term $-4b$.

Example 5

Simplify the following expressions completely.
(a) $3a + 5b + 3b + a$ (b) $5p + 3q - 2p + q$
(c) $5a + 7 - 3a - 4$

(a) $3a + 5b + 3b + a = 4a + 8b$
(b) $5p + 3q - 2p + q = 3p + 4q$
(c) $5a + 7 - 3a - 4 = 2a + 3$

You can simplify algebraic expressions by **collecting like terms** together.

Exercise 3D

Simplify these expressions completely by collecting like terms.

1 $3a + 4b + 4a + 2b$ 2 $6m + 5n + 3m + 2n$

3 $2p + 3q - p + 2q$ 4 $8e + 6c + 8e$

5 $5y + 7p - 3y + 5p$ 6 $2a + 8g + 3a + 5g - a$

7 $4k + 3q + 5k - 2q$ 8 $9d + 7f - 8d + 3f$

9 $5h + 8 - 2h + 2$ 10 $3f + 2f + 4e - 2e$

11 $7g + 8n - 3g - n$ 12 $5 + g + 2 + 3g - 3 - 2g$

13 $2a + 3a + 4a + 5a$ 14 $3b + b + 5b - 4b$

15 $7c + 8c - 5c - 6c$ 16 $5d + 4d - 3d + 6d - 7d$

17 $2a + 7b + 5a - 6b$ 18 $2c + 4b + 6c - 3b + 7b - 2c$

19 $3p + 2p - 4p + 3 - 2$ 20 $7y + 4z + 2y - 3z + 5y + 3z$

21 $12a - 7a + 9a - 2a + 5a$ 22 $3p + 4p + 5p - 8p - 4p$

23 $6s + 4s - 3s + 5s - 5s$ 24 $3a + 2 + 5a - 1 - 7a - 1$

3.5 Multiplying with letters and numbers

Remember: $2a$ is $a + a$ and $3a$ is $a + a + a$. But:

 $2a$ also means 2 lots of a or 2 multiplied by a or $2 \times a$
 $3a$ means   3 lots of a or 3 multiplied by a or $3 \times a$

In algebra, when you want to multiply two items you just write them next to each other, like this:

 $2 \times a$ is written $2a$ $c \times d$ is written cd
 $a \times b$ is written ab $3 \times e \times f$ is written $3ef$

> Don't forget that $12ab$ is $12 \times a \times b$ not $1 \times 2 \times a \times b$!

Exercise 3E

Use multiplication signs to write these expressions out in a longer form. The first one is done for you.

1 $pq = p \times q$ 2 rst 3 $2ef$

4 $5abc$ 5 $7klm$ 6 $9ab$

7 $15abc$ 8 $3pqrs$ 9 $16st$

10 $6yz$ 11 $8defg$ 12 $20abcd$

Write these expressions in a simpler form. The first one is done for you.

13 $p \times q = pq$ **14** $e \times f \times g$ **15** $r \times s \times t$

16 $2 \times e \times f$ **17** $2 \times c \times d$ **18** $h \times d \times s$

19 $2 \times s \times f$ **20** $3 \times d \times e \times f$ **21** $4 \times p \times q$

22 $3 \times h \times j$ **23** $5 \times k \times v$ **24** $12 \times r \times s \times t$

3.6 Multiplying algebraic expressions

Sometimes you can simplify an algebraic expression, such as $2a \times 3b$, by multiplying the terms by each other:

Multiply the numbers.

$$2a \times 3b = 2 \times a \times 3 \times b$$

Multiply the letters.

$$= 6 \times ab$$

$$= 6ab$$

___ **Example 6** ___

Simplify (a) $5a \times 4b$ (b) $3p \times 4q$

(a) $5a \times 4b$ so $5 \times 4 = 20$
$a \times b = ab$ and $20 \times ab = 20ab$

(b) $3p \times 4q$ so $3 \times 4 = 12$
$p \times q = pq$ and $12 \times pq = 12pq$

Exercise 3F

Simplify these expressions by multiplying the terms by each other. The first one is done for you.

1 $2a \times 4b = 8ab$ **2** $3c \times 5d$

3 $3p \times 4q$ **4** $5s \times 4t$

5 $6f \times 5g$ **6** $7p \times 4q$

7 $9m \times 4n$ **8** $3a \times 4b \times 2c$

9 $3r \times 4s \times 2t$ **10** $5p \times 4q$

11 $2a \times 6b$ **12** $5p \times 4q \times 2r$

13 $3t \times 4s$ **14** $4p \times 7t$

15 $9e \times 5c$ **16** $8g \times 4q \times 2r$

17 $4d \times 12r$ **18** $12s \times 5t$

19 $5y \times 6t$ **20** $2s \times 4t \times 5r$

3.7 Dividing algebraic expressions

You will sometimes need to divide algebraic expressions. To do this you will need to divide the numbers, and cancel the letters if possible.

Example 7

Simplify (a) $12a \div 4$ (b) $\dfrac{20ab}{5b}$

(a) $12a \div 4$ or $\dfrac{12a}{4}$ so $12 \div 4 = 3$ and $3 \times a = 3a$

(b) $\dfrac{20ab}{5b}$ or $20ab \div 5b$ so $20 \div 5 = 4$

$ab \div b = a$ and $4 \times a = 4a$

Exercise 3G

Simplify these expressions by dividing them by each other. The first one is done for you.

1 $12pq \div 3q = 4p$ **2** $3p \div 3$

3 $5a \div a$ **4** $12n \div 3$

5 $4e \div 2$ **6** $15s \div s$

7 $24b \div 6$ **8** $14ab \div 2b$

9 $18st \div 3t$ **10** $\dfrac{30xy}{5x}$

11 $\dfrac{30pq}{pq}$ **12** $\dfrac{12abc}{3c}$

13 $\dfrac{18ac}{6a}$ **14** $\dfrac{30xy}{2y}$

15 $\dfrac{36pq}{6}$

3.8 Calculating powers

There is a short way of writing repeated multiplication by the same number.

	How you write it:	How you say it:	
3×3	3^2	3 to the power 2	usually called 3 squared
$3 \times 3 \times 3$	3^3	3 to the power 3	usually called 3 cubed
$3 \times 3 \times 3 \times 3$	3^4	3 to the power 4	often called 3 to the fourth

Example 8

Work out (a) 3^2 (b) 5^3 (c) 2^6

(a) $3^2 = 3 \times 3 = 9$

(b) $5^3 = 5 \times 5 \times 5 = 125$

(c) $2^6 = 2 \times 2 \times 2 \times 2 \times 2 \times 2 = 64$

> Use the power button on your calculator to work out numbers raised to a power.

Example 9

Work out (a) $3^3 \times 4^2$ (b) $\dfrac{8^3}{2^3}$ (c) $5^2 + 3^3$

(a) $3^3 \times 4^2 = 27 \times 16 = 432$

(b) $\dfrac{8^3}{2^3} = \dfrac{512}{8} = 64$

(c) $5^2 + 3^3 = 25 + 27 = 52$

> A power is also known as an index. The plural of index is indices.

Example 10

Find the value of x.

(a) $8^x = 64$ (b) $3^x = 81$

(a) $8 \times 8 = 64$ so $8^2 = 64$ and $x = 2$

(b) $3 \times 3 \times 3 \times 3 = 81$ so $3^4 = 81$ and $x = 4$

Exercise 3H

1 Find the values of these powers:

(a) 3^2 (b) 2^3 (c) 1^4 (d) 5^4

(e) 2^5 (f) 4^3 (g) 2^4 (h) 2^7

(i) 6^3 (j) 5^3 (k) 5^2 (l) 10^5

> For example:
> $6^2 = 6 \times 6 = 36$

Work out the values of the powers in questions **2–4**.

2 (a) 3^6 (b) 5^5 (c) 0^2 (d) 9^4

3 (a) 4^2 (b) 10^3 (c) 9^5 (d) $4^3 + 3^2$

4 (a) 12^3 (b) 3^4 (c) 14^2 (d) $8^4 \div 2^3$

Find the value of x in questions **5–8**.

5 (a) $3^x = 27$ (b) $2^x = 8$ (c) $10^x = 100\,000$

6 (a) $6^x = 1296$ (b) $5^x = 125$ (c) $4^x = 256$

7 (a) $13^x = 169$ (b) $4^x = 4096$ (c) $11^x = 1331$

8 (a) $2^x = 1024$ (b) $9^x = 729$ (c) $15^x = 225$

There are 2^6 small squares on a chessboard.

3.9 Multiplying and dividing powers of the same number

Sometimes you need to write the product of two or more powers of a number as a single power of the same number.

$2^2 \times 2^3 = (2 \times 2) \times (2 \times 2 \times 2) = 2^5$

$3^3 \times 3^4 = (3 \times 3 \times 3) \times (3 \times 3 \times 3 \times 3) = 3^7$

> Notice that:
> $2^2 \times 2^3 = 2^{2+3} = 2^5$
> $3^3 \times 3^4 = 3^{3+4} = 3^7$

To **multiply** powers of the same number, add the indices:
$3^3 \times 3^4 = 3^{3+4} = 3^7$

You can use a similar method when you divide one power of a number by another power of the same number.

$5^6 \div 5^2 = \dfrac{5 \times 5 \times 5 \times 5 \times 5 \times 5}{5 \times 5} = 5 \times 5 \times 5 \times 5 = 5^4$

$4^5 \div 4^2 = \dfrac{4 \times 4 \times 4 \times 4 \times 4}{4} = 4 \times 4 \times 4 = 4^3$

> Notice that:
> $5^6 \div 5^2 = 5^{6-2} = 5^4$
> $4^5 \div 4^2 = 4^{5-2} = 4^3$

To **divide** powers of the same number, subtract the indices:
$4^5 \div 4^2 = 4^{5-2} = 4^3$

Example 11

Write these expressions as a single power of the number.

(a) $3^2 \times 3^3$ (b) $5^3 \times 5$

(c) $3^4 \times 3^2 \times 3^6$ (d) $7^5 \div 7^4$

(a) $3^2 \times 3^3 = 3^{2+3} = 3^5$

(b) $5^3 \times 5 = 5^{3+1} = 5^4$

(c) $3^4 \times 3^2 \times 3^6 = 3^{4+2+6} = 3^{12}$

(d) $7^5 \div 7^4 = 7^{5-4} = 7^1$

Raising a number to the power 1

Notice that $\dfrac{3^3}{3^2} = \dfrac{3 \times 3 \times 3}{3 \times 3} = 3$ and $\dfrac{3^3}{3^2} = 3^{3-2} = 3^1$

So $3^1 = 3$.

Any number raised to the **power 1** is equal to the number itself:
$3^1 = 3$

Raising a number to the power 0

Notice too that $\dfrac{3^2}{3^2} = 1$ and $\dfrac{3^2}{3^2} = 3^{2-2} = 3^0$

So $3^0 = 1$.

> Any non-zero number, raised to the **power 0** is equal to 1:
> $3^0 = 1$

Raising the power of a number to a further power

$(10^2)^3 = 10^2 \times 10^2 \times 10^2$
$\qquad\quad = (10 \times 10) \times (10 \times 10) \times (10 \times 10) = 10^6$

> Notice that:
> $(10^2)^3 = 10^{2\times3} = 10^6$

To raise a power of a number to a **further power**, multiply the indices:
   $(10^2)^3 = 10^{2\times3} = 10^6$

Exercise 3I

Simplify these expressions by writing as a single power of the number.

1 (a) $6^8 \times 6^3$ (b) $8^3 \times 8^5$ (c) $2^4 \times 2^2$

2 (a) $4^3 \div 4^2$ (b) $6^6 \div 6^3$ (c) $7^5 \div 7$

3 (a) $4^2 \times 4^3$ (b) $5^3 \div 5$ (c) $3^9 \div 3^8$

4 (a) $5^6 \times 5^4 \times 5^3$ (b) $2^3 \times 2^7 \times 2$

5 (a) $10^2 \times 10^2 \times 10$ (b) $9^4 \div 9^4$

6 (a) $6^3 \times 6^7 \times 6$ (b) $5^2 \times 5^2 \times 5^2$

7 (a) $3^5 \times 3 \times 3^2$ (b) $\dfrac{4^7 \times 4^5}{4^6}$

8 (a) $\dfrac{6^8}{6^2 \times 6^3}$ (b) $\dfrac{5^8 \times 5^4}{5^7}$ (c) $\dfrac{4^9}{4^2 \times 4^5}$

9 (a) $(5^2)^3$ (b) $(7^4)^2$

3.10 Using powers to multiply letters

When you want to multiply together two letters that are the same, you can write them as powers:

	How you write it:	How you say it:	
$a \times a$	a^2	a to the power 2	usually called a squared
$a \times a \times a$	a^3	a to the power 3	usually called a cubed
$a \times a \times a \times a$	a^4	a to the power 4	often called a to the fourth
$a \times a \times a \times a \times a$	a^5	a to the power 5	often called a to the fifth

Exercise 3J

1 Write these expressions in a simpler way using powers.

(a) $b \times b \times b$

(b) $p \times p$

(c) $r \times r \times r \times r \times r \times r \times r$

(d) $s \times s \times s \times s \times s$

(e) $q \times q \times q \times q$

(f) $c \times c \times c \times c \times c$

> For example: $d \times d = d^2$

2 Simplify these expressions using powers.

(a) $a \times a \times a \times a$

(b) $s \times s \times s$

(c) $t \times t \times t \times t \times t \times t$

(d) $v \times v \times v$

(e) $f \times f \times f \times f \times f$

(f) $y \times y \times y \times y \times y$

3 Write out these expressions in full.

(a) a^3

(b) a^4

(c) d^2

(d) e^5

(e) f^4

(f) p^5

(g) a^7

(h) s^2

(i) k^6

(j) n^3

(k) n^7

(l) a^{12}

> For example: $c^2 = c \times c$

4 Write these in a simpler form.

(a) a to the power 5

(b) b to the power 6

(c) c squared

(d) d cubed

(e) e to the power 7

3.11 Using powers to simplify

Section 3.9 showed how to multiply and divide with powers of numbers. You can use similar ideas in algebra.

$$x^4 \times x^3 = (x \times x \times x \times x) \times (x \times x \times x) = x^7$$

> Notice that:
> $x^4 \times x^3 = x^{4+3} = x^7$

To **multiply** powers of the same letter add the indices:
$$x^a \times x^b = x^{a+b}$$

$$x^6 \div x^2 = \frac{x \times x \times x \times x \times x \times x}{x \times x} = x \times x \times x \times x = x^4$$

> Notice that:
> $x^6 \div x^2 = x^{6-2} = x^4$

To **divide** powers of the same letter subtract the indices:
$$x^a \div x^b = x^{a-b}$$

Sometimes you will be asked to simplify an expression containing different powers of the same letter multiplied or divided.

To **simplify** an expression containing different powers of the same letter multiplied or divided, write the expression as a single power of the letter.

Example 12

Simplify (a) $x^8 \times x^3$ (b) $x^{16} \div x^2$ (c) $x^4 \times x^3 \times x^5$

(a) $x^8 \times x^3 = x^{8+3} = x^{11}$

(b) $x^{16} \div x^2 = x^{16-2} = x^{14}$

(c) $x^4 \times x^3 \times x^5 = x^{4+3+5} = x^{12}$

Example 13

Simplify (a) $3y^2 \times 4y^3$ (b) $12y^8 \div 4y^3$

(a) $3y^2 \times 4y^3 = 3 \times 4 \times y^2 \times y^3 = 12 \times y^{2+3} = 12y^5$

(b) $12y^8 \div 4y^3 = \dfrac{12y^8}{4y^3} = \dfrac{12}{4} \times \dfrac{y^8}{y^3} = 3 \times y^{8-3} = 3y^5$

Exercise 3K

Simplify these expressions.

1 (a) $x^8 \times x^2$ (b) $y^3 \times y^8$ (c) $w^9 \times w^5$

2 (a) $a^5 \times a^3$ (b) $b^3 \times b^3$ (c) $d^7 \times d^4$

3 (a) $p^5 \div p^2$ (b) $q^{12} \div q^2$ (c) $t^8 \div t^4$

4 (a) $j^9 \div j^3$ (b) $k^5 \div k^4$ (c) $n^{25} \div n^{23}$

5 (a) $x^5 \times x^2 \times x^2$ (b) $y^2 \times y^4 \times y^3$ (c) $z^3 \times z^5 \times z^2$

6 (a) $3x^2 \times 2x^3$ (b) $5y^9 \times 3y^{20}$ (c) $6z^8 \times 4z^2$

7 (a) $12p^8 \div 4p^3$ (b) $15q^5 \div 3q^3$ (c) $6r^5 \div 3r^2$

Raising a letter to the power 1 or 0

Notice that $\dfrac{x^3}{x^2} = \dfrac{x \times x \times x}{x \times x} = x$ and $\dfrac{x^3}{x^2} = x^{3-2} = x^1$

Any letter raised to the **power 1** is equal to the letter itself:
  $x^1 = x$

Notice too that $\dfrac{y^2}{y^2} = 1$ and $\dfrac{y^2}{y^2} = y^{2-2} = y^0$

Any letter raised to the **power 0** is equal to 1:
  $y^0 = 1$

Raising a power to a further power

$$(x^2)^3 = x^2 \times x^2 \times x^2$$
$$= (x \times x) \times (x \times x) \times (x \times x) = x^6$$

To raise a power of a letter to a **further power**, multiply the indices:

$$(x^a)^b = x^{ab}$$

Example 14

Simplify: (a) $(x^4)^5$ (b) $(3y^5)^3$

(a) $(x^4)^5 = x^{4 \times 5} = x^{20}$

(b) $(3y^5)^3 = 3^3 \times (y^5)^3 = 27 \times y^{5 \times 3} = 27y^{15}$

Exercise 3L

Simplify these expressions.

1 (a) $(d^3)^4$ (b) $(e^5)^2$ (c) $(f^3)^3$ (d) $(g^7)^9$

2 (a) $(g^6)^4$ (b) $(h^2)^2$ (c) $(k^4)^0$ (d) $(m^0)^{56}$

3 (a) $(3d^2)^7$ (b) $(4e)^3$ (c) $(3f^{129})^0$

4 (a) $\dfrac{a^4 \times a^5}{a^9}$ (b) $\dfrac{b^7 \times b}{b^4}$ (c) $\dfrac{c^3 \times c^4}{c^2 \times c^5}$

5 (a) $4d^9 \times 2d$ (b) $8e^8 \div 4e^4$ (c) $(4f^2)^2$

3.12 Putting in the punctuation

In maths, brackets help show the order in which you should carry out the operations $\div$, $\times$, $+$ and $-$. For example:

$$2 + (3 \times 4) = 2 + 12 = 14 \quad \text{and} \quad (2 + 3) \times 4 = 5 \times 4 = 20$$

So $2 + (3 \times 4)$ is different from $(2 + 3) \times 4$ even though they both use the same numbers and the $+$ and $\times$ symbols in the same order.

Always deal with the operations in brackets first.
Then $\div$ and $\times$. Then $+$ and $-$.

BIDMAS is a made-up word to help you remember the order of operations:

BIDMAS

| Brackets | Indices | Divide | Multiply | Add | Subtract |

When the operations are the same, you do them in the order they appear.

Example 15

Work out   (a) $(3 \times 2) - 1$ (b) $3 \times (2 - 1)$

(a) $(3 \times 2) - 1 = 6 - 1 = 5$
(b) $3 \times (2 - 1) = 3 \times 1 = 3$

> Work out the Brackets first.

Example 16

Work out   (a) $3 + 2 \times 5 - 1$ (b) $24 \div 4 \div 2$

(a) $3 + 2 \times 5 - 1$

  $= 3 + 10 - 1$

  $= 13 - 1$
  $= 12$

(b) $24 \div 4 \div 2$
  $= 6 \div 2$
  $= 3$

> There is no Bracket or Divide, so start with Multiply, then Add, then Subtract.

> Operations are the same so do them in the order they appear.

Example 17

Work out   (a) $(2 + 3)^2$ (b) $2^2 + 3^2$

(a) $(2 + 3)^2 = 5^2 = 25$
(b) $2^2 + 3^2 = 4 + 9 = 13$

Notice that the answers are different: $(2 + 3)^2$ is not the same as $2^2 + 3^2$.

> Brackets first, then Indices.

> Indices first, then Add.

Exercise 3M

1   Use BIDMAS to help you find the value of these expressions:

(a) $5 + (3 + 1)$ (b) $5 - (3 + 1)$
(c) $5 \times (2 + 3)$ (d) $5 \times 2 + 3$
(e) $3 \times (4 + 3)$ (f) $3 \times 4 + 3$
(g) $20 \div 4 + 1$ (h) $20 \div (4 + 1)$
(i) $6 + 4 \div 2$ (j) $(6 + 4) \div 2$
(k) $24 \div (6 - 2)$ (l) $24 \div 6 - 2$
(m) $7 - (4 + 2)$ (n) $7 - 4 + 2$
(o) $((15 - 5) \times 4) \div ((2 + 3) \times 2)$

$9 + 2 \times 5 = 19$, not 55. Can you explain why?

2   Make these expressions correct by replacing the • with
+ or − or × or ÷ and using brackets if you need to.
The first one is done for you.

(a) $4 • 5 = 9$ becomes $4 + 5 = 9$ (b) $4 • 5 = 20$
(c) $2 • 3 • 4 = 20$ (d) $3 • 2 • 5 = 5$
(e) $5 • 2 • 3 = 9$ (f) $4 • 2 • 8 = 10$
(g) $5 • 4 • 5 • 2 = 27$ (h) $5 • 4 • 5 • 2 = 23$

3   Work out

(a) $(3 + 4)^2$ (b) $3^2 + 4^2$ (c) $3 \times (4 + 5)^2$
(d) $3 \times 4^2 + 3 \times 5^2$ (e) $2 \times (4 + 2)^2$ (f) $2^3 + 3^2$

(g) $2 \times (3^2 + 2)$ (h) $\dfrac{(2 + 5)^2}{3^2 - 2}$ (i) $\dfrac{5^2 - 2^2}{3}$

(j) $4^2 - 2^4$ (k) $2^5 - 5^2$ (l) $4^3 - 8^2$

3.13 Using brackets in algebra

Brackets are often used in algebra. For example:

$2 \times (a + b)$ means   add a to b *before* multiplying by 2

Usually this is written: $2(a + b)$, without the $\times$. This avoids
confusion with the letter x which is used a lot in algebra.

$2(a + b)$ means $2 \times a + 2 \times b = 2a + 2b$

Working this out is called **expanding the brackets**. Actually
the brackets disappear!

Example 18

Expand the brackets in these expressions:
(a) $3(b + c)$ (b) $3(2a − b)$

(a) $3(b + c) = 3 \times b + 3 \times c = 3b + 3c$
(b) $3(2a − b) = 3 \times 2a + 3 \times −b = 6a − 3b$

Expanding the brackets means multiplying to remove the
brackets.

Exercise 3N

Expand the brackets in these expressions.

1 $2(p + q)$ **2** $3(c + d)$ **3** $5(y − n)$

4 $3(t + u)$ **5** $7(2p + q)$ **6** $2(3a − 2b)$

7 $4(2a + b)$ **8** $3(a − 2b)$ **9** $3(4r − 5s)$

10 $10(a − 7b)$ **11** $4(6s + 4t)$ **12** $5(6p + 4q − 2r)$

13 $12(3a + 4b)$ **14** $7(4s − 5t)$ **15** $3(5a − 4b + 2c)$

Adding expressions with brackets

You can simplify an expression by first expanding the brackets and then collecting like terms.

___ Example 19 ___

Simplify $2(a + 3b) + 5(2a - b)$

$2(a + 3b) + 5(2a - b)$

$= 2 \times a + 2 \times 3b + 5 \times 2a + 5 \times -b$

$= 2a + 6b + 10a - 5b$

$= 2a + 10a + 6b - 5b$

$= 12a + b$

> First expand the brackets.

> Now collect like terms.

Exercise 30

Expand the brackets in these expressions and then collect like terms.

> Remember:
> $4a$ means $a + a + a + a$
> and $4 \times a$
> $3ab$ means $3 \times a \times b$
> $3(c + d)$ means $3c + 3d$

1 $2(a + b) + 3(a + b)$

2 $3(a - 2b) + 4(2a + 3b)$

3 $5(2a - b) + 4(2a + b)$

4 $3(p + q) + 4(p + q)$

5 $4(5a + c) + 2(3a - c)$

6 $3(p + 2q) + 3(5p - 2q)$

7 $5(4t - 3s) + 8(3t + 2s)$

8 $7(2d + 3e) + 6(2e - 2d)$

9 $5(3z + b) + 4(b - 2z)$

10 $2(a + b + 2c) + 3(2a + 3b - c)$

11 $3(4a - 2b) + 5(a + b)$

12 $6(p + 2q + 3r) + 2(3p - 4q - 9r)$

13 $4(3a + 5b) + 5(2a - 4b)$

14 $5(5g + 4h) + 4(h - 5g)$

15 $2(a + 2b - 3c) + 3(5a - b + 4c) + 4(a + b + c)$

Subtracting expressions with brackets

___ Example 20 ___

Expand the brackets in the expression $15 - (6 + 2)$

The minus sign belongs with the term in brackets.

$15 - (6 + 2)$ means $15 + -1 \times (6 + 2)$

$= 15 \quad - 6 \quad - 2$

$= 7$

> Remember:
> When you multiply:
> like signs give +
> $2 \times 3 = 6$
> $-2 \times -3 = 6$
> unlike signs give −
> $2 \times -3 = -6$
> $-2 \times 3 = -6$

Example 21

Expand   (a) $-(a + b)$ (b) $-(a - b)$

(a) $-(a + b)$ means $-1 \times (a + b) = -a - b$

(b) $-(a - b)$ means $-1 \times (a - b) = -a + b$

> $-1 \times +b = -b$

> $-1 \times -b = +b$

Exercise 3P

1 Work out

    (a) $10 - (3 + 2)$ (b) $20 - (5 - 2)$ (c) $12 - (6 - 4)$
    (d) $10 - (3 + 4)$ (e) $12 - (5 + 3)$ (f) $6 - (7 - 5)$
    (g) $14 - (8 + 6)$ (h) $15 - (3 - 2)$

2 Expand the bracket in these expressions.

    (a) $-(p + q)$ (b) $-(p - q)$ (c) $-(a + b + c)$
    (d) $-(a + b - c)$ (e) $-(r + s)$ (f) $-(r - s)$
    (g) $-(p + q - r)$ (h) $-(p - q + r)$

Example 22

Write $3a + 2b - (a + b)$ as simply as possible.

$$3a + 2b - (a + b) = 3a + 2b - a - b$$
$$= 2a + b$$

Exercise 3Q

Write these expressions as simply as possible.

1 $4a + 3b - (a + b)$ **2** $5p + 2q - (p + q)$

3 $3(2a + 4) - (3a + 5)$ **4** $2y - 3z - (y + z)$

5 $3(3r + 4s) - 2(r + s)$ **6** $3(2a + 5) - 2(3a + 4)$

7 $5(2s + 3t) - 4(s + 2t)$ **8** $4(3a + b) - 3(2a + 5b)$

9 $2(m + 3n) - (2m + n)$ **10** $5(8h - 3k) - 4(7h + 2k)$

11 $3(c + 2d) - 2(c + 3d)$ **12** $4a - (3a + 5b)$

Example 23

> Watch out for the $-$ sign inside the bracket.

Write $3a + 2b - 2(a - b)$ as simply as possible.

> Multiplying gives $-2 \times -b = +2b$

$$3a + 2b - 2(a - b) = 3a + 2b - 2a + 2b$$
$$= a + 4b$$

Exercise 3R

Simplify these expressions. They *all* have − signs inside brackets.

1 $4a + 3b - (a - b)$ **2** $5p + 2q - (p - q)$

3 $3(2a + 4) - (3a - 5)$ **4** $2y - 3z - (y - z)$

5 $3(3r + 4s) - 2(r - s)$ **6** $3(2a + 5) - 2(3a - 4)$

7 $5(2s + 3t) - 4(s - 2t)$ **8** $4(3a + b) - 3(2a - 5b)$

9 $2(m + 3n) - (2m - n)$ **10** $5(8h - 3k) - 4(7h - 2k)$

11 $3(c + 2d) - 2(c - 3d)$ **12** $4a - (3a - 5b)$

More about expanding brackets

You can expand an expression such as $a(x + y)$ in the same way as $2(a + b)$ on page 60.

___ **Example 24** _____

Expand $a(x + 2y)$

$$a(x + 2y) = a \times (x + 2y)$$
$$= a \times x + a \times 2y$$
$$= ax + 2ay$$

> In algebra letters are usually put in alphabetical order.

___ **Example 25** _____

Expand $b^2(3a + b)$

$$b^2(3a + b) = b^2 \times 3a + b^2 \times b$$
$$= 3ab^2 + b^3$$

Exercise 3S

1 Expand

  (a) $x(a + 2)$ (b) $y(3 - x)$
  (c) $ax(b + 2c)$ (d) $a(2a^2 + 1)$
  (e) $ab(a + b)$ (f) $a^2(x + y)$
  (g) $2p(3p - 4q)$ (h) $3a(2a + 3b)$
  (i) $abc(3 - a - bc)$ (j) $q(p + pr)$

2 Expand and simplify

  (a) $a(b + c) + c(a + b)$ (b) $b(3 - b) + 2(b^2 - b)$
  (c) $2x(x + 3) - 5(x^2 + x)$ (d) $r^2(3s - r) 2s(rs r^2)$
  (e) $2p(q + 1) + 3q(2 - p)$ (f) $p(x - y) - y(x - p)$

3.14 Factorising algebraic expressions

The opposite process to multiplying out brackets is called **factorising**. Factorising means splitting an expression into parts.

You can factorise numbers:

$12 = 4 \times 3$ 4 and 3 are both factors of 12.

$12 = 2 \times 6$ 2 and 6 are factors of 12 as well.

You can also factorise algebraic expressions:

$ab = a \times b$ a and b are factors of ab

$2pq = 2 \times p \times q$ 2, p and q are factors of $2pq$

$x^2 = x \times x$ x and x are factors of x^2

To factorise a more complex expression you need to find factors common to all the terms.

___

Example 26

Factorise $12a + 4b$

$12a + 4b = ④ \times 3 \times a + ④ \times b$ ——— 4 is common to both terms.

$ = 4(\qquad)$ ———————— Place 4 outside a bracket.

$ = 4(3a + b)$ ———————— Work out what is missing from inside the bracket.

This process is called factorising.

$4(3a + b) = 12a + 4b$ —————————— Check that the factorised expression is equivalent to the original.

___

Example 27

Factorise $2x^2 + 5x$

This can be written as:

$2 \times ⓧ \times x + 5 \times ⓧ$ ———— x is common to both terms.

$= x(\qquad)$ ———————————— Place x outside a bracket.

$= x(2x + 5)$ ———————————— Now make the expression equivalent to the original.

___

Example 28

Factorise $12a^2 - 4ab$

This can be written as:

$④ \times 3 \times ⓐ \times a - ④ \times ⓐ \times b$ — 4 and a are common to both terms.

$= 4a(\qquad)$ ———————————— Place $4a$ outside a bracket.

$= 4a(3a - b)$ ——————————— Now make the expression equivalent to the original.

You won't be splitting us up...

Factorising means splitting up an expression using brackets.

Exercise 3T

1 Factorise
(a) $x^2 + 3x$
(b) $a^2 - ab$
(c) $p^2 + pq$
(d) $3a + 12b$
(e) $5a + 10$
(f) $2b - 4c$
(g) $4 + 8a$
(h) $2a - 2$
(i) $3a + 9$
(j) $5p + 25$
(k) $4a + 16$
(l) $4p - 8$
(m) $7x - 14$
(n) $7y + 7$
(o) $7y^2 + y$
(p) $5q - 15$
(q) $x^2 + 2x$
(r) $y^2 + 3y$
(s) $3a - 3$
(t) $2a^4 + 3a$
(u) $3xy - 4xz$
(v) $4a^2 - 5a$
(w) $5a^5 - 4a$
(x) $5x^2 + 4x$

Factorise each of the expressions in questions **2–7**.

2 (a) $2x + 6$
(b) $6y + 2$
(c) $15b - 5$
(d) $4r - 2$
(e) $3x + 5xy$
(f) $12x + 8y$
(g) $12x - 16$
(h) $9 - 3x$
(i) $9 + 15g$

3 (a) $3x^2 + 4x$
(b) $5y^2 - 3y$
(c) $2a^2 + a$
(d) $5b^2 - 2b$
(e) $7c - 3c^2$
(f) $d^2 + 3d$
(g) $6m^2 - m$
(h) $4xy + 3x$
(i) $n^3 - 8n^2$

4 (a) $8x^2 + 4x$
(b) $6p^2 + 3p$
(c) $6x^2 - 3x$
(d) $3b^2 - 9b$
(e) $12a + 3a^2$
(f) $15c - 10c^2$
(g) $21x^4 + 14x^3$
(h) $16y^3 - 12y^2$
(i) $6d^4 - 4d^2$

5 (a) $ax^2 + ax$
(b) $pr^2 - pr$
(c) $ab^2 - ab$
(d) $qr^2 - q^2$
(e) $a^2x + ax^2$
(f) $b^2y - by^2$
(g) $6a^3 - 9a^2$
(h) $8x^3 - 4x^4$
(i) $18x^3 + 12x^5$

6 (a) $12a^2b + 18ab^2$
(b) $4x^2y - 2xy^2$
(c) $4a^2b + 8ab^2 + 12ab$
(d) $4x^2y + 6xy^2 - 2xy$
(e) $12ax^2 + 6a^2x - 3ax$
(f) $a^2bc + ab^2c + abc^2$

7 (a) $5x + 20$
(b) $12y - 10$
(c) $3x^2 + 5x$
(d) $4y - 3y^2$
(e) $8a + 6a^2$
(f) $12b^2 - 8b$
(g) $cy^2 + cy$
(h) $3dx^2 - 6dx$
(i) $9c^2d + 15cd^2$

Mixed exercise 3

1 (a) Simplify
  (i) $c + c + c + c$
  (ii) $p \times p \times p \times p$
  (iii) $3g + 5g$
  (iv) $2r \times 5p$
(b) Expand $5(2y - 3)$
(c) Factorise $15a + 10$ [E]

2 Audrey sells packets of sweets.
There are three sizes of packets.

There are n sweets in the small packet.
There are twice as many sweets in the medium packet as there are in the small packet.

(a) Write down an expression, in terms of n, for the number of sweets in the medium packet.

There are 15 more sweets in the large packet than in the medium packet.

(b) Write down an expression, in terms of n, for the number of sweets in the large packet.

A small packet of sweets costs 20p.
Sebastian buys q small packets of sweets.

(c) Write down an expression, in terms of q, for the cost in pence of the sweets. [E]

3 Eggs are sold in boxes.
A small box holds 6 eggs.

Hina buys x small boxes of eggs.

(a) Write down in terms of x, the total number of eggs in these small boxes.

A large box holds 12 eggs.
Hina buys 4 less of the large boxes of eggs than the small boxes.

(b) Write down, in terms of x, the number of large boxes she buys.

(c) Find, in terms of x, the total number of eggs in the large boxes that Hina buys.

(d) Find, in terms of x, the total number of eggs that Hina buys.
Give your answer in its simplest form. [E]

4 (a) Simplify $y + y$
(b) Simplify $p^2 + p^2 + p^2$
(c) Factorise $x^2 - 3x$
(d) Expand the bracket $5(2q + 7)$ [E]

5 Factorise each of these expressions.
(a) $5x + 10$ (b) $6y - 9$ (c) $4a + 9ab$
(d) $10xy - 11y$ (e) $2xy + 4x$ (f) $6a - 9ab$
(g) $4x^2 - 8x$ (h) $12xy^2 + 4x^2y - 2xy$

6 Simplify fully
    (a) $x^5 \times x^3$ **(b)** $4y^3 \times 5y^5$ **(c)** $12p^5 \div 3p^2$

7 Work out
    (a) $5^6 \div 5^4$ **(b)** $64 \div 2^4$ **(c)** $\dfrac{9^2 \times 3^3}{27}$

8 Find the value of x when $2^x \times 2^2 = 2^8$

Summary of key points

1 An **algebraic expression** is a collection of letters, symbols and numbers:

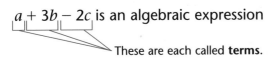

    $a + 3b - 2c$ is an algebraic expression

                        These are each called **terms**.

    Terms which use the same letter or arrangement of letters are called **like terms**.
        a and $3a$ are like terms $2g$ and $8g$ are like terms

2 You can combine **like terms** by adding or subtracting them:
    $2a + 3a = 5a$ and $3b + 4b - b = 6b$

3 You can simplify algebraic expressions by **collecting like terms** together:
    $2a - 4b + 3a + 5b$ simplifies to $5a + b$

4 The ^{2} in 7^2 is called an **index** or **power**. It tells you how many times the given number must be multiplied by itself.

5 To **multiply** powers of the same number or letter, add the indices:
    $3^3 \times 3^4 = 3^{3+4} = 3^7$ $x^a \times x^b = x^{a+b}$

6 To **divide** powers of the same number or letter, subtract the indices:
    $4^5 \div 4^2 = 4^{5-2} = 4^3$ $x^a \div x^b = x^{a-b}$

7 Any number or letter raised to the **power 1** is equal to the number or letter itself:
    $3^1 = 3$ $x^1 = x$

    Any non-zero number or letter, raised to the **power 0** is equal to 1:
    $3^0 = 1$ $y^0 = 1$

8 To raise a power of a number or letter to a **further power**, multiply the indices:
    $(10^2)^3 = 10^{2 \times 3} = 10^6$ $(x^a)^b = x^{ab}$

9 To **simplify** an expression containing different powers of the same letter multiplied or divided, write the expression as a single power of the letter.

10 BIDMAS is a made-up word to help you remember the order of operations:

11 When the operations are the same you do them in the order they appear.

$10 \div 2 \div 5 = 5 \div 5 = 1$

12 Expanding the brackets means multiplying to remove the brackets:

$4(3a + b) = 12a + 4b$

13 Factorising means splitting up an expression using brackets:

$12a + 4b = 4(3a + b)$

4 Patterns and sequences

4.1 Number patterns

Sometimes you will need to find the missing numbers in a number pattern like this one:

2, 4, 6, 8, 10, —, —, 16, 18

Algebra can help you do this. But first let's explore some number patterns.

2, 4, 6, 8, 10, —, —, 16, 18

The two missing numbers are 12 and 14.

The rule for this pattern is: **add 2 each time**.

> This pattern is also the two times table, and all the numbers are multiples of 2.

0, 4, 8, 12, 16, —, —, 28, 32

The two missing numbers are 20 and 24.

The rule for this pattern is: **add 4 each time**.

> This pattern is also the four times table, and all the numbers are multiples of 4.

In a number pattern or **sequence** there is a **rule** to get from one number to the next.

Exercise 4A

Find the two missing numbers in these number patterns.
Write down the rule for each pattern too.

1 3, 6, 9, —, —, 18, 21   **2** 5, 10, 15, 20, —, —, 35, 40

3 1, 2, 3, 4, —, —, 7, 8   **4** 7, 14, 21, 28, —, —, 49, 56

5 0, 6, 12, —, —, 30, 36   **6** 10, 20, 30, —, —, 60, 70

7 5, 7, 9, 11, —, —, 17, 19   **8** 4, 7, 10, 13, —, —, 22, 25

9 3, 8, 13, 18, —, —, 33, 38   **10** 1, 5, 9, 13, —, —, 25, 29

Smaller and smaller

Sometimes the numbers in a pattern get smaller each time.

Example 1

Find the missing numbers in this number pattern:

18, 16, 14, 12, —, —, 6, 4, 2, 0

The missing numbers are 10 and 8.

The rule for this pattern is: **take away 2 each time**.

Exercise 4B

Find the two missing numbers in these number patterns.
Write down the rule for each pattern too.

1 21, 18, 15, 12, —, —, 3   **2** 24, 20, 16, —, —, 4, 0

3 30, 25, 20, —, —, 5, 0   **4** 49, 42, 35, 28, —, —, 7

5 28, 25, 22, 19, 16, —, —, 7   **6** 37, 32, 27, 22, —, —, 7

7 19, 17, 15, —, —, 9, 7   **8** 25, 21, 17, —, —, 5, 1

9 33, 28, 23, —, —, 8, 3   **10** 45, 38, 31, 24, —, —, 3

Larger and larger

Example 2

Find the missing numbers in this number pattern:

1, 2, 4, 8, —, —, 64, 128

The missing numbers are 16 and 32.

The rule for this pattern is: **multiply by 2 each time**.

The numbers in the pattern are also all powers of 2:

$$1 = 1 \qquad\qquad = 2^0$$
$$2 = 2 \qquad\qquad = 2^1$$
$$4 = 2 \times 2 \qquad = 2^2$$
$$8 = 2 \times 2 \times 2 \qquad = 2^3$$
$$16 = 2 \times 2 \times 2 \times 2 = 2^4$$

etc.

Exercise 4C

Find the missing numbers in these number patterns.
Write down the rule for each pattern too.

1 1, 3, 9, —, —, 243   **2** 1, 4, 16, —, 256

3 1, —, 25, 125, —, 3125   **4** 1, 10, 100, —, —, 100 000

5 3, 6, 12, —, —, 96   **6** 2, 6, 18, —, —, 486

7 2, 8, 32, —, —, 2048   **8** 2, 20, 200, —, —, 200 000

9 2, 10, 50, —, 1250   **10** 3, 15, 75, —, 1875

Example 3

Find the missing number in this number pattern:

   243, 81, 27, —, 3, 1

The rule for this pattern is: **divide by 3 each time.**

The missing number is 9.

> The numbers in the pattern are also all powers of 3:
>
> $243 = 3 \times 3 \times 3 \times 3 \times 3 = 3^5$
> $81 = 3 \times 3 \times 3 \times 3 \quad = 3^4$
> $27 = 3 \times 3 \times 3 \quad\quad = 3^3$
> $9 = 3 \times 3 \quad\quad\quad = 3^2$
> $3 = 3 \quad\quad\quad\quad = 3^1$
> $1 = 3 \div 3 \quad\quad\quad = 3^0$

Exercise 4D

Find the missing numbers in these number patterns.
Write down the rule for each pattern too.

1   128, 64, 32, —, 8, 4, —, 1

2   256, 64, —, 4, 1

3   100 000, 10 000, —, —, 10

4   625, 125, —, 5, 1

5   96, 48, 24, —, —, 3

6   486, 162, 54, —, —, 2

7   2048, 512, 128, —, —, 2

8   200 000, 20 000, 2000, —, —, 2

9   1250, 250, 50, —, 2

10   1875, 375, 75, —, 3

4.2 Finding the rule for a number pattern

Examples 4, 5 and 6 have some more difficult number patterns, with some hints on how to find their rules.

Example 4

Pattern ——————— 1,   4,   7,   10,   13,   ...

Differences between —— +3   +3   +3   +3
pairs of numbers

> The dots mean the pattern continues.

The rule is: **add 3 each time.**
So the next number is 16.

Example 5

Pattern ——— 1, 4, 9, 16, 25, ...

Differences ——— +3 +5 +7 +9

The rule is: **add the next odd number each time.**
The *difference* goes up by 2 each time.

Example 6

Pattern ——— 1, 1, 2, 3, 5, 8, 13, ...

Differences ——— +0 +1 +1 +2 +3 +5

The rule is: **add the previous two numbers each time.**
The *differences have the same pattern* as the pattern itself.

This is called the Fibonacci sequence. It is named after a
famous Italian mathematician.

Fibonacci numbers
(1, 1, 2, 3, 5, 8, 13, 21, 34, ...)
often appear in nature.
Ordinary field daisies have
34 petals.

Exercise 4E

Write out each pattern in the same way as in Examples 4, 5
and 6. Find the differences and rule for each one, and the
next number.

1 1, 3, 5, 7, 9, ...   **2** 1, 5, 9, 13, 17, ...

3 1, 8, 27, 64, 125, ...   **4** 2, 4, 6, 8, 10, ...

5 2, 5, 8, 11, 14, ...   **6** 3, 7, 11, 15, 19, ...

7 2, 2, 4, 6, 10, 16, ...   **8** 3, 3, 6, 9, 15, 24, ...

9 3, 5, 7, 9, 11, 13, ...   **10** 4, 7, 10, 13, 16, ...

11 2, 7, 12, 17, 22, ...   **12** 3, 8, 13, 18, 23, ...

4.3 Using algebra to write the rule for a number pattern

You can use algebra to write a rule to find any number in a
pattern or sequence.

A sequence is a set of
numbers in order.

Each number in a pattern is called a **term.**

Here is a pattern made with crosses.

```
 ×       ××      ×××     ××××     ×××××
 ×       ××      ×××     ××××     ×××××
```

Pattern number 1 | Pattern number 3 | Pattern number 5

Pattern number 2 | Pattern number 4

To find the number of crosses in pattern number 20 you need a rule to find the **20th term**.

> The number of crosses in pattern number 20 is the 20th term.

Step 1 Make a table. Fill in the pattern numbers and numbers of crosses.

Step 2 Find the differences between the numbers of crosses.

Pattern number	Number of crosses
1	2
2	4
3	6
4	8
5	10
⋮	

Pattern number	Number of crosses	Difference
1	2	
2	4	+2
3	6	+2
4	8	+2
5	10	+2
⋮		

It is easy to use the rule **+2** to find the next term, but not so easy to find the 20th term.

You can use the difference (2) to help you find another rule:

   1st term $= 1 \times 2 = 2$
   2nd term $= 2 \times 2 = 4$
   3rd term $= 3 \times 2 = 6$

The new rule is: **multiply the term number by 2**.

This is the **general rule** for this pattern: the nth term is $2n$.

You can use the general rule to find any term:

   20th term $= 20 \times 2 = 40$

When you know the nth term of a pattern, you can calculate any term in the pattern by replacing 'n' with the pattern number.

Example 7

(a) Find the general rule for the nth term in this pattern:

   1, 4, 7, 10, 13, ...

(b) Use the general rule to find the 20th term.

(a) Make a table:

Term number	Term	Difference
1	1	
2	4	+3
3	7	+3
4	10	+3
5	13	+3

> The rule is add 3. So the number in front of the n is 3.

1st term $= 1 \times 3 - 2 = 1$
2nd term $= 2 \times 3 - 2 = 4$
3rd term $= 3 \times 3 - 2 = 7$

The nth term is $n \times 3 - 2$
The general rule is $3n - 2$

(b) The 20th term is $(3 \times 20) - 2 = 58$

> When you have multiplied the term number by 3, you then need to subtract 2 in order to get the number in the sequence.

Exercise 4F

1

4 matches   7 matches   10 matches

(a) Draw the next two patterns.
(b) Complete this table.

Term number	1	2	3	4	5
Matches used	4	7	10		

(c) Write down the rule to find the 6th term.
(d) Find the general rule for the nth term.

2 For these patterns:
(a) Draw the next two patterns.
(b) Write down the rule to find the next pattern.
(c) Find the nth term in the pattern.
(d) Use your rule to find the 10th term.

   (i) $\begin{matrix} \times \\ \times \end{matrix}$ $\begin{matrix} \times\times \\ \times\times \end{matrix}$ $\begin{matrix} \times\times\times \\ \times\times\times \end{matrix}$ $\begin{matrix} \times\times\times\times \\ \times\times\times\times \end{matrix}$

  (ii)

 (iii)

 (iv)    [E]

  (v) $\begin{matrix} & \times \\ \times & \times\times \end{matrix}$ $\begin{matrix} \times\times \\ \times\times\times \end{matrix}$ $\begin{matrix} \times\times\times \\ \times\times\times\times \end{matrix}$ $\begin{matrix} \times\times\times\times \\ \times\times\times\times\times \end{matrix}$

 (vi) $\begin{matrix} \times \\ \times\times \end{matrix}$ $\begin{matrix} \times\times \\ \times\times\times \end{matrix}$ $\begin{matrix} \times\times\times \\ \times\times\times\times \end{matrix}$ $\begin{matrix} \times\times\times\times \\ \times\times\times\times\times \end{matrix}$

3 Find the general rule for the number of matches needed to make the *n*th pattern in this sequence:

4 Write each pattern in a table in the same way as in Example 7. Find the general rule for the *n*th term. Then use your rule to find the 20th term.

(a) 3, 6, 9, 12, 15, 18, 21, ...

(b) 5, 10, 15, 20, 25, 30, 35, 40, ...

(c) 1, 2, 3, 4, 5, 6, 7, 8, ...

(d) 7, 14, 21, 28, 35, 42, 49, 56, ...

(e) 0, 6, 12, 18, 24, 30, 36, ...

(f) 10, 20, 30, 40, 50, 60, 70, ...

(g) 5, 7, 9, 11, 13, 15, 17, 19, ...

(h) 4, 7, 10, 13, 16, 19, 22, 25, ...

(i) 3, 8, 13, 18, 23, 28, 33, 38, ...

(j) 1, 5, 9, 13, 17, 21, 25, 29, ...

(k) 1, 3, 5, 7, 9, 11, ...

(l) 3, 5, 7, 9, 11, 13, ...

(m) 2, 5, 8, 11, 14, 17, ...

(n) 5, 8, 11, 14, 17, 20, ...

(o) 1, 5, 9, 13, 17, 21, ...

(p) 2, 6, 10, 14, 18, 22, ...

(q) 2, 7, 12, 17, 22, 27, ...

(r) 4, 9, 14, 19, 24, 29, ...

(s) 40, 35, 30, 25, 20, ...

(t) 38, 36, 34, 32, 30, ...

To find the general term of a sequence that gets smaller, you subtract a multiple of *n* from a fixed number. For example, $15 - 2n$ is the general term for 13, 11, 9, 7, 5, ...

4.4 Is a number part of a sequence?

Sometimes you will be asked: *How do you know if a number is part of a pattern or sequence?*

You have to find out if the number is in the sequence or not, and then explain how you know this.

Example 8

Here is a number pattern:

2, 7, 12, 17, 22, ...

(a) Explain why 422 is in the pattern.
(b) Explain why 325 is not in the pattern.

There are different ways of answering questions like these.
Here are some possibilities:

(a)   (i) Every even term ends in 2 and they go up 2, 12,
          22, ..., so 422 will be in the pattern as it ends in a 2.
     (ii) The nth term is $5n - 3$, so if 422 is in the pattern
          $$5n - 3 = 422$$
          $$5n = 425$$
          $$n = 85,$$ so 422 is the 85th term in the pattern.
(b)   (i) 325 ends in a 5 and every member of the pattern
          ends in either a 2 or a 7, so 325 cannot be in the
          pattern.
     (ii) The nth term is $5n - 3$ so if 325 is in the pattern
          $$5n - 3 = 325$$
          $$5n = 328$$
          $$n = 65.6$$
          If 325 is in the pattern n must be a whole
          number. But 65.6 is not a whole number so 325 is
          not in the pattern.

Exercise 4G

For each of these number patterns, explain whether the
numbers in brackets are members of the number pattern.

1   1, 3, 5, 7, 9, 11, ...   (21, 34)

2   3, 5, 7, 9, 11, 13, ...   (63, 86)

3   2, 5, 8, 11, 14, 17, ...   (50, 66)

4   5, 8, 11, 14, 17, 20, ...   (101, 98)

5   1, 5, 9, 13, 17, 21, ...   (101, 150)

6   2, 6, 10, 14, 18, 22, ...   (101, 98)

7   2, 7, 12, 17, 22, 27, ...   (97, 120)

8   4, 9, 14, 19, 24, 29, ...   (168, 169)

9   40, 35, 30, 25, 20, ...   (85, 4)

10 38, 36, 34, 32, 30, ...   (71, 82)

4.5 Using a graphical calculator to produce number sequences

You can use the **Ans** and **EXE** keys together to generate number sequences. For example:

Press **1** **EXE**

Press **Ans** **+** **1** **EXE** **EXE** **EXE** … Keep pressing **EXE**

The calculator appears to be 'counting'.

Each time **EXE** is pressed, 'Ans + 1' is calculated, where Ans is the *last answer displayed*.

> **Ans** recalls the most recent answer.

> **EXE** performs (or repeats) the most recent calculation(s).

```
1
                        1.
Ans + 1
                        2.
                        3.
                        4.
                        5.
```

Example 9

(a) Use the **Ans** and **EXE** keys to produce the even numbers, starting with 2.

(b) Show how the **Ans** and **EXE** keys can be used to produce the sequence 2, 6, 18, 54, …

(a) **2** **EXE** **Ans** **+** **2** **EXE** **EXE** **EXE** …

(b) **2** **EXE** **Ans** **×** **3** **EXE** **EXE** **EXE** …

Exercise 4H

Write down the key presses, including **Ans** and **EXE**, which will generate the following sequences.

1 1, 3, 5, 7, 9, …   **2** 5, 10, 15, 20, 25, …

3 2, 4, 8, 16, 32, …   **4** 3, 9, 27, 81, 243, …

5 10, 9, 8, 7, 6, …   **6** 16, 8, 4, 2, 1, …

7 200, 20, 2, 0.2, 0.02, …   **8** $-5, -7, -9, -11, -13, …$

4.6 Investigating number sequences with a spreadsheet

You can generate many number sequences on the same spreadsheet and compare them.

Before you start Exercise 4I, you need to find out, for your spreadsheet package:

- how to enter numbers and formulae in the cells of your spreadsheet
- how to copy a formula from one cell to other cells.

Now work through the exercise to practise these skills.

Exercise 4I

1 Generate the whole numbers from
1 to 10 in column A:
   Put the number 1 in cell A1.
   Put the formula = A1 + 1 in cell A2.
   Copy the formula in A2 down
   column A as far as A10.

2 Generate the even numbers in
column B:
   Put the number 2 in cell B1.
   Put the formula = B1 + 2 in cell B2.
   Copy the formula in B2 down
   column B as far as B10.

3 Generate the odd numbers in
column C:
   Put the number 1 in cell C1.
   Put the formula = C1 + 2 in cell C2.
   Copy the formula in C2 down
   column C as far as C10.

Formula: = A1 + 1	Formula: = B1 + 2	Formula: = C1 + 2	
	A	**B**	**C**	**D**
1	1	2	1	
2	2	4	3	
3	3	6	5	
4	4	8	7	
5	5	10	9	
6	6	12	11	
7	7	14	13	
8	8	16	15	
9	9	18	17	
10	10	20	19	

4 Generate the triangular numbers in
column D:
   Put the number 1 in cell D1.
   Put the formula = D1 + A2 in cell
   D2.
   Copy the formula in D2 down
   column D as far as D10.

5 Add consecutive odd numbers and
put the answers in column E:
   Put the formula = C1 + C2 in cell E2.
   Copy the formula in E2 down
   column E as far as E10.
   What do you notice about the
   numbers in column E?

6 Add consecutive triangular
numbers and put the answers in
column F:
   Put the formula = D1 + D2 in cell F2.
   Copy the formula in F2 down
   column F as far as F10.
   What is the name of the sequence of numbers in
   column F?

Formula: = D1 + A2	Formula: = C1 + C2	Formula: = D1 + D2	
C	**D**	**E**	**F**	**G**
1	1			
3	3	4	4	
5	6	8	9	
7	10	12	16	
9	15	16	25	
11	21	20	36	
13	28	24	49	
15	36	28	64	
17	45	32	81	
19	55	36	100	

Mixed exercise 4

1   The table shows some rows in a number pattern.

Row 1	1	$= \dfrac{1 \times 2}{2}$
Row 2	1 + 2	$= \dfrac{2 \times 3}{2}$
Row 3	1 + 2 + 3	$= \dfrac{3 \times 4}{2}$
Row 4	1 + 2 + 3 + 4	
Row 8		

(a) Copy the table and complete row 4 and row 8.
(b) Work out the sum of the first 100 whole
     numbers.   [E]

2   Here are the first five terms of a number sequence:
        3   8   13   18   23
(a) Write down the next **two** terms of the sequence.
(b) Explain how you found your answer.
(c) Explain why 387 is **not** a term of the sequence.   [E]

3   Here are some patterns made up of dots:

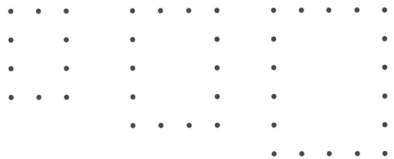

Pattern number 1   Pattern number 2   Pattern number 3

(a) Draw Pattern number 4.
(b) Copy and complete the table.

Pattern number	1	2	3	4	5
Number of dots	10	14	18		

(c) How many dots are used in Pattern number 10?   [E]

4   Here are some patterns made with crosses:

| Pattern number 1 | Pattern number 2 | Pattern number 3 | Pattern number 4 |

(a) Draw pattern number 5.

(b) Copy and complete the table for pattern number 5
     and pattern number 6.

Pattern number (n)	1	2	3	4	5	6
Number of crosses (C)	5	8	11	14		

(c) Work out the pattern number that has 26 crosses.

(d) Work out the number of crosses in pattern number 10.

(e) Write down a formula for the number of crosses, C,
     in terms of the pattern number, n.   [E]

Summary of key points

1 In a number pattern or **sequence** there is always a **rule** to get from one number to
   the next.
   For example:

4, 7, 10, 13, ...	The rule is: add 3
50, 46, 42, 38, ...	The rule is: take away 4
2, 4, 8, 16, ...	The rule is: multiply by 2
100 000, 10 000, 1000, ...	The rule is: divide by 10

2 When you know the nth term of a pattern, you can calculate any term in the pattern
   by replacing 'n' with the pattern number

3 To find the nth term of a number pattern, use a table of values.
   For example

Pattern number	Term	Difference
1	1	The rule is add 3 so the number in front of the n is 3.
2	4	
3	7	Check for the plus or minus number by putting the value of the term number into the nth term
4	10	
n	$3n - 2$	

5 Decimals

5.1 Understanding place value

Some things in life can only have whole number values. For example, the number of people in a party is always a whole number.

Here there are *whole* numbers of people and animals.

Other items can also have other values. For example, the weight of a packet of sugar is 2.2 lbs and the height of a person may be 1.76 metres.

These are *decimal* numbers. Values that are not whole numbers can be recorded using decimals (with differing degrees of accuracy).

In a decimal number, the **decimal point** separates the whole number from the part that is smaller than 1.

> 2.2 is read as two point two.
> 1.76 is read as one point seven six.

Example 1

A Formula One Grand Prix driver has his lap time recorded as 53.398 seconds.

You can better understand what 53.398 seconds really means by drawing a decimal place value diagram.

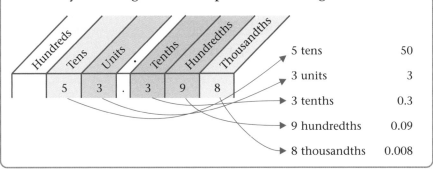

5 tens	50
3 units	3
3 tenths	0.3
9 hundredths	0.09
8 thousandths	0.008

> Read the whole number and then read the digits in order:
> fifty-three point three nine eight.

Example 2

A woman 400 m hurdler's time is 54.08 seconds.
Draw up a place value table.

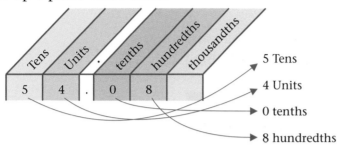

5 Tens

4 Units

0 tenths

8 hundredths

Even though there are no *tenths* the 0 has to be recorded
to keep the 8 in its correct place value position.

Example 3

Write down the place value of the underlined digit in each
number.

(a) 3<u>2</u>.8   (b) 0.38<u>5</u>   (c) 10.<u>0</u>3   (d) 4.2<u>9</u>0

(a) 2 units   (b) 5 thousandths
(c) 0 tenths   (d) 9 hundredths

Exercise 5A

1 Draw a place value diagram like the ones in Examples 1
and 2 and write in these numbers:
(a) 41.6   (b) 4.16   (c) 34.6   (d) 1.463
(e) 0.643   (f) 1.005   (g) 5.01   (h) 0.086

2 What is the place value of the underlined digit in each
number?
(a) 2<u>5</u>.4   (b) 2.<u>5</u>4   (c) 25.4<u>6</u>   (d) 3.5<u>4</u>6
(e) <u>1</u>8.07   (f) 9.66<u>9</u>   (g) 216.0<u>3</u>1   (h) 2.135<u>7</u>
(i) 9.1<u>0</u>2   (j) 3.<u>3</u>36   (k) 2.59<u>1</u>   (l) 0.0<u>2</u>7

5.2 Writing decimal numbers in order of size

To arrange decimal numbers in order of size you need to have
a good understanding of place value.

> Sort decimal numbers in order of size by first comparing the
> whole number parts, then the digits in the tenths place, then
> the digits in the hundredths place, and so on.

Example 4

Write these decimal numbers in order of size, starting with the largest: 3.069, 5.2, 3.4, 3.08, 7.0

Step 1 Look at the whole number parts:
7 is bigger than 5; 5 is bigger than 3
Ordered: 7.0, 5.2   Unordered: 3.069, 3.4, 3.08

Step 2 Look at the tenths place:
4 is bigger than 0
Ordered: 7.0, 5.2, 3.4   Unordered: 3.069, 3.08

Step 3 Look at the hundredths place:
8 is bigger than 6
So the order is: 7.0, 5.2, 3.4, 3.08, 3.069

Exercise 5B

1 Rearrange these decimal numbers in order of size, starting with the largest.
(a) 0.62, 0.71, 0.68, 0.76, 0.9
(b) 3.4, 3.12, 3.75, 2.13, 2.09
(c) 0.42, 0.065, 0.407, 0.3, 0.09
(d) 3.0, 6.52, 6.08, 3.58, 3.7
(e) 0.06, 0.13, 0.009, 0.105, 0.024
(f) 2.09, 1.08, 2.2, 1.3, 1.16

2 Put these decimal numbers in order of size, smallest first.
(a) 4.85, 5.9, 5.16, 4.09, 5.23
(b) 0.34, 0.09, 0.37, 0.021, 0.4
(c) 5, 7.23, 5.01, 7.07, 5.009
(d) 1.001, 0.23, 1.08, 1.14, 0.07

3 The table gives the price of a pack of Sudso soap powder in different shops.

Shop	Stall	Corner	Market	Main	Store	Super
Price	£1.29	£1.18	£1.09	£1.31	£1.20	£1.13

Remember:
£1.80 means 1 pound and 80 pence.
£1.08 means 1 pound and 8 pence.
The position of the zero is important!

Write the list of prices in order, starting with the lowest price.

4   The table gives the heights in metres of six girls.

Rachel	Ira	Sheila	Naomi	Latif	Jean
1.56	1.74	1.78	1.65	1.87	1.7

Write the list of names in descending order of height, starting with the tallest.

5   The fastest lap times (in seconds) of six drivers were:

Ascarina	53.072	Bertolini	53.207
Rascini	52.037	Alloway	57.320
Silverman	53.027	Killim	53.702

Write down the drivers' times in order, starting with the fastest.

6   A new cereal gives these weights per 100 g of vitamins and minerals:

Fibre	1.5 g	Iron	0.014 g
Vitamin B6	0.002 g	Thiamin B1	0.0014 g
Riboflavin B2	0.0015 g	Sodium	0.02 g

Write down the weights in order, starting with the lowest.

5.3 Rounding decimal numbers

As with ordinary numbers, it is sometimes helpful to round a decimal number and give the result correct to the nearest whole number, or correct to so many decimal places (d.p.).

To round a decimal to the nearest whole number, look at the digit in the tenths column (or first decimal place). If it is 5 or more, round the whole number up. If it is less than 5, do not change the whole number.

Example 5

Round £5.11 to the nearest pound.

In this example the first decimal place is **less** than 5 so you do not change the whole number.

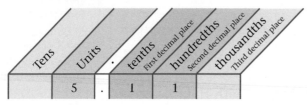

£5.11 to the nearest pound is £5.

Example 6

Round 7.815 to the nearest whole number.

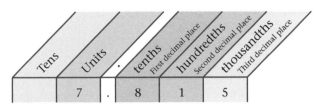

		.			
	7	.	8	1	5

7 is in the units column
8 is in the first decimal place
1 is in the second decimal place
5 is in the third decimal place

8 in the first decimal place is more than 5 so you round up.

7.815 rounded to the nearest whole number is 8.

Example 7

Terry spent £37.52 on a new computer game.
Round the cost to the nearest pound.

Because the digit in the first decimal place is 5, the whole number is rounded up to £38.

To round a decimal to one decimal place (1 d.p.), look at the second decimal place. If it is 5 or more round up. If it is less than 5, leave it and any remaining digits in the decimal part out.

Example 8

Round the following numbers to *one* decimal place.

(a) 25.27   (b) 25.72   (c) 25.55   (d) 25.528

(a) The second decimal place is 7 which is 5 or more so round the 2 up to 3. The answer is 25.3.
(b) The second decimal place is 2 which is less than 5 so leave this digit out. The answer is 25.7.
(c) The second decimal place is 5 so round the 5 in the first decimal place up to 6. The answer is 25.6.
(d) The second decimal place is 2 which is less than 5 so leave this and any other digits in the decimal part out. The answer is 25.5.

Exercise 5C

1 Round these numbers to the nearest whole number.
    (a) 7.8   (b) 13.29   (c) 14.361   (d) 5.802
    (e) 10.59   (f) 19.62   (g) 0.771   (h) 20.499
    (i) 0.89   (j) 100.09   (k) 19.55   (l) 1.99

2 Round these numbers to one decimal place.
    (a) 3.6061   (b) 5.3391   (c) 0.0901   (d) 9.347
    (e) 10.6515   (f) 7.989   (g) 2.0616   (h) 0.4999
    (i) 2.45   (j) 125.67   (k) 0.05   (l) 9.890

3 Round
    (a) 13.6 mm to the nearest mm
    (b) 80.09 m to the nearest m
    (c) 0.907 kg to the nearest kg
    (d) £204.49 to the nearest £
    (e) 3.601 lb to the nearest lb
    (f) 2.299 tonne to the nearest tonne
    (g) 10.5001 g to the nearest g
    (h) 8.066 min to the nearest min

5.4 Rounding to a number of decimal places

There are times when you work something out on your
calculator and the number fills the whole display. The answer
is far more accurate than you need. Instead of using all the
digits you can round the number to a given number of
decimal places.

Reminder: $14.576 = 14 + 0.5 + 0.07 + 0.006$

Each of the digits 5,
7 and 6 in the number
14.576 represents a
quantity which is
less than 1. They
are decimal values.

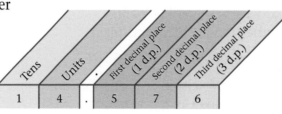

$14.57\vert6 = 14.58$
(correct to 2 d.p.).

Does 6.25 round to 6.2 or 6.3?

6.3, as a 5 is normally rounded up.

You can round (or correct) numbers to a given number of
decimal places (d.p.). Count the number of places from the
decimal point. Look at the next digit after the one you want.
If it is 5 or more, you need to round up.

Example 9

Round these numbers (i) to 3 d.p. (ii) to 2 d.p.
(a) 4.4315   (b) 7.3962

(a) (i) In the number 4.4315 the next digit after the
3rd d.p. is 5. So round up and the 1 becomes 2.
So 4.4315 rounded to 3 d.p. is 4.432

(ii) In the number 4.4315 the next digit after the
2nd d.p. is 1, so you round down and the 3 remains
the same.
So 4.4315 rounded to 2 d.p. is 4.43

(b) (i) 7.3962 to 3 d.p. is 7.396

(ii) 7.3962 to 2 d.p. is 7.40
The 6 makes the 9 round up to 10 and this changes
the 3 to a 4.

> You can write either
> 4.4315 = 4.432
> (correct to 3 decimal
> places) or
> 4.4315 = 4.432 (to 3 d.p.)

> Note: the final zero is
> important because 2 d.p.
> means that two decimal
> digits need to be shown.
> In this case the 4 and the
> 0 must both be included.

Exercise 5D

In questions **1** to **4** round the numbers
(i) to 3 d.p.   (ii) to 2 d.p.

1 (a) 4.2264   (b) 9.7868
  (c) 0.4157   (d) 0.058 38

2 (a) 10.5167   (b) 7.5034
  (c) 21.7295   (d) 9.088 95

3 (a) 15.5978   (b) 0.4081
  (c) 7.2466   (d) 6.050 77

4 (a) 29.1582 cm   (b) 0.054 86 kg
  (c) 13.3785 km   (d) £5.9976

5 Round each number to the number of decimal places
given in brackets.
  (a) 5.6166 (3 d.p.)   (b) 0.0112 (1 d.p.)
  (c) 0.923 98 (4 d.p.)   (d) 0.8639 (2 d.p.)
  (e) 9.6619 (1 d.p.)

5.5 Rounding to a number of significant figures

In Chapter 1 you looked at rounding numbers to '1 significant
figure'. You will also often be asked to round answers to
'2 significant figures' or '3 significant figures'. 'Significant'
means 'important'.

When you are estimating the number of people at a hockey match you don't need to say that there were exactly 8742 people there. You can give your answer to 2 significant figures:

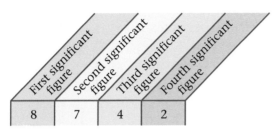

There were about 8700 people (to 2 s.f.).
This is called 'rounding to 2 significant figures'.

You can round (or correct) numbers to a given number of **significant figures (s.f.)**. The first significant figure is the first non-zero digit in the number, counting from the left.

Rounding to a significant figure which is on the right of the decimal point is like the process you used in rounding to decimal places. You look at the next digit after that significant figure.

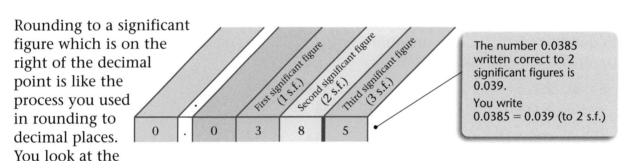

The number 0.0385 written correct to 2 significant figures is 0.039.

You write
0.0385 = 0.039 (to 2 s.f.)

Example 10

Round 642.803
(a) to 1 s.f.   **(b)** to 2 s.f.   **(c)** to 3 s.f.   **(d)** to 4 s.f.   **(e)** to 5 s.f.

You need the zeros to show the place value of the 6.

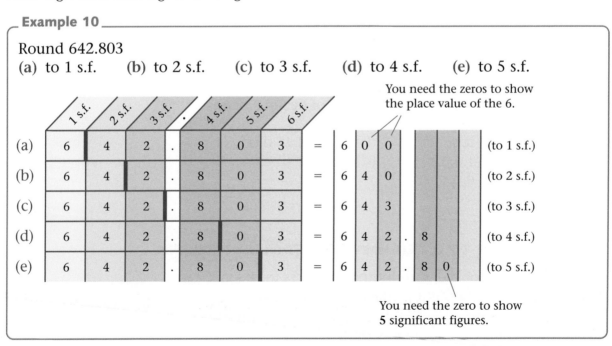

You need the zero to show **5 significant figures**.

Exercise 5E

In questions **1** to **5** round the numbers
(i) to 1 s.f.   (ii) to 3 s.f.

1 (a) 0.061 75   (b) 0.1649   (c) 96.303   (d) 41.475

2 (a) 734.56   (b) 0.079 47   (c) 5.6853   (d) 586.47

3 (a) 0.014 48   (b) 2222.8   (c) 76.249   (d) 0.3798

4 (a) 8.3846   (b) 35.959   (c) 187.418   (d) 0.066 63

5 (a) 94.746 cm   (b) 851.126 m*l*
    (c) 6.2534 g   (d) 0.062 62 mg

6 Round each number to the number of significant figures
    given in brackets.
    (a) 0.098 12 (2 s.f.)   (b) 54.875 (4 s.f.)
    (c) 7.6542 (1 s.f.)   (d) 3125.4 (2 s.f.)
    (e) 5942.7 (1 s.f.)   (f) 52.973 (3 s.f.)

5.6 Adding and subtracting decimals

Example 11

Two children weigh 24.5 kg and 35.75 kg. What is their
combined weight?

Combined weight is 24.5 kg + 35.75 kg

Put the decimal points
under each other.

Keep digits in their
columns as in a place
value diagram.

$$24.5$$
$$35.75$$
$$\overline{\quad.\quad}$$

Decimal point in the
answer should be in
line.

Then add:

$$\begin{array}{r} 24.5 \\ +35.75 \\ \hline 60.25 \\ \hline \end{array}$$
$$\small 1\ 1$$

Example 12

Add 13.6 and 125.403

$$\begin{array}{r} 13.6 \\ +125.403 \\ \hline 139.003 \\ \hline \end{array}$$
$$\small 1$$

When working out a decimal addition or subtraction, always
put the decimal points under each other.

Exercise 5F

Work these out, showing all your working.

1	1.5 + 4.6	**2**	3 + 0.25
3	26.7 + 42.2	**4**	125.7 + 0.32
5	0.1 + 0.9	**6**	16.1 + 2.625
7	9.9 + 9.9	**8**	10 + 1.001
9	0.005 + 1.909	**10**	117 + 1.17
11	6.3 + 17.2 + 8.47	**12**	13.08 + 9.3 + 6.33
13	0.612 + 3.81 + 14.7	**14**	8.6 + 3.66 + 6.066
15	7 + 3.842 + 0.222	**16**	23.43 + 5.36 + 2.216
17	3.07 + 12 + 0.0276	**18**	5.02 + 31.5 + 142.065

Example 13

Fiona buys a kettle costing £12.55. She pays with a £20 note. How much change should she receive?

£20 − £12.55

$$\begin{array}{r} {}^1 2 {}^9\!\!\!\!\diagup 0 \; . \; {}^9\!\!\!\!\diagup 0 \; {}^1\!\!\!\!\diagup 0 \\ - \; 1 \, 2 \; . \; 5 \, 5 \\ \hline 7 \; . \; 4 \, 5 \end{array}$$

You need to write 20 as 20.00

She receives £7.45 change.

Shopkeepers often give change by counting on:
£12.55 +   5p = £12.60
£12.60 + 40p = £13.00
£13.00 + £7   = £20.00
Change is
    £7 + 40p + 5p = £7.45

Example 14

Bill earns £124.65 per week but needs to pay £33.40 in tax and national insurance. What does he take home?

£124.65 − £33.40

$$\begin{array}{r} {}^1\!\!\!\!\diagup 2 \, 4 \; . \; 6 \, 5 \\ - \; 3 \, 3 \; . \; 4 \, 0 \\ \hline 9 \, 1 \; . \; 2 \, 5 \end{array}$$

Remember to put the decimal points under each other.

Bill takes home £91.25

Exercise 5G

1 Work out these money calculations, showing all your working. (Amounts are given in £s.)

Use the shopkeepers' 'counting on' method for some of these questions.

(a)	19.90 − 13.70	(b)	5.84 − 1.70	(c)	23.50 − 9.40
(d)	100.70 − 3.40	(e)	0.59 − 0.48	(f)	1 − 0.65
(g)	16.90 − 10.71	(h)	21.64 − 10.50	(i)	2.50 − 1.60
(j)	5.84 − 1.77	(k)	23.50 − 9.47	(l)	14 − 0.75

2 Work out these calculations, showing all your working.

(a)	6.125 − 4.9	(b)	14.01 − 2.361
(c)	3.29 − 1.036	(d)	204.06 − 35.48

5.7 Multiplying decimals

When multiplying decimals, the answer must have the same number of decimal places as the total number of decimal places in the numbers being multiplied.

Example 15

Find the cost of 5 books at £4.64 each.

$$
\begin{array}{r}
4\,6\,4 \\
\times\quad 5 \\
\hline
2\,3\,2\,0 \\
\hline
{\scriptstyle 3\ 2}
\end{array}
$$

Multiply the numbers together ignoring the decimals.

$$5 \times 4.64$$

0 d.p. + 2 d.p. = 2 d.p.

Count the total number of decimal places (d.p.) in the numbers you are multiplying.

The answer must have 2 d.p.
So the cost is £23.20

The answer must have the same number of decimal places.

Example 16

Work out 0.52×0.4

$$
\begin{array}{r}
5\,2 \\
\times\quad 4 \\
\hline
2\,0\,8
\end{array}
$$

$$0.52 \times 0.4$$

2 d.p. + 1 d.p. = 3 d.p.

The answer must have 3 d.p. so it is 0.208

Example 17

Find the cost of 25 books at £5.75 each.

Long multiplication

$$
\begin{array}{r}
5\,7\,5 \\
\times\quad 2\,5 \\
\hline
2\,8\,7\,5 \quad {\scriptstyle 575 \times 5} \\
+1\,1\,5\,0\,0 \quad {\scriptstyle 575 \times 20} \\
\hline
1\,4\,3\,7\,5
\end{array}
$$

£143.75

Decimal point is placed to give 2 decimal places.

Napier's Bones

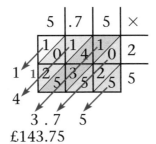

£143.75

Adding method

£	5 . 7 5	
+£	5 . 7 5	
£	1 1 . 5 0	2 lots
£	1 1 . 5 0	2 lots
£	5 . 7 5	1 lot
£	2 8 . 7 5	5 lots
£1 1 5 . 0 0		20 lots
£1 4 3 . 7 5		

Remember the different ways of multiplying shown in Chapter 1.

Exercise 5H

Work these out, showing all your working.

1 Find the cost of
   (a) 6 books at £2.25 each
   (b) 4 tins of biscuits at £1.37 each
   (c) 8 ice creams at £0.65 each
   (d) 1.5 kilos of pears at £0.80 per kilo.

2 (a) 7.6×4 (b) 0.76×4 (c) 0.76×0.4
   (d) 2.25×5 (e) 2.25×0.5 (f) 0.225×0.5
   (g) 22.5×0.05 (h) 2.25×0.005 (i) 0.225×0.005

3 (a) $24.6 \times 7\,\text{kg}$ (b) 3.15×0.03 seconds
   (c) $0.12 \times 0.12\,\text{m}$ (d) 0.2×0.2 miles
   (e) $1.5 \times 0.6\,l$ (f) 0.03×0.04 hours

4 (a) 6.42×10 (b) 64.2×10 (c) 0.642×10
   (d) 56.23×10 (e) 5.623×10 (f) $0.056\,23 \times 10$

Look carefully at your answers to question **4**.
What do you notice?

5 (a) 0.045×100 (b) 0.45×100 (c) 4.5×100
   (d) 0.0203×100 (e) 0.203×100 (f) 2.03×100

What do you notice about your answers to question **5**?

6 A book costs £4.65. Work out the cost of buying
   (a) 25 copies   (b) 36 copies   (c) 55 copies.

7 It costs £7.85 for one person to enter the Fun Beach.
   How much does it cost
   (a) 15 people   (b) 25 people   (c) 43 people?

8 A bucket holds 4.55 litres of water. How much water is
   contained in
   (a) 15 buckets   (b) 25 buckets   (c) 65 buckets?

5.8 Division with decimals

Example 18

Five friends win £216.35 in a charity lottery. They share
the money equally. How much do they each get?

$216.35 \div 5$

Put the decimal
points in line.

$$\begin{array}{r} 4\ 3\,.\,2\ 7 \\ \hline 5\,)\,2\ 1^16\,.\,1^33^35 \end{array}$$

Because 5 is a whole
number, divide straight
away.

Example 19

Work out   (a) $5.215 \div 7$ (b) $4.5 \div 6$

(a) $\begin{array}{r} 0.745 \\ \overline{7)5.^52^31^35} \end{array}$

(b) $\begin{array}{r} 0.75 \\ \overline{6)4.^45^30} \end{array}$

> 6 divides into 45, 7 times remainder 3.

> Add a zero in the next decimal place. Place the 3 remainder next to the zero.

> 6 into 30 goes 5 times.

Exercise 5I

Work these out, showing all your working.

1   (a) $64.48 \div 4$ (b) $3.165 \div 5$ (c) $133.56 \div 9$
    (d) $205.326 \div 6$ (e) $35.189 \div 7$ (f) $0.0368 \div 8$

2   (a) $34.5 \div 10$ (b) $3.45 \div 10$ (c) $0.345 \div 10$
    (d) $78 \div 10$ (e) $7.8 \div 10$ (f) $0.78 \div 10$
    (g) $65 \div 10$ (h) $65 \div 100$ (i) $65 \div 1000$

Write down anything you notice about your answers to question **2**.

3   (a) $5 \div 2$ (b) $6 \div 5$ (c) $3.5 \div 4$
    (d) $0.72 \div 3$ (e) $1.56 \div 3$ (f) $1.24 \div 8$
    (g) $14.4 \div 12$ (h) $1.3 \div 8$

4   Seven people share £107.80 equally.
    How much will each receive?

5   How many 3 litre jugs would be needed to hold
    43.5 litres of lemonade?

Example 20

Work out $70 \div 8$

$$\begin{array}{r} 8.75 \\ \overline{8)7^70.^60^40} \end{array}$$

Example 21

1.2 metres of fabric costs £1.56. What is the cost per metre?

   $1.56 \div 1.2$ —————— not a whole number

To change 1.2 to a whole number multiply by 10:

   $1.2 \times 10 = 12$

Do the same to 1.56: $1.56 \times 10 = 15.6$
The division becomes $15.6 \div 12$

$\begin{array}{r} 1.3 \\ \overline{12)15.^36} \end{array}$ The answer is 1.3 or £1.30

> If the number you are dividing by is **not** a whole number, change it to a whole number. Remember to do the same to the number that is to be divided.

Exercise 5J

Work these out, showing all your working.

1 $7.75 \div 2.5$ 2 $7.92 \div 2.2$ 3 $9.86 \div 5.8$

4 $18.9 \div 12.6$ 5 $0.129 \div 0.03$ 6 $0.27 \div 0.1$

7 $6.634 \div 0.62$ 8 $0.2121 \div 0.21$ 9 $3.5 \div 1.4$

10 (a) $12 \div 20$ (b) $9 \div 12$ (c) $4 \div 16$ (d) $10 \div 50$
     (e) $6 \div 30$ (f) $5 \div 25$ (g) $25 \div 8$ (h) $16 \div 40$

11 Benni wins £5050. He splits the £5050 equally between
    12 charities.
    How much does each charity receive?

12 Rodney cuts a 3 m long plank of wood into 12 equal parts.
    How long is each of the 12 pieces of wood?

13 How many books each costing £3.50 can be bought for £20?

Mixed exercise 5

1 Write these numbers to 3 significant figures.
   (a) 345 750   (b) 3478
   (c) 3.5784   (d) 0.004 503

2 Write these numbers to 2 decimal places.
   (a) 3.476   (b) 0.0576
   (c) 23.875   (d) 456.7523

3 Find the value of
   (a) $2.6 + 34.56 + 5$ (b) $3.75 + 20 + 36.2$
   (c) $7.54 - 3.22$ (d) $5.67 - 0.84$
   (e) $5 - 3.55$ (f) 3.24×6
   (g) 4.56×0.8 (h) 5.75×2.5
   (i) $12.5 \div 5$ (j) $18 \div 50$
   (k) $24.6 \div 0.4$ (l) $12.5 \div 50$

4 Write the following numbers in order of size, starting
   with the largest:
        0.606, 9.253, 0.727, 3.510, 0.660

5 Work out the following, and then round your answers to
   2 significant figures.
   (a) Jean has a 5.3 mile round trip to work. If she travels
        to work on 21 days in a month, how far does she
        travel?

'Round trip' means Jean
travels to and from work
a total of 5.3 miles each
day.

(b) In the four weeks in May, Michael manages to save £3.92, £6.51, £9.12 and £1.77. How much does he save altogether in May?

(c) Manik starts the day with £50. After buying a shirt for £11.99, he splits the change equally between his three children. How much does each receive?

6   Natasha has one pound sixty pence. Her friend Kelly has two pounds five pence. Write down, in figures, how much money each girl has.

Summary of key points

1   In a decimal number, the **decimal point** separates the whole number from the part that is smaller than 1.

2   Sort decimal numbers in order of size by first comparing the whole number parts, then the digits in the tenths place, then the digits in the hundredths place, and so on.

3   To round a decimal to the nearest whole number, look at the digit in the tenths column (or first decimal place). If it is 5 or more, round the whole number up. If it is less than 5, do not change the whole number.

4   To round a decimal to one decimal place (1 d.p.), look at the second decimal place. If it is 5 or more, round up. If it is less than 5, leave it and any remaining digits in the decimal part out.

5   You can round (or correct) numbers to a given number of **decimal places (d.p.)**. Count the number of places from the decimal point. Look at the next digit after the one you want. If it is 5 or more, you need to round up.

6   You can round (or correct) numbers to a given number of **significant figures (s.f.)**. The first significant figure is the first non-zero digit in the number, counting from the left. For example, 5.245 is 5.2 to 2 s.f.

7   When working out a decimal addition or subtraction, always put the decimal points under each other.

8   When multiplying decimals, the answer must have the same number of decimal places as the total number of decimal places in the numbers being multiplied.

9   When dividing decimals by decimals make sure you always divide by a whole number. You do this by multiplying both numbers by 10 or 100 or 1000 etc.

6 Angles and turning

6.1 Turning

The London Eye is turning ...

You can show clockwise ◌ and anticlockwise ◌ turns like this:

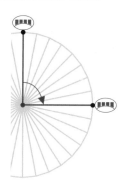

$\frac{1}{4}$ turn clockwise

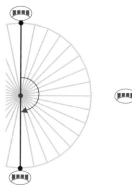

$\frac{1}{2}$ turn clockwise

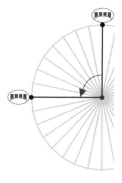

$\frac{1}{4}$ turn anticlockwise

Example 1

An aeroplane is flying North. In which direction will it be flying after:

(a) a $\frac{1}{4}$ turn clockwise   (b) a $\frac{1}{2}$ turn clockwise   (c) a $\frac{1}{4}$ turn anticlockwise?

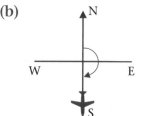

(a)   It will be flying East.

(b)   It will be flying South.

(c)   It will be flying West.

Example 2

Sam is standing in a market square facing North.
What building will he be facing after

(a) a $\frac{1}{4}$ turn clockwise   (b) a $\frac{1}{2}$ turn anticlockwise

(c) a $\frac{3}{4}$ turn clockwise   (d) a $\frac{1}{4}$ turn anticlockwise

(e) a $\frac{3}{4}$ turn anticlockwise

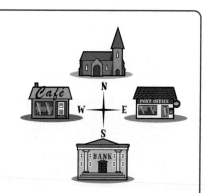

(a) Post Office   (b) Bank

(c) Café   (d) Café

(e) Post Office

Exercise 6A

1 Write down which of these are turning movements:
  (a) a car door opening
  (b) a ship changing direction
  (c) opening a book
  (d) a person crossing the road
  (e) a skier skiing straight down a mountain
  (f) a weather vane as the wind changes.

2 Lisa is facing East. Which way will she be facing after
  (a) a $\frac{1}{4}$ turn clockwise   **(b)** a $\frac{1}{4}$ turn anticlockwise
  (c) a $\frac{1}{2}$ turn clockwise   **(d)** a $\frac{1}{2}$ turn anticlockwise?
  What do you notice about your answers to **(c)** and **(d)**?

3 Ajay is walking South-West. Which direction is he
  walking in after
  (a) a $\frac{1}{4}$ turn clockwise   **(b)** a $\frac{1}{2}$ turn
  (c) a $\frac{1}{4}$ turn anticlockwise?

4 How much does the hour hand of a clock turn between
  (a) 3pm and 6pm   **(b)** 1pm and 7pm
  (c) 11am and 2pm?

6.2 Measuring angles

An **angle** is a measure of *turn*. It is a change of direction.
There is no change of position.

An angle can be measured as a turn or using degrees.

There are 360 degrees or 360° in a full turn.
The sign for a degree is °.

That makes 90° in a $\frac{1}{4}$ turn, 180° in a $\frac{1}{2}$ turn and
270° in a $\frac{3}{4}$ turn.

An angle that is a $\frac{1}{4}$ turn
is called a **right angle**.
A right angle has 90°.

An angle that is less than
a $\frac{1}{4}$ turn or 90° is called an
acute angle.

An angle that is more than
a $\frac{1}{4}$ turn or 90° and less
than a $\frac{1}{2}$ turn or 180° is
called an **obtuse angle**.

An angle that is a
$\frac{1}{2}$ turn or 180° is called a
straight line or **straight
angle**.

An angle that is more than a $\frac{1}{2}$ turn or 180° and
less than a full turn or 360° is called a **reflex angle**.

Example 3

Name the different types of angles in this diagram:

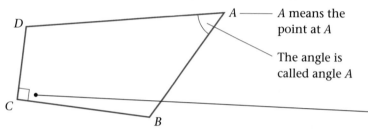

A ——— *A* means the
point at *A*

The angle is
called angle *A*

⌐ is the symbol for a
right angle.

Angle *A* is less than a $\frac{1}{4}$ turn. It is an acute angle.

Angle *B* is more than a $\frac{1}{4}$ turn and less than a $\frac{1}{2}$ turn. It is
an obtuse angle.

Angle *C* is a $\frac{1}{4}$ turn. It is a right angle. Lines BC and CD are
perpendicular.

Angle *D* is more than a $\frac{1}{4}$ turn and less than a $\frac{1}{2}$ turn. It is
an obtuse angle.

Exercise 6B

In questions **1–8** write down whether the marked angles are
acute, obtuse, right or reflex.

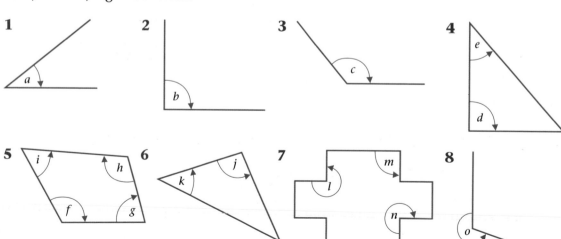

In questions **9–16** estimate the size of the marked angles in degrees.

9

10

q

11

r

12

s

13

t

14

u

15

v

w

16

x

6.3 Naming angles

You can use letters to name the sides and angles of shapes. This shape is named *ABCD* using the letters for the corners and going round clockwise:

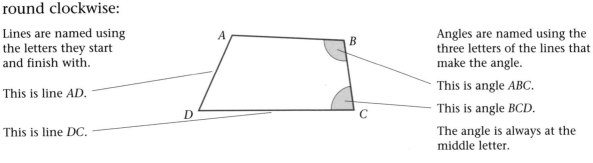

Lines are named using the letters they start and finish with.

This is line *AD*.

This is line *DC*.

Angles are named using the three letters of the lines that make the angle.

This is angle *ABC*.

This is angle *BCD*.

The angle is always at the middle letter.

Exercise 6C

Use letters to identify all the lines and shaded angles in each diagram.

1

2

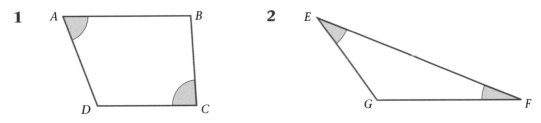

3

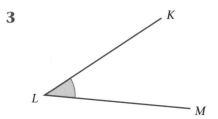

4

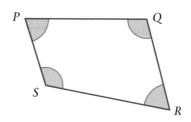

5

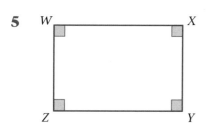

6

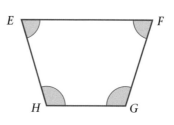

6.4 Measuring angles with a protractor

You can use a **protractor** to measure angles accurately.

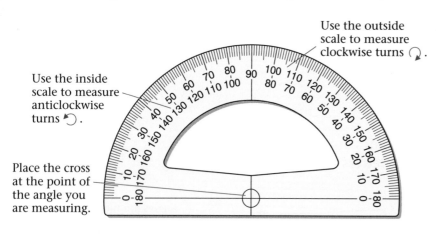

Use the inside scale to measure anticlockwise turns ↶.

Use the outside scale to measure clockwise turns ↷.

Place the cross at the point of the angle you are measuring.

Angle measurer

You can use an angle measurer instead of a protractor.

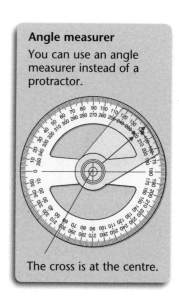

The cross is at the centre.

Example 4

Use a protractor to measure the angle CBA.

Here the lines of angle CBA are long enough to reach the outer edge of the protractor.

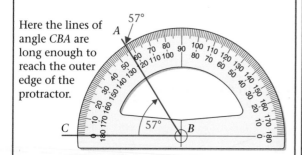

The angle is 57°.

Example 5

Use a protractor to measure the angle BCD.

Use the inside scale to measure angle BCD.

When the line is too short to reach the scale, extend it with a straight edge like this piece of paper.

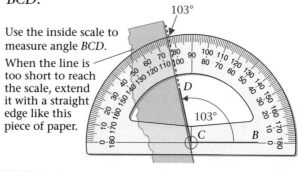

The angle is 103°.

Exercise 6D

Measure and name the angles in each diagram.

1

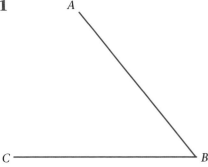

2

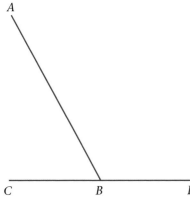

3

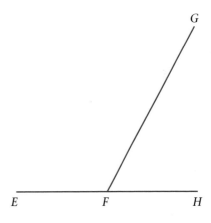

4

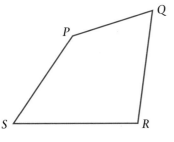

5

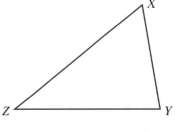

6

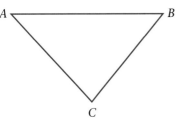

7

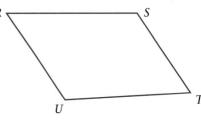

8

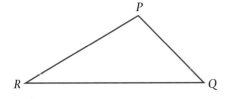

9

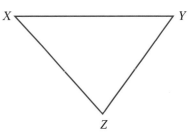

10

6.5 Drawing angles

You need to be able to draw angles which are accurate to within 2°.

Example 6

Draw these two angles on a line DE which is 8 cm long:

(a) a clockwise angle $DEF = 79°$ (b) an anticlockwise angle $EDC = 123°$

(a) Drawing angle DEF:

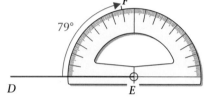

D ————— E   D ————— E   D ————— E

Draw DE 8 cm long.

Put the protractor cross at E.
Mark the point F at a clockwise
turn of 79°.

Join the points E and F
to give the angle DEF.

(b) Drawing angle EDC:

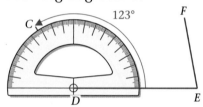
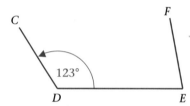

Put the protractor cross at D.
Mark the point C at an
anticlockwise turn of 123°.

Join the points D and C
to give the angle EDC.

When you have to draw a reflex angle it is a good idea to use a circular protractor.

Example 7

Draw angle $CBA = 270°$

Step 1 Put the circular protractor
with centre on B and 0° on
the line BC.

Step 2 Count around to 270°.

Step 3 Mark the point A.

Step 4 Join A to B.

Example 8

Draw angle $PQR = 300°$

Step 1 $360 - 300 = 60$

Step 2   Draw an angle of 60°.

Step 3   Mark the 300° angle.

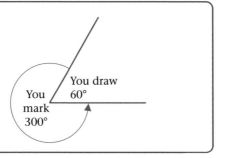

You draw 60°

You mark 300°

Exercise 6E

You need a protractor, ruler and pencil.

1   Draw and label these angles:
    (a) $ABC = 40°$ (b) $DEF = 65°$ (c) $GHK = 125°$ (d) $LMN = 34°$
    (e) $OPQ = 136°$ (f) $RST = 162°$ (g) $UVW = 78°$ (h) $XYZ = 97°$
    (i) $PQR = 185°$ (j) $XYZ = 330°$ (k) $ABC = 240°$ (l) $RST = 305°$

2   Make accurate drawings of these diagrams:

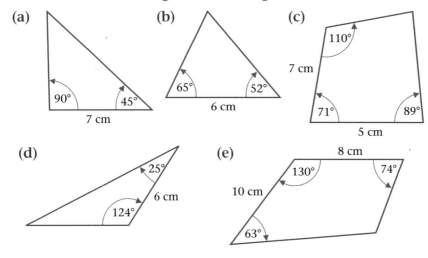

(a)   90°   45°   7 cm

(b)   65°   52°   6 cm

(c)   110°   7 cm   71°   89°   5 cm

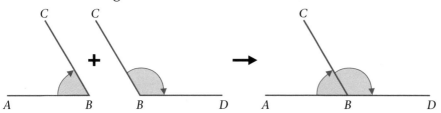

(d)   25°   6 cm   124°

(e)   130°   8 cm   74°   10 cm   63°

6.6 Angles on a straight line

Here are two angles ABC and CBD:

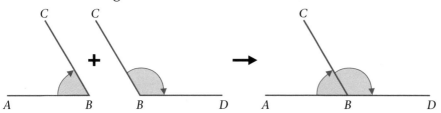

Joined together they make the angle ABD which is a straight line.
These two angles add up to 180°:
    angle ABC + angle $CBD = 180°$

The angles on a straight line add up to 180°.

Example 9

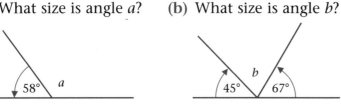

(a) What size is angle *a*?   (b) What size is angle *b*?

(a) The angles make a
straight line so:
$58° + a = 180°$
$a = 180° - 58° = 122°$

(b) The 3 angles make a
straight line so:
$45° + b + 67° = 180°$
$b = 180° - (45° + 67°) = 68°$

The letter *a* must equal 122
because $58 + 122 = 180°$

The letter *b* must equal 68
because $45 + 68 + 67 = 180°$

Exercise 6F

Find the angles represented by letters in these questions.
Give reasons for your answers.

1   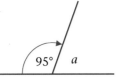   **2**   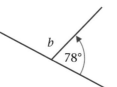   **3**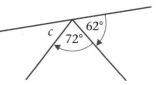

4   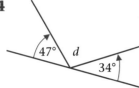   **5**   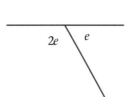   **6**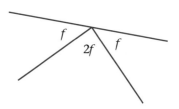

6.7 Angles meeting at a point

The angles at a point add up to 360°.

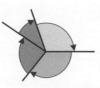

Where two straight lines cross, the
opposite angles are equal. They are
called **vertically opposite angles**.

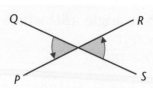

The shaded angles opposite
each other are the same.

To see why, imagine that
line *QS* has turned
anticlockwise to give line
PR. Both 'ends' of the line
have moved through the
same angle.

Example 10

Find all the angles in this diagram. Give reasons for your answers.

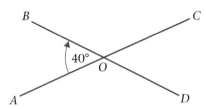

Angle $AOB = 40°$

So angle $COD = 40°$ (vertically opposite angle AOB)

Angle $AOD = 180 - 40 = 140°$ (the angles make a straight line)

So angle $BOC = 140°$ (vertically opposite angle AOD)

Give reasons for your answers when you can.

Exercise 6G

Find the angles represented by letters in these questions.
Give reasons for your answers.

1

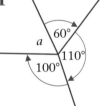

2

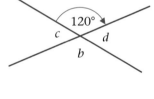

3

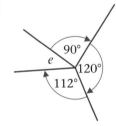

4

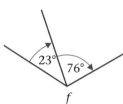

5

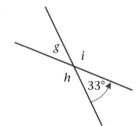

6

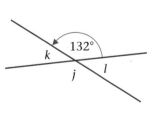

7

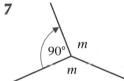

8

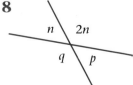

9

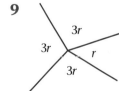

6.8 Sums of angles for triangles and quadrilaterals

The interior angles of a triangle always add up to 180°.

You can see this by checking that the angles in these triangles add up to 180°.

 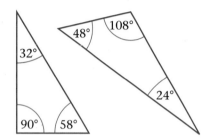

Another way to see this is to cut out a triangle and tear the corners off like this:

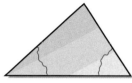

Tear these corners off.

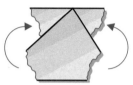

Put all three corners together. They make a straight line which is an angle of 180°.

The interior angles of a quadrilateral (a four-sided shape) always add up to 360°.

You can see this by measuring the angles...

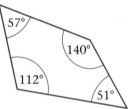

... or by dividing the quadrilateral into two triangles...

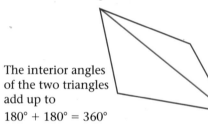

The interior angles of the two triangles add up to 180° + 180° = 360°

... or by tearing off the four corners:

Put the angles together. They make a full turn of 360°.

Example 11

(a) Work out the missing angle in this triangle:

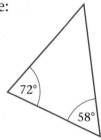

(b) Find the missing angle of this quadrilateral:

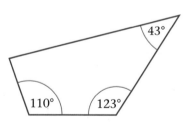

(a) Two of the angles add up to 130°. The third angle must be

180° − 130° = 50°

(b) The 3 angles marked add up to 276° So the missing angle must be

360° − 276° = 84°

Exercise 6H

Work out the missing angles in these triangles and
quadrilaterals. Give reasons for your answers.

1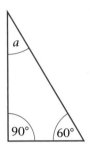

2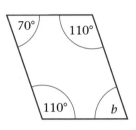

3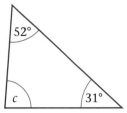

4

5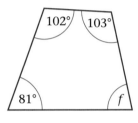

6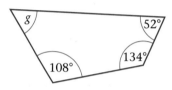

7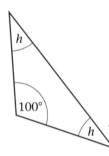

8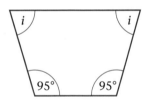

9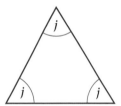

Worked examination question 1

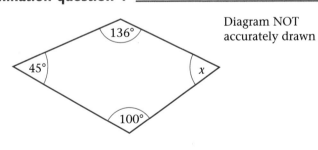

Diagram NOT
accurately drawn •——

> This means that you
> cannot measure the
> angles with a
> protractor.

Work out the value of x. [E]

$x + 136° + 45° + 100° = 360°$ (sum of angles of quadrilateral)

$\qquad x + 281° = 360°$

so $\qquad\qquad x = 360° - 281° = 79°$

Worked examination question 2

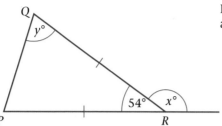

Diagram NOT
accurately drawn

$PR = QR$ and angle $PRQ = 54°$.

(a) Work out the value of x.

Triangle PQR is a special type of triangle.

(b) Write down the mathematical name of this type of triangle.

(c) Work out the value of y.   [E]

Remember:
Sides marked in the same
way are the same length.

(a) $x° = 180° - 54°$ (angles on a straight line)

$x = 126$

(b) Triangle PQR has two equal sides so it is an isosceles triangle.

(c) angle $P + y° + 54° = 180°$ (sum of angles of triangle)

so   angle $P + y° = 180° - 54° = 126°$

angle $P = y°$ (base angles of isosceles triangle)

so $y° = 126° ÷ 2$

$y = 63$

The base angles of an
isosceles triangle are
equal.

For more about isosceles
triangles see Section 7.1.

Exercise 6I

Work out the lettered angles, giving reasons for your answers.

1

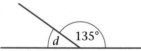

2

3

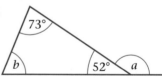

4

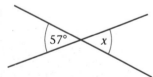

5

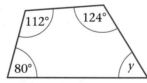

6   In triangle ABC, $AC = BC$ and angle $CAB = 25°$.
Work out

(a) angle CBA

(b) angle ACB.

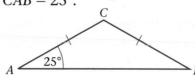

7 In triangle *PQR*, *PQ* = *QR* and angle *PQR* = 116°. Work out the size of angle *QPR*.

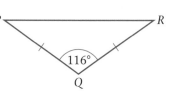

8 The arrowhead shape *PQRS* is a type of kite. *PQ* = *QR* and *PS* = *SR*. Angle *PSQ* = 115° and angle *QPS* = 23°. Calculate angle *PQR*.

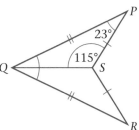

9 *ABCD* is a kite in the shape of an arrowhead. *AD* = *DC* = *BD* and *AB* = *BC*. Angle *DBC* = 34°.

Calculate
(a) angle *ABC*
(b) angle *BDC*
(c) angle *ADC*.

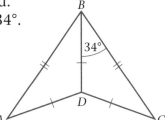

10 Work out the sizes of all the angles marked with letters.

(a)
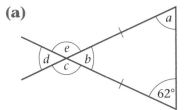

(b)
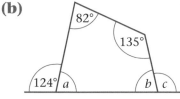

(c)
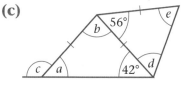

(d)
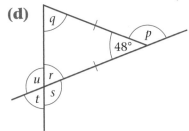

(e)
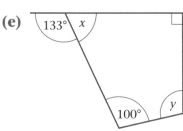

(f)
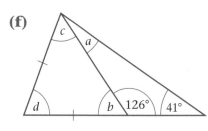

6.9 Alternate and corresponding angles

Parallel lines

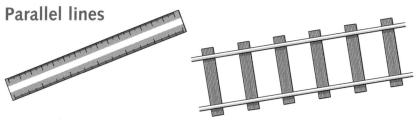

The distance between the two edges of a ruler is the same all the way along it. Similarly the distance between the two rails of a train track is the same wherever it is measured.

Lines which remain the same distance apart are called **parallel lines**. On diagrams this is shown by marking the parallel lines with arrows.

If there is a second pair of parallel lines in one diagram these are marked with double arrows.

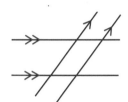

When a straight line crosses a pair of parallel lines it makes angles which are the same size.

Alternate angles

The shaded angles are equal.
They are called **alternate angles**.

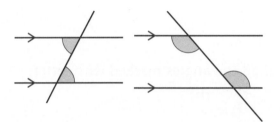

Alternate angles are sometimes called 'Z' angles.

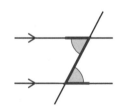

Corresponding angles

The shaded angles are equal.
They are called **corresponding angles**.

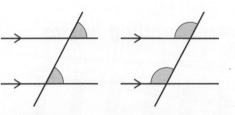

Corresponding angles are sometimes called 'F' angles.

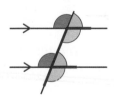

Exercise 6J

1 Find and name as many pairs of parallel lines as you can in this diagram:

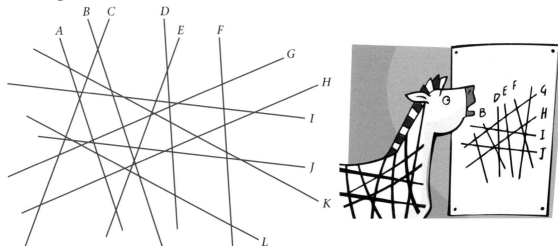

2 Here is the logo of the 'Flying A' pizza company. On a copy of the drawing mark

(a) a right angle with an R

(b) two parallel lines each with a P

(c) an obtuse angle with an O.

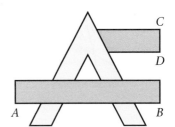

[E]

3 In the diagram, which pair of angles are alternate angles?

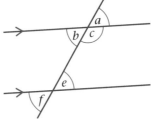

4 In the diagram, which pair of angles are corresponding angles?

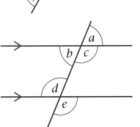

5 Find the size of each angle marked with a letter. Give reasons for your answers.

(a)

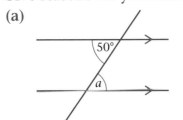

(b)

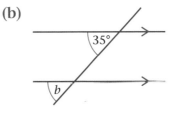

(c)

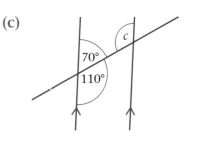

(d)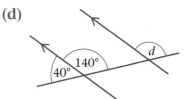

(e)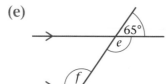

(f)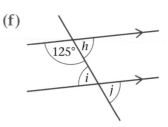

6 Calculate the named angles, giving reasons for your answers.

(a)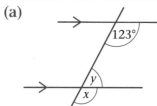

(b)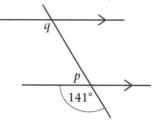

(c)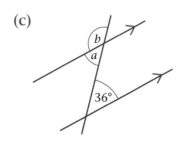

(d)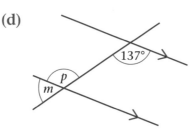

(e)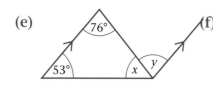

(f)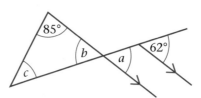

(g)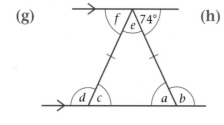

(h)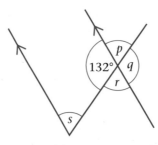

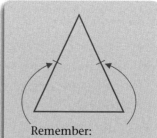

Remember:
Sides marked in the same way are the same length.

7 The diagram shows the following information:
BA is parallel to *CD*, *CA* = *CB*, angle *ACD* = 64°.
Find the size of **(a)** angle *BAC* **(b)** angle *BCA*.

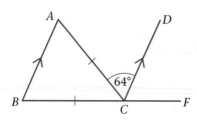

[E]

8

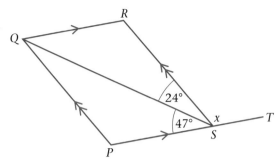

PQRS is a parallelogram.

Angle *QSP* = 47°   Angle *QSR* = 24°   *PST* is a straight line.

(a) (i) Find the size of the angle marked *x*.
     (ii) Give a reason for your answer.

(b) (i) Work out the size of angle *PQS*.
     (ii) Give a reason for your answer.   [E]

6.10 Proof in geometry

Extend each side of a triangle.

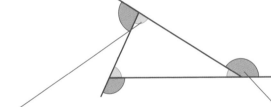

The angles inside are called the **interior angles**.

The angles outside are called the **exterior angles**.

You need to be able to prove that the exterior angle is the sum of the two interior and opposite angles:

> To prove something in maths you have to explain *why it is true*.

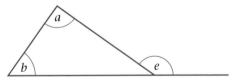

Through the point of angle *e* draw a line parallel to the opposite side of the triangle.
Angle *e* is now divided into two angles, *c* and *d*.

> $e = a + b$

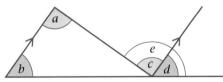

$a = c$ (alternate angles)
$b = d$ (corresponding angles)

So $a + b = c + d = e$

Proving that the angles of a triangle add up to 180°

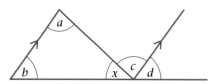

You might be asked to do this in your exam.

The angles of the triangle are *a*, *b* and *x*.

Angle *a* = angle *c*   (alternate angles)
Angle *b* = angle *d*   (corresponding angles)
$c + d + x = 180°$ (sum of angles in a straight line is 180°)
$a + b + x = 180°$ (replace *c* with *a* and *d* with *b*)

Therefore the angle sum of a triangle is 180°.

Exercise 6K

1 Prove that the angle marked *x* is 45° in each diagram.
   (a)   **(b)**

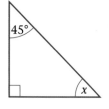

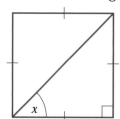

2 Prove that the angle marked *y* is 30° in each diagram.
   (a)   **(b)**

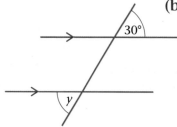

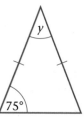

3 Prove that triangle *ABC* is isosceles in each diagram.
   (a)   **(b)**

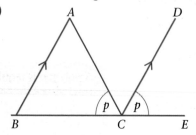

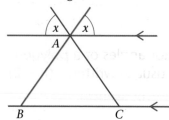

6.11 Calculating angles in polygons

Sum of exterior angles

Step 1 Draw a polygon (with each angle less than 180°) on paper.
Step 2 Extend each side of the polygon to form the exterior angles.
Step 3 Label each exterior angle with a different letter.
Step 4 Cut out each exterior angle leaving some extra paper.
Step 5 Place the angles together at a point.
Step 6 Write down what you notice.

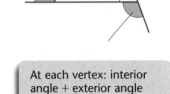

extending each side forms the **exterior angles**

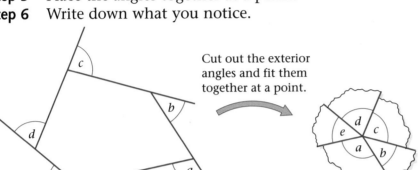

Cut out the exterior angles and fit them together at a point.

At each vertex: interior angle + exterior angle = 180°

The exterior angles fit together at a point with no gaps, so they add to 360°.

Try this yourself with a polygon with a different number of sides.

The sum of the exterior angles of any polygon is 360°.

At each vertex (point) of a polygon the sum of the interior angle and the exterior angle is 180°.

Sum of interior angles

In this hexagon the six vertices are joined to a point inside to make six triangles.

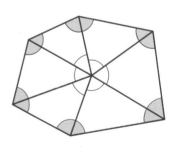

The sum of the interior angles of the hexagon and the angles at the point inside equals the sum of the angles of six triangles, so

sum of interior angles of a hexagon + 360° = 6 × 180°

so   sum of interior angles of a hexagon = (6 × 180°) − 360°
= 720°

To find the sum of the interior angles of a polygon with n sides join all the vertices to a point in the centre to make n triangles.

The sum of the interior angles of a polygon with n sides is
$(n \times 180°) - 360°$,   usually written $(n - 2) \times 180°$

A polygon is regular if its sides are all the same length and its angles are all the same size.

If the polygon is regular, each interior angle is the sum of all the interior angles divided by the number of sides.

Example 12

Work out the size of an interior angle of a regular nonagon.

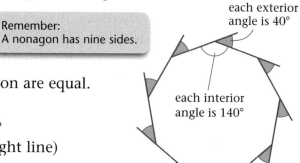

each exterior angle is 40°

Method 1: Using exterior angles

> Remember:
> A nonagon has nine sides.

The nine exterior angles add to 360°.

All the exterior angles of a regular nonagon are equal.

One exterior angle is 360° ÷ 9 = 40°.

So one interior angle is 180° − 40° = 140°

(angles on a straight line)

An interior angle of a regular nonagon is 140°.

each interior angle is 140°

Method 2: Using interior angles

A regular nonagon has nine equal sides.

Join all the vertices to the centre, O, of the nonagon.

The sum of all the angles at O is 360°

so   angle AOB = 360° ÷ 9 = 40°

Angle ABO + angle BAO = 180° − 40° = 140°

(sum of angles of triangle)

Angle ABO = angle BAO = 140° ÷ 2 = 70°

(base angles of isosceles triangle)

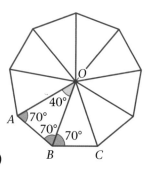

Angle CBO = 70° (by symmetry) so angle ABC is 140°.

An interior angle of a regular nonagon is 140°.

Method 3: Using the formula

A regular nonagon has 9 equal sides, so $n = 9$.

Sum of 9 interior angles $= (n - 2) \times 180°$

$$= (9 - 2) \times 180°$$

$$= 7 \times 180°$$

$$= 1260°$$

One interior angle = 1260° ÷ 9 = 140°

Example 13

Calculate x.

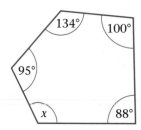

Method 1: Using exterior angles

interior angle + exterior angle = 180°

Four of the exterior angles are:

$180° - 88° = 92°$ $180° - 100° = 80°$
$180° - 134° = 46°$ $180° - 95° = 85°$

These four angles add to 303°.
The exterior angles of a polygon add to 360°.
So the exterior angle next to x is $360° - 303° = 57°$
and $x = 180° - 57° = 123°$.

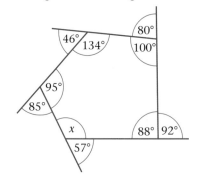

Method 2: Using interior angles

Join all the vertices to a point inside the pentagon to make five triangles.

The sum of all the angles in five triangles is
$5 \times 180° = 900°$.
This includes 360° at the point.

So the sum of all the interior angles of the pentagon is
$900° - 360° = 540°$.

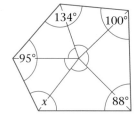

Adding all the interior angles:

$$88° + 100° + 134° + 95° + x = 540°$$

so $x = 540° - 417° = 123°$

Exercise 6L

1 Work out the size of each of the exterior angles of a
   (a) regular pentagon   **(b)** regular hexagon
   (c) regular octagon.

2 Work out the size of each of the interior angles of a
   (a) regular pentagon   **(b)** regular hexagon
   (c) regular octagon.

3 The diagrams show the exterior angles of some regular
   polygons. How many sides has each of the polygons?
   (a)   **(b)**   **(c)**

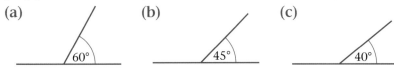

4 The diagrams show the interior angles of some regular
   polygons. How many sides has each of the polygons?
   (a)   **(b)**   **(c)**

In questions **5–7** give reasons for your answers.

5 Calculate: **(a)** p **(b)** q.

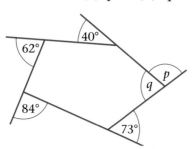

6 Calculate m.

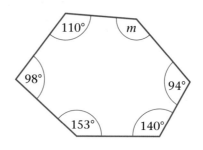

7 Calculate the size of one interior angle of a regular decagon.

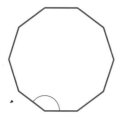

6.12 Bearings

Bearings are used to describe directions with angles.

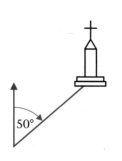

If you begin facing North and then turn clockwise until you face the monument, you have turned through 50°.

The angle you turn is called the **bearing**.

It is always written as a three-figure number.

> When there are less than three digits in the angle you need to add zeros to make a three-figure number. For example a bearing of 9° is written 009°.

You write the bearing of the monument as 050°.

On the map the bearing of Birmingham from London is 315°. The bearing of London from Birmingham is 135°.

A **bearing** is the angle measured from facing North and turning clockwise. It is always a three-figure number.

When you measure a bearing you always put the centre of your protractor on the point where the bearing is taken *from*. You put the zero of the protractor on the North line and measure the angle clockwise. It is a good idea to use a circular protractor to do this.

Example 14

Find the bearing of B from A.

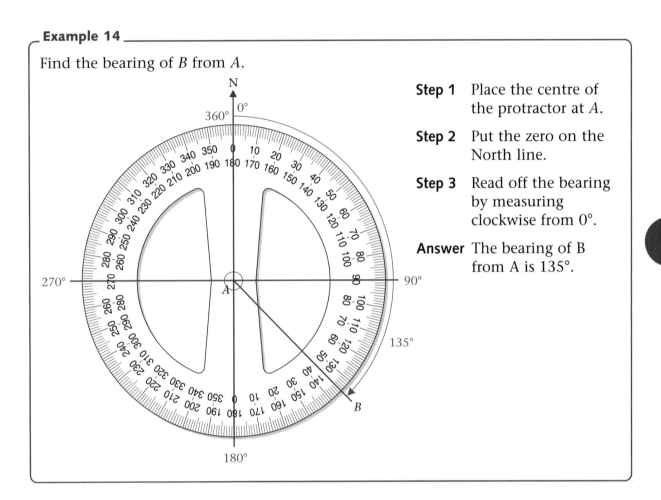

Step 1 Place the centre of the protractor at A.

Step 2 Put the zero on the North line.

Step 3 Read off the bearing by measuring clockwise from 0°.

Answer The bearing of B from A is 135°.

Exercise 6M

1 Write down the bearing of B from A.

(a)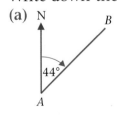

(b)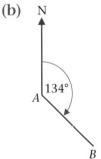

(c)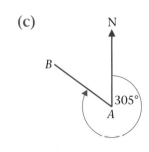

(d)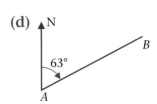

(e)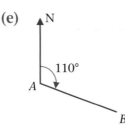

(f)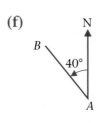

(g)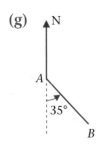

(h)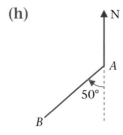

(i)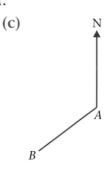

2 Measure and write down the bearing of B from A.

(a)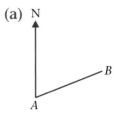

(b)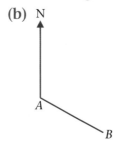

(c)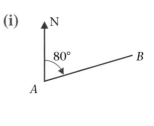

3 Draw these bearings of B from A.

    (a) 050°   **(b)** 125°   **(c)** 300°   **(d)** 250°

4 Work out the bearing of

    (a) B from A

    (b) A from B

    (c) C from B

    (d) B from C.

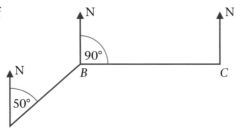

N lines are parallel.

Mixed exercise 6

1 The lines in the diagram are straight.

    (a) Mark with arrows (>>) a pair of parallel lines.

    (b) Mark with the letter R, a right angle.

    (c) What type of angle is shown by the letter?

        (i) x   **(ii)** y?

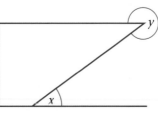

[E]

2 *PQ* is a straight line.

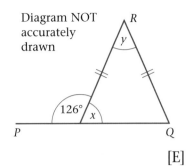

Diagram NOT accurately drawn

   (a) Work out the size of the angle marked *x*.

   (b) **(i)** Work out the size of the angle marked *y*.
   (ii) Give reasons for your answer.

   [E]

3 **(a)** Find the size of angle *C*.

   (b) Triangle ABC is equilateral. Explain why.

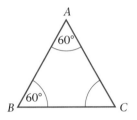

> Remember:
> An equilateral triangle has all three sides the same length and all three angles the same size.

   [E]

4 *PQR* is a straight line.
   SQ = *SR*

   (a) Work out the size of the angle marked *x*.

   (b) Give reasons for your answer.

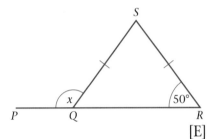

   [E]

5 *DE* is parallel to *FG*. Find the size of the angle marked *y*. Give the reason for your answer.

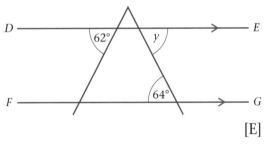

   [E]

6 Here is a regular polygon.

   (a) Write down the name of the polygon.

   (b) Work out the number of degrees in the exterior angle.

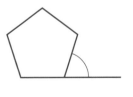

   [E]

7 **(a)** Write down the special name for these types of angles:

   (i)   **(ii)**   **(iii)**

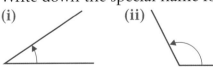

   (b) This diagram is wrong. Explain why.

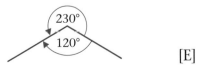

   [E]

8 Use a protractor to find the bearing of:

(a) Q from P

(b) P from R

(c) R from Q.

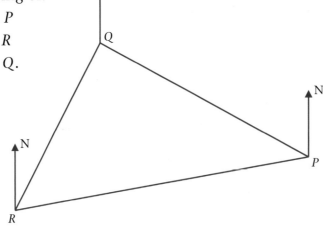

Summary of key points

1 An **angle** is a measure of *turn*. It is a change of direction. There is no change of position.

2 There are 360 degrees or 360° in a full turn. The sign for a degree is °.

3 An angle that is a $\frac{1}{4}$ turn is called a **right angle**. A right angle has 90°.

4 An angle that is less than a $\frac{1}{4}$ turn or 90° is called an **acute angle**.

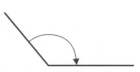

5 An angle that is more than a $\frac{1}{4}$ turn or 90° and less than a $\frac{1}{2}$ turn or 180° is called an **obtuse angle**.

6 An angle that is a $\frac{1}{2}$ turn or 180° is called a **straight line** or **straight angle**.

7 An angle that is more than a $\frac{1}{2}$ turn or 180° and less than a full turn or 360° is called a **reflex angle**.

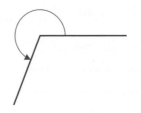 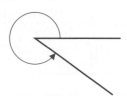

8 The angles on a straight line add up to 180°.

9 The angles at a point add up to 360°.

10 Where two straight lines cross, the opposite angles are equal.
They are called **vertically opposite angles**.

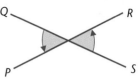

11 The interior angles of a triangle always add up to 180°.

12 The interior angles of a quadrilateral always add up to 360°.

13 Lines which remain the same distance apart are called **parallel lines**.
On diagrams this is shown by marking the parallel lines with arrows.

14 The shaded angles are equal.
They are called **alternate angles**.

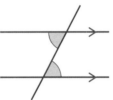

15 The shaded angles are equal.
They are called **corresponding angles**.

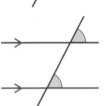

16 The sum of the exterior angles of any
polygon is 360°.

17 At each vertex (point) of a polygon the sum of the interior angle and the exterior
angle is 180°.

18 The sum of the interior angles of a polygon with n sides is $(n \times 180°) - 360°$,
usually written $(n - 2) \times 180°$

19 A **bearing** is the angle measured from
facing North and turning clockwise.
It is always a three-figure number.

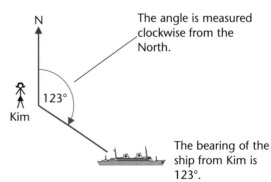

The angle is measured clockwise from the North.

The bearing of the ship from Kim is 123°.

7 2-D shapes

This chapter looks at 2-D shapes. It shows you how to use their properties to solve problems.

You should know some of these properties already:

A straight line is **one-dimensional** (1-D). It has only **length**.

A **line segment** is a section of a line. It is named using letters, for example, the line segment *AB*:

A ——————— *B*

An **angle** is a measure of *turn* (or change of direction).

The darker geo strip has turned through an angle.

A rectangle and a circle are **two-dimensional** (2-D) shapes. They have *area*.
All points on 2-D shapes are in the same **plane** (or flat surface).

Two lines are **parallel** if they are in the same direction.

The arrows mean the lines are parallel.

A cube and a football are **three-dimensional** (3-D) objects. They have *volume* (or capacity).

Two lines are **perpendicular** if they are at right angles to each other.

This line is horizontal. This line is vertical.

The square sign means the lines are perpendicular because this is a right angle.

7.1 Some reminders about polygons

A **polygon** is a 2-D shape with any number of straight sides.

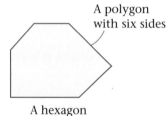

A polygon with six sides

A hexagon

Number of sides	Name of polygon
3	triangle
4	quadrilateral
5	pentagon
6	hexagon
7	heptagon
8	octagon
9	nonagon
10	decagon

The table shows the special names used for polygons with different numbers of sides.

A polygon is **regular** if all its sides and all its angles are equal.

You can show that sides are equal on a shape by using the same mark on the equal sides.

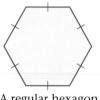

The marks show this shape has six equal sides

A regular hexagon

- The point where two sides meet is called a corner or **vertex**. The plural of vertex is **vertices**.
- The **angle** at a vertex is a measure of the turn between the two sides that meet there. Angles are usually measured in **degrees**.

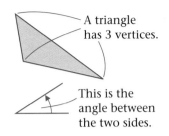

A triangle has 3 vertices.

This is the angle between the two sides.

Special triangles

Name	Shape	Properties
Triangle		• three sides • angles that add up to 180°
Isosceles triangle	2 equal sides 2 equal angles	• two equal sides • two equal angles
Equilateral triangle	3 equal sides The 3 angles are each 60°	• three equal sides • three 60° angles
Right-angled triangle		• a right angle as one of its angles
Scalene triangle		• no equal sides • no equal angles
Obtuse-angled triangle		• one obtuse angle

Special quadrilaterals

Name	Shape	Properties
Quadrilateral		• four sides • angles that add up to 360°
Trapezium	parallel sides	• one pair of opposite sides parallel

Name	Shape	Properties
Parallelogram		• both pairs of opposite sides parallel • opposite sides equal • opposite angles equal • diagonals that bisect each other Bisect means 'divides exactly into two equal parts'.
Rhombus		• all sides equal • both pairs of opposite sides parallel • opposite angles equal • diagonals that bisect each other at right angles • diagonals that bisect the angles at the vertices
Rectangle		• both pairs of opposite sides parallel • four 90° angles • equal diagonals that bisect each other • opposite sides equal
Square		• all sides equal • four 90° angles • both pairs of opposite sides parallel • equal diagonals that bisect each other at right angles • diagonals that bisect the angles at the vertices
Kite		• two pairs of adjacent sides equal • one pair of opposite angles equal • diagonals that cross at right angles • one of its diagonals bisected by the other diagonal

Naming angles

Angles can be named using letters. For example:

The angle marked is angle *BAC* or in short form $\widehat{BAC}$ or $\angle BAC$.
It could also be called angle *CAB* or in short $\widehat{CAB}$ or $\angle CAB$.

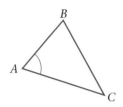

Exercise 7A

1 Copy and complete these sentences. Use numbers and/or
   the correct word chosen from these:

       equal   opposite   parallel   sides

   The first two have been done for you.

   (a) A triangle has __3__ sides and __3__ angles.

   (b) An **equilateral triangle** has <u>equal</u> sides. Each angle
   measures <u>60°</u>.

   (c) An **isosceles triangle** has ____ equal sides and ____
   angles which are equal.

   (d) The largest angle in a **right-angled triangle** always
   measures ____ .

   (e) **Quadrilaterals** have ____ sides and angles.

   (f) The angles in a rectangle are all ____ . Opposite sides
   are ____ .

   (g) All the sides of a **square** are ____ and the angles are
   all ____ .

   (h) A **kite** has two pairs of equal ____ and one pair of
   ____ angles.

   (i) ____ sides and angles of a **parallelogram** are ____ .
   ____ sides are parallel.

   (j) A **rhombus** has four equal ____ and opposite angles
   are ____ . ____ sides are parallel.

   (k) A **trapezium** has one pair of ____ sides.

Patterns in a 19th century
rug, woven by Navajo Native
Americans.

2 Name these special quadrilaterals:

   (a)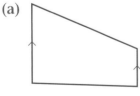

   (b)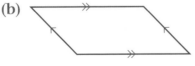

   (c)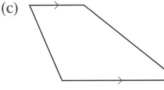

   (d)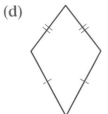

   (e)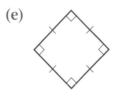

   (f)

3 You will need a ruler and a protractor.

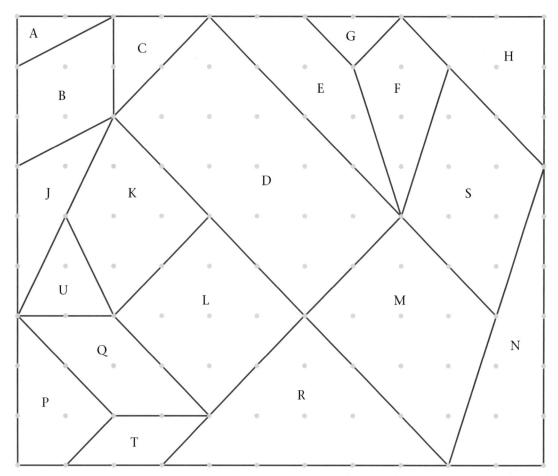

Copy and complete these statements about the 2-D shapes in the diagram.

Use a ruler and protractor to help you.

The first one has been done for you.

(a) Shapes <u>A, C, G, H, N and R</u> are all right-angled triangles.

(b) Shape ____ is a square.

(c) Shapes ____ are all parallelograms.

(d) Shape D is a ____ .

(e) Shapes ____ and ____ are trapeziums.

(f) The kites are shapes ____ and ____ .

(g) Shape ____ is an ordinary quadrilateral.

(h) Shape U is an ____ triangle.

(i) The only square in the picture is shape ____ .

(j) Shapes ____ are isosceles triangles.

4 Here is a list of the names of some shapes:

hexagon	rhombus	isosceles triangle
rectangle	trapezium	parallelogram
octagon	pentagon	right-angled triangle
square	kite	equilateral triangle

Use the list to help you write down the names of these:

(a)   (b)  (c)

(d)  (e)  (f)

(g) 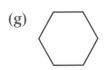 (h)   (i)

5 Write down the special names of these shapes.
  (a) a triangle with all its sides equal
  (b) a polygon with five sides
  (c) a polygon with eight equal sides and all its angles equal
  (d) a triangle with two of its sides equal
  (e) a polygon with ten vertices.

6 Write down the name of a quadrilateral with
  (a) all its sides and all its angles equal
  (b) only one pair of opposite sides parallel
  (c) only one diagonal bisected by the other diagonal.

7 Write down the names of all the quadrilaterals which have
  (a) all their angles equal
  (b) two pairs of opposite sides parallel
  (c) all their sides equal
  (d) two pairs of equal sides but not all their sides equal.

8 Write down the names of all the quadrilaterals which have
  (a) the diagonals equal
  (b) the diagonals bisecting each other
  (c) the diagonals meeting at right angles
  (d) the diagonals bisecting each other at right angles
  (e) at least one pair of opposite sides parallel.

9 In the parallelogram
  (a) write down the value of a
  (b) calculate
      (i) b (ii) c.

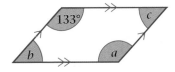

Remember:
The angles of a
quadrilateral add to 360°.

10 In the kite *PQRS* angle *QPR* = 58°.
Calculate
   (a) angle *PQS*
   (b) angle *PQR*.

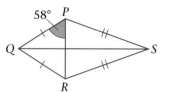

11 In the rhombus, *AC* = 6 cm and
BD = 10 cm.
Work out the area of
   (a) triangle *ABD*
   (b) the rhombus *ABCD*.

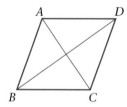

> Note:
> The area of a triangle is
> $\frac{1}{2}$ × base × height. You
> can read more about this
> in Chapter 19 (in Book 2).

7.2 Drawing 2-D shapes on grid paper

There are occasions when it is a good idea to use grid paper to
draw shapes.
Squared paper is very common but you may also use
isometric grid paper. The grid on isomeric paper is made up
from equilateral triangles.

Shapes based on right angles are easy to draw on squared paper.

Example 1

Draw a parallelogram, a square and a right-angled triangle on squared paper.

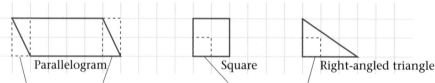

Parallelogram   Square   Right-angled triangle

You can see the sloping sides   You can easily see the
are parallel and equal because   right angles because
they are both diagonals of   of the square grid.
2 by 1 rectangles.

Shapes based on equilateral triangles or with 60° angles are
easier to draw on isometric paper.

Example 2

Draw an equilateral triangle, a regular hexagon and an arrowhead on isometric paper.

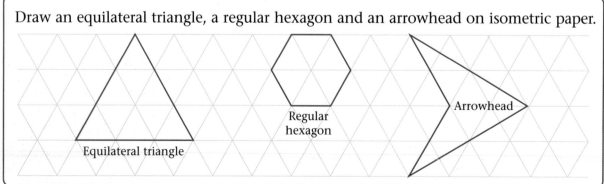

Regular
hexagon

Arrowhead

Equilateral triangle

Exercise 7B

You will need squared paper and isometric paper.

1 On squared paper draw
  (a) a rectangle with sides 2 cm and 3 cm
  (b) a right-angled triangle with base 3 cm and height 2 cm
  (c) a square with sides 3 cm long.

2 On squared paper draw
  (a) an isosceles triangle with a base of 5 cm and a height of 3 cm
  (b) a parallelogram with the longest sides 5 cm
  (c) a trapezium with parallel sides that add up to 9 cm and with height 3 cm.

3 On isometric paper draw
  (a) an equilateral triangle with sides of 5 cm
  (b) a regular hexagon with sides of 4 cm
  (c) a parallelogram with opposite sides of 5 cm and 3 cm
  (d) an isosceles trapezium with parallel sides of 5 cm and 7 cm and slant sides 3 cm.

An isosceles trapezium has equal base angles.

4 Design some square tiles using quadrilaterals and triangles. Do not use too many different shapes in any one design.

Here are two designs from the floor of a Roman villa.

7.3 Congruent shapes

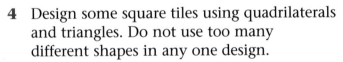

These three shapes are facing different ways but their sides are the same length and their angles are the same size.

Shapes which are exactly the same size and shape are **congruent**.

Example 3

Which of these shapes are congruent?

A   B   C   D

Shapes A and C are **congruent**. They have the same length sides and the same size angles.

Reflected shapes are still the same size and shape. These shapes are congruent.

Exercise 7C

Write down the letters of the shapes which are congruent.

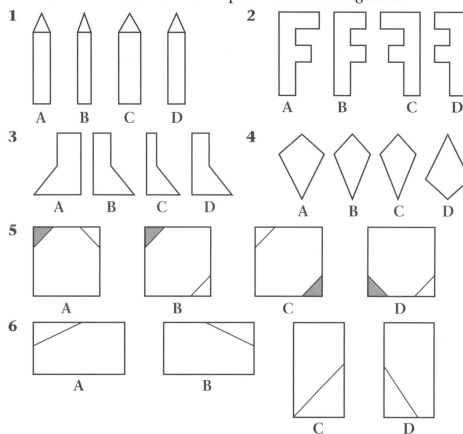

You need a ruler, protractor and squared paper to answer questions **7–8**.

7 Copy the shape on to squared paper. On the same paper draw two shapes that are congruent to the given one, but turned round into a different position.

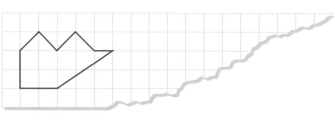

8

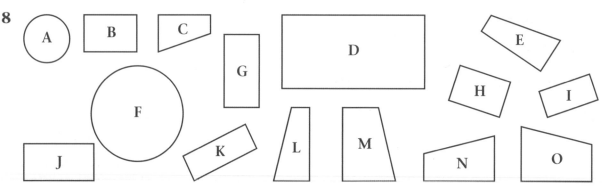

Write down the letters of two pairs of congruent shapes.

7.4 Tessellations

A pattern of shapes which fit together without leaving gaps or overlapping is called a **tessellation**.

Tessellating shapes are often used to make tiles or patterns.

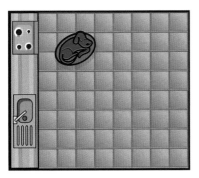

Square floor tiles

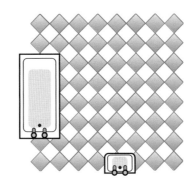

Squares rotated

Rectangular bricks

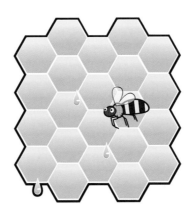

Hexagons

Example 4

Tessellate this trapezium on a grid.

There are three possible ways of doing this.

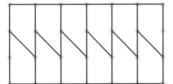  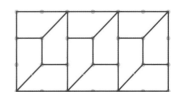

Exercise 7D

You will need dotted grid paper.

1 Show how each of these shapes tessellates.

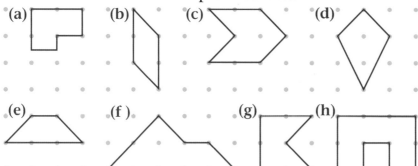

2 Using an isometric grid or dotted isometric paper show how these shapes tessellate.

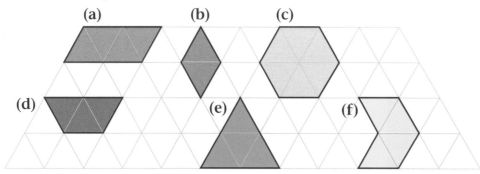

3 Show how you can make a regular octagon and a square tessellate. See if you find two other regular polygons that tessellate together.

4 Here is one shape with curved sides that tessellates. Find three more shapes with curved sides that tessellate. You must show at least eight of your shapes tessellating.

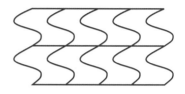

5 Make some interesting patterns using combinations of different shapes that tessellate.

7.5 Making accurate drawings

Line segments

A straight line can be continued forever in both directions. It has infinite length.

The part of the straight line that is between X and Y is called the **line segment** XY.

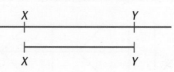

Sometimes you will be asked to make an accurate drawing from given measurements.

Example 5

Make an accurate drawing of triangle *ABC*
with *AB* = 6 cm, *BC* = 5 cm and *CA* = 4 cm.

Make a rough sketch first, to get an idea of
what your finished drawing should be like.

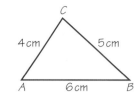

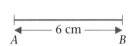

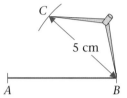

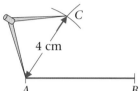

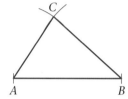

Start with the longest
side. Draw a line
segment 6 cm long
and label its ends *A*
and *B*.

Set your compasses to
a radius of 5 cm. Put
the point at *B* and
draw an arc near
where you think *C*
will be.

Set your compasses
to 4 cm. Put the point
at *B* and draw a
second arc. Point *C*
is where the two arcs
cross.

Join *C* to *A* and *B* to
complete the triangle.

Leave in the arcs.

Example 6

Make an accurate drawing of triangle
PQR with *PQ* = 5 cm, angle *P* = 40°
and angle *Q* = 60°.

Make a rough sketch first.

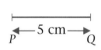

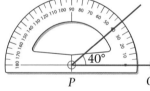

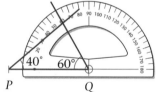

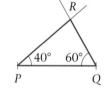

Draw a line segment
5 cm long and label
its ends *P* and *Q*.

Place your protractor over
point *P*. Mark a point at
40° (anticlockwise) and
join it to *P* with a line.

Place your protractor
over point *Q*. Mark a
point at 60° (clockwise)
and join it to *Q* with
a line.

The new lines cross
at *R* completing
the triangle *PQR*.

Example 7

(a) Make an accurate drawing of quadrilateral *PQRS* with *PQ* = 6.4 cm,
PS = 3.5 cm, *SR* = 4.7 cm, *QR* = 5.3 cm and angle *P* = 112°.
(b) Measure angle *QRS*.

(a) Make a rough sketch with the longest side at the bottom.
The vertices *P*, *Q*, *R* and *S* should be in that order
around the quadrilateral.

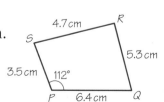

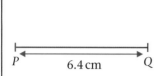

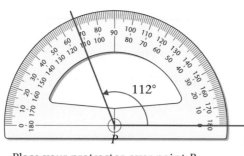

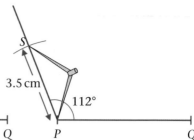

Draw a line segment 6.4 cm long and label the ends *P* and *Q*.

Place your protractor over point *P*. Mark a point at 112° (anticlockwise) and join it to *P* with a line.

Set your compasses to 3.5 cm and use them to mark point *S* 3.5 cm along the line from *P*.

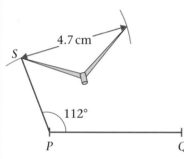

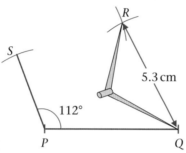

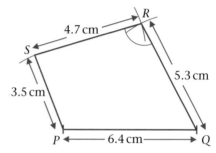

Set your compasses to 4.7 cm. With the point at *S* draw an arc near where you expect *R* to be.

Set your compasses to 5.3 cm. With the point at *Q* draw another arc near where you expect *R* to be. The two arcs cross at *R*.

Join *R* to *S* and *Q* to complete the quadrilateral *PQRS*. Use a protractor to measure angle *QRS*.

(b) If you have made an accurate drawing, angle *QRS* should be about 115°.

You can construct regular polygons inscribed in a circle by dividing the circle equally.

> This means a polygon whose vertices all touch the circle's circumference.

Example 8

Draw a circle with radius 5 cm.
Construct an inscribed regular polygon with nine sides.
The polygon is regular, so the angles at the centre are equal.
$9a = 360°$ so $a = 360° \div 9 = 40°$
Draw a sketch to help you.

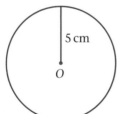

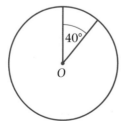

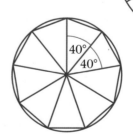

Draw a circle with radius 5 cm. Draw any radius.

Draw another radius at 40° to the first radius. Continue drawing radii at 40° to the previous radius.

Join up the points where the radii meet the circle with nine lines. These lines will form the regular polygon.

Exercise 7E

You need a ruler, compasses and a protractor.

1 Make accurate full-size drawings of these triangles:

(a)

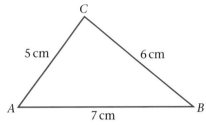

(b)

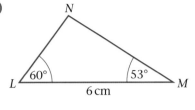

(c)

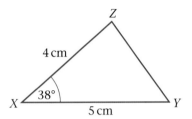

(d)

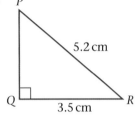

2 (a) Make an accurate drawing of the quadrilateral *ABCD*.
  (b) Measure and write down the size of angle *BAD*.

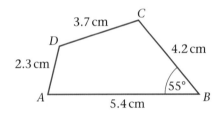

3 (a) Make an accurate drawing of the quadrilateral *PQRS*.
  (b) Measure and write down the length of *RS*.

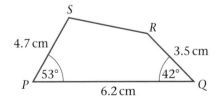

4 Draw a circle with radius 6 cm. Construct an inscribed regular polygon with nine sides.

5 Try to make accurate drawings of triangles with these measurements:
  (a) *ABC* with *AB* = 9 cm, angle *A* = 30° and *BC* = 3 cm
  (b) *LMN* with LM = 9 cm, angle *L* = 30° and *MN* = 5 cm
  (c) *XYZ* with XY = 9 cm, angle *X* = 30° and *YZ* = 4.5 cm.

> It may be possible to draw more than one triangle, or no triangle at all for some measurements.

7.6 Using scales in accurate drawings

Maps and plans are accurate drawings from which measurements can be made.

> There is more about ratios in Chapter 17 (in Book 2).

A **scale** is a ratio which shows the relationship between a length on a drawing and the actual length in real life.

Ordnance Survey Pathfinder maps used by hill walkers are on a scale of 1 to 25 000, written 1 : 25 000.

1 cm on the map represents 25 000 cm in real life, which is 250 m or a quarter of a kilometre.

Example 9

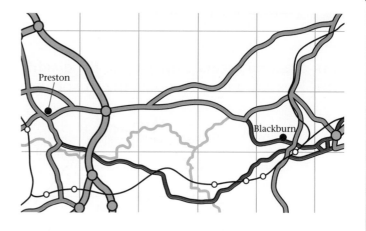

The scale on a road map is 1 : 200 000.
Preston and Blackburn are 8 cm apart on the map.
(a) Work out the real distance, in km, between Preston and Blackburn.

York is 37 km in a straight line from Leeds.
(b) Work out the distance of York from Leeds on the map.

(a) The distance on the map is 8 cm.
The real distance is 8 cm × 200 000 = 1 600 000 cm
Divide by 100 to change cm to m:

> Remember:
> 1 m = 100 cm
> 1 km = 1000 m

   real distance = 16 000 m

Divide by 1000 to change m to km:
The real distance between Preston and Blackburn is 16 km.

(b) The real distance is 37 km.
Multiply by 1000 to change km to m:

   real distance = 37 × 1000 = 37 000 m

Multiply by 100 to change m to cm:
   real distance = 37 000 × 100 = 3 700 000 cm
Divide by 200 000 to find the distance on the map:

   Distance on the map = $\dfrac{3\,700\,000}{200\,000}$ = 18.5 cm

Scale drawings and bearings

Sometimes you will have to draw diagrams to scale and use bearings so that you can measure and calculate missing angles and distances.

> Remember:
> A bearing is a three-figure angle measured from the North.
>
>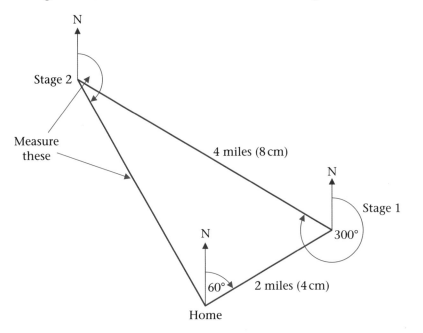
>
> The bearing of Chris from Louise is 070°.

___ **Example 10** _____

Sam walks for 2 miles on a bearing of 060° from home.
He then walks a further 4 miles on a bearing of 300°.
How far is Sam from home? What bearing must Sam walk
on to get back home? Use a scale of 2 cm to represent 1 mile.

Step 1 Draw the bearing of 060° from home.
Step 2 Make the line 4 cm long. •
Step 3 Put in a new North line at the end of Stage 1.
Step 4 Draw the bearing of 300° from Stage 1.
Step 5 Make the line 8 cm long (4 miles is 4 × 2 cm).
Step 6 Put in a new North line at the end of Stage 2.
Step 7 Measure the distance from Stage 2 to home.
Step 8 Measure the bearing from Stage 2 to home.
Answer Sam is about 3.5 miles from home and must walk
on a bearing of 150°.

> As the scale is 2 cm for 1 mile, you need to draw a line that is 4 cm long.

Exercise 7F

You will need a ruler and protractor.

1   The scale of a map is 1 cm to 2 km.
    The distance between Axton and Dixiville is 5.5 cm on the map.
    How many kilometres apart are Axton and Dixiville in real life?

2 A map is drawn on a scale of 3 cm to 1 km.

(a) Work out the real length of a lake which is 4.2 cm long on the map.

(b) The distance between the church in Canwick and the town hall in Barnton is 5.8 km. Work out the distance between them on the map.

> **Scale: 3 cm to 1 km**
> This means that a real length of 1 km is represented on the map by a length of 3 cm.

3 Jane walks for 10 miles on a bearing of 060°. Use a scale of 1 cm to represent 1 mile to show the journey.

4 Sam runs for 4 km on a bearing of 120°. Use a scale of 1 cm to represent 2 km to show the journey.

5 A plan of a rectangular playing field is drawn using a scale of 1 : 2500.

The width of the field on the plan is 5 cm.

(a) (i) Work out the real width of the field in centimetres.

(ii) Change your answer to metres.

The area of the field on the plan is 31.5 cm².

(b) (i) Work out the length, in centimetres, of the playing field on the plan.

(ii) Work out the real length, in metres, of the playing field.

6 On the map the scale is 1 : 50 000. Use the map to find

(a) the distance of the church with a tower at Rampton from the church with a tower at Cottenham

(b) the bearing of the church at Rampton from the church with a tower at Cottenham.

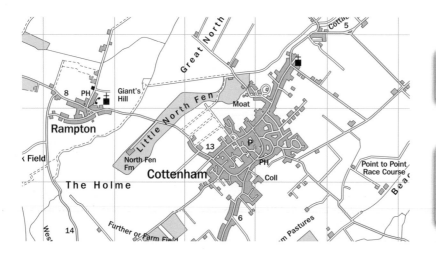

> The sign ⌖ on this map represents a church with a tower.

> Use the straight edge of a piece of paper to join the two churches to help you measure the bearing. (See Example 5 on page 100).

7   Witley is 2 km due South of Milford. The bearing of
    Hydestile from Milford is 125° and the distance from
    Milford to Hydestile is 2.8 km.

    (a) Make a scale drawing to show the three villages.
         Use a scale of 1 : 25 000.
    (b) Use your drawing to find
         (i) the distance of Hydestile from Witley
         (ii) the bearing of Hydestile from Witley.

> **Scale: 1 : 25 000**
> This means that 1 cm on
> the scale drawing
> represents a real length of
> 25 000 cm. This is the
> scale on maps often used
> by walkers.

8   Ian sails his boat from the Isle of Wight for 20 km on a
    bearing of 135°. He then sails on a bearing of 240° for
    10 km. How far is Ian from his starting point? What
    bearing does he need to sail on to get back to the start?
    Use a scale of 1 cm to represent 2 km.

9   Peg Leg the pirate buried his treasure 100 yards from
    the big tree on a bearing of 045°. One-Eyed Rick dug up
    the treasure and moved it 50 yards on a bearing of 310°
    from where it had been buried.
    How far is the treasure from the big tree now?
    What bearing is the new hiding place of the treasure?
    Use a scale of 1 cm to represent 10 yards.

10 Ray flew his plane on a bearing of 300° for 200 km.
    He then changed direction and flew on a bearing of 150°
    for 100 km. What bearing must Ray fly on to get back to
    the start? How far is he away from the start?

7.7 Constructing angles without a protractor

You will be expected to be able to draw some angles without
using a protractor. You will need a pair of compasses and a
straight edge (ruler).

Angle of 60°

	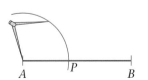	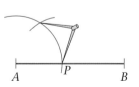	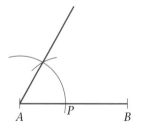
Draw a line segment *AB*.	Put your compass point at *A* and draw an arc that crosses the line segment. Make sure your compass setting does not change.	Put your compass point at *P* and draw an arc to cut the first arc.	Then draw a line from *A* through the point where the two arcs meet.

Bisecting an angle (cutting an angle in half)

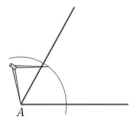

Put your compass point at *A*. Draw an arc that crosses both lines.

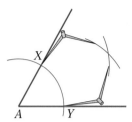

Put your compass point at *X* and then *Y* and draw two arcs that cross.

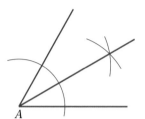

Draw a line to bisect the angle.

You can now use this technique of bisecting an angle to bisect a 60° angle and get a 30° angle.

Drawing an angle of 90°

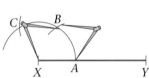

Draw a line segment *XY*. Put your compass point at *X*. Draw an arc that crosses *XY* at *A*. Move the compass point to *A*. Draw an arc at *B*

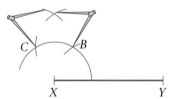

Put your compass point at *B* and then *C*. Draw arcs to cross above *X*.

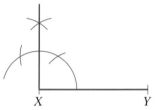

Draw a line from *X* through the point where the two arcs cross.

Bisecting a line

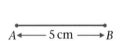

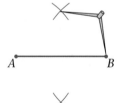

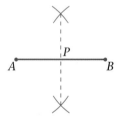

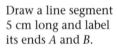

Draw a line segment 5 cm long and label its ends *A* and *B*.

Set your compasses to any radius greater than 2.5 cm (5 cm ÷ 2). With the point at *A* draw arcs on each side of the line segment where you expect the bisector to be.

Keep the compasses at the same radius but move the point to *B* and draw two new arcs.

Draw a line segment joining the points where the arcs cross. This is the perpendicular bisector of *AB*. Mark with a *P* the point where this perpendicular bisector crosses the line segment *AB*.

Exercise 7G

Use the ideas of starting with 60° and bisecting angles to construct the angles in questions 1–8.

1 60°   **2** 30°   **3** 120°   **4** 90°

5 45°   **6** 75°   **7** 15°   **8** 135°

9 Draw a line that is 6 cm long and bisect it.
Check that each part is 3 cm long.

10 Draw a triangle that has sides 10 cm, 8 cm and 8 cm.
Bisect each of the sides. The bisectors should meet at a point. Use that point as the centre to draw a circle. The circle should pass through all the vertices of the triangle.

11 Draw a triangle that has sides 15 cm, 10 cm and 8 cm.
Bisect each of the angles. The bisectors should meet at a point. Use that point as the centre to draw a circle. The circle should touch each of the sides of the triangle.

7.8 Finding the locus of a point

To enter the harbour safely this boat must follow the path shown by the red dotted line.

All the points on the path obey a rule:

Each point is always equidistant (the same distance) from *A* and *B*.

This path is called the **locus** of the points.

A **locus** is a set of points that obey a given rule.

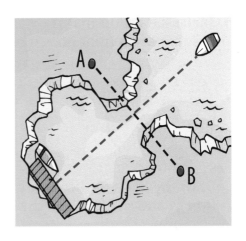

Here are the main ideas behind the loci you need to know.

> Loci is the plural of locus.

The locus of points equidistant from **one point** is a circle.

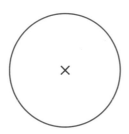

The locus of points equidistant from **two points** is the perpendicular bisector of the line joining the two points.

The locus of points equidistant from **one line** is made from two semicircles and two parallel lines.

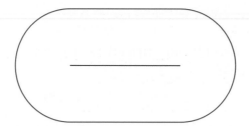

The locus of points equidistant from **two lines** is made by bisecting the angles formed by *AB* and *CD*.

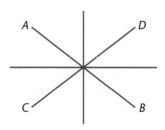

Regions

Sometimes the locus is a **region** of space.

The key words here are 'greater than', 'less than', 'nearer to'.

> Remember these signs:
> < less than
> > greater than

Example 11

(a) Shade the region that is less than 3 cm from *A*.

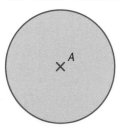

Draw the locus of the points 3 cm from *A* and shade inside the circle.

(b) Shade the region that is nearer to *BC* than to *AB*.

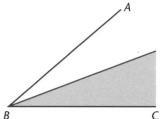

Bisect angle *ABC* and shade the part that is nearer to *BC* than it is to *AB*.

Worked examination question

A, *B* and *C* represent three radio masts on a plan.

Signals from mast *A* can be received 300 km away, those from mast *B* 350 km away and those from mast *C* 200 km away.

Show, by shading, the region in which signals can be received from all three masts.   [E]

B
•

•A

•
C

Scale: 1 cm represents 100 km

Signals from *A* can be received inside a circle with centre *A* and radius 300 km.

1 cm represents 100 km so 3 cm represents 300 km. Draw a circle with centre *A* and radius 3 cm.

In the same way draw circles with centre *B* and radius 3.5 cm and with centre *C* and radius 2 cm.

The region in which all three signals can be received must be inside all the circles, so it is the region shaded in the diagram.

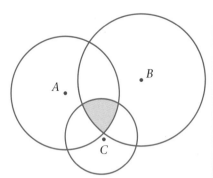

This is a scaled-down sketch.

Exercise 7H

1. Draw the locus of all points that are 5 cm from a point *P*.

2. Draw the locus of all points that are 5 cm from a line *AB* that is 8 cm long.

3. Points *P* and *Q* are 8 cm apart. Draw the locus of all points that are the same distance from *P* as they are from *Q*.

4. *AB* and *CD* are two perpendicular lines. Draw the locus of all points that are the same distance from *AB* as they are from *CD*.

5. Draw a square with sides of length 4 cm. Draw the locus of all points that are 5 cm from the sides of the square.

6. Here is a diagram of a rectangular garden. Copy it into your book using a scale of 1 cm to 1 m.

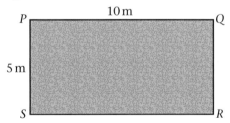

A tree is to be planted nearer to *PQ* than to *PS* and less than 4 metres from *P*. Shade the region within the garden where the tree could be planted.

7. Two marker buoys *A* and *B* are in the sea near the town of Barry. *B* is 250 m due East of *A*.
   (a) Using a scale of 1 cm to 50 m make an accurate drawing to show the positions of *A* and *B*.

   Juliet sails her boat so that she is always the same distance from *A* as from *B*.
   (b) Construct accurately the course along which Juliet sails.

8   In triangle *DEF*, *DE* = 7 cm, angle *D* = 42° and angle *E* = 57°.
    (a)   Make an accurate drawing of triangle *DEF*.
    (b)   Draw accurately the locus of all points that are the
          same distance from *D* as from *E*.
    (c)   Draw the locus of all points that are 4 cm from *D*.
    (d)   Mark the points *P* and *Q* which are on both loci.

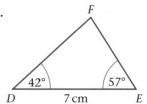

9   The map shows part of a coastline and a coastguard
    station. 1 cm on the map represents 2 km.
    A ship is 12 km from the coastguard station on a bearing
    of 160°.
    (a)   Use tracing paper to make a copy of the map. Plot
          the position of the ship from the coastguard station.
    It is not safe for ships to come within 6 km of the
    coastguard station.
    (b)   Shade the area on the map which is less than 6 km
          from the coastguard station.

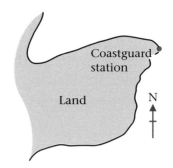

Mixed exercise 7

1   Write down the name of each of these shapes:
    (a)   (b)   (c)

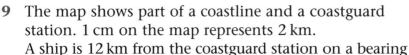

2   Write down the letters of the shapes that are congruent.

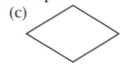

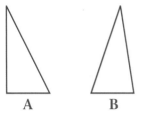

Floor pattern in an Italian
church.

3   Use a grid made of centimetre squares to show how these
    shapes will tessellate. You must draw at least eight shapes.
    (a)   (b)   (c)

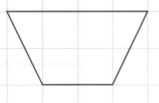
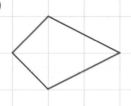
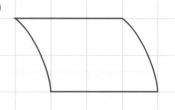

4 The diagram shows a sketch of triangle *ABC*.
BC = 7.3 cm
AC = 8 cm
Angle *C* = 38°
(a) Make an accurate drawing of triangle *ABC*.
(b) Measure the size of angle *A* on your diagram.   [E]

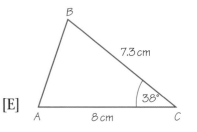

5 On a copy of the grid below, draw a line from the point *C*
perpendicular to the line *AB*.

[E]

6 This is a map of Northern England.

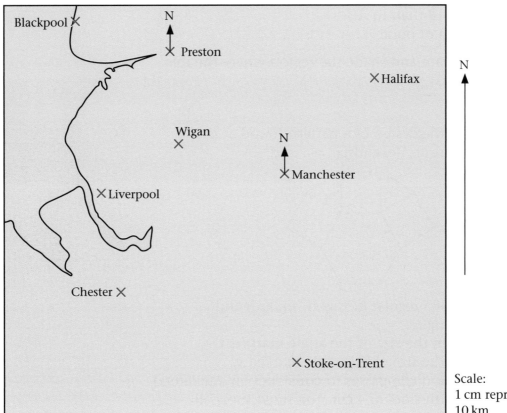

Scale:
1 cm represents
10 km

A plane flies in a straight line from Preston to Stoke-on-Trent.
(a) How far does it fly?
Give your answer in kilometres.
(b) Measure and write down the bearing of Preston from
Manchester.   [E]

7 Using ruler and compasses **construct** an angle of 45°.
You must show **all** construction lines.   [E]

8 The diagram represents a triangular garden *ABC*.

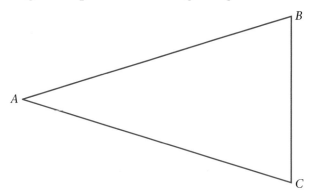

The scale of the diagram is 1 cm to represent 1 m. A tree
is to be planted in the garden so that it is

    nearer to *AB* than to *AC*
    within 5 m of point *A*.

Trace the diagram and shade the region where the tree
may be planted.   [E]

9 This is part of the design of a pattern found at the
theatre of Diana at Alexandria.

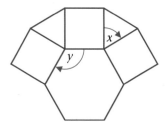

It is made up of a regular hexagon, squares and
equilateral triangles.
(a) Write down the size of the angle marked *x*.
(b) Work out the size of the angle marked *y*.
(c) Use ruler and compasses to **construct** an equilateral
    triangle with sides of 4 cm. You must show all
    construction lines.

10 Draw triangle *PQR* with *PQ* = 10 cm, *QR* = 8 cm and
RP = 6 cm.
Bisect the lines *PQ, QR* and *RP*.

Summary of key points

1   A **polygon** is a 2-D shape
    with any number of
    straight sides.

A pentagon

2   A polygon is **regular**
    if all its sides and all
    its angles are equal.

A regular pentagon

3   Shapes which are exactly
    the same size and shape are
    congruent.

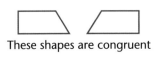

These shapes are congruent

4   A pattern of shapes which fit together without
    leaving gaps or overlapping is called a **tessellation**.

5   A straight line can be continued forever in
    both directions. It has infinite length. The part
    of the straight line that is between X and Y is
    called the **line segment** XY.

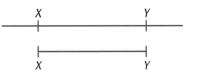

6   A **scale** is a ratio which shows the relationship between
    a length on a drawing and the actual length in real life.

7   Using a pair of compasses and a ruler you can construct
    an angle of 60°, bisect an angle and bisect a line without
    using a protractor.

8   A **locus** is a set of points that obey a given rule.

9   The locus of points equidistant from **one
    point** is a circle.

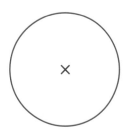

10 The locus of points equidistant from **two
    points** is the perpendicular bisector.

11   The locus of points equidistant from **one line**
     is made from two semicircles and two parallel
     lines.

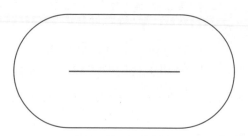

12   The locus of points equidistant from **two lines**
     is made by bisecting the angles formed by
     AB and *CD*.

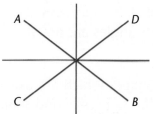

13   Sometimes the locus is a **region** of space.

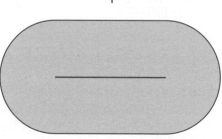

8 Fractions

8.1 Fractions from pictures

All these things can be divided into parts called **fractions**:

This football pitch has two halves.

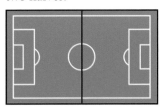

One part is **one half** or $\frac{1}{2}$ of the pitch.

This DVD has eight sectors.

One part is **one eighth** or $\frac{1}{8}$ of the DVD.

This chessboard has 64 small squares.

One part is **one sixty-fourth** or $\frac{1}{64}$ of the board.

Using numbers to represent fractions

I am going to eat three quarters or $\frac{3}{4}$ of this omelette.

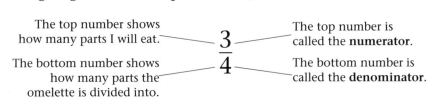

The top number shows how many parts I will eat.

$\frac{3}{4}$

The top number is called the **numerator**.

The bottom number shows how many parts the omelette is divided into.

The bottom number is called the **denominator**.

Two thirds or $\frac{2}{3}$ of these parking spaces are occupied.

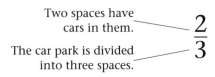

Two spaces have cars in them.

$\frac{2}{3}$

The car park is divided into three spaces.

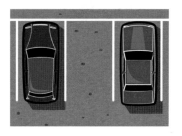

Exercise 8A

1 Copy these shapes into a table like the one on the right. Complete the table. The first shape has been done for you.

Shape	Fraction shaded	Fraction not shaded
(circle)	$\frac{1}{2}$	$\frac{1}{2}$

2 Make four copies of this rectangle.
Shade them to show these fractions:

(a) $\frac{1}{16}$ (b) $\frac{3}{16}$ (c) $\frac{8}{16}$ (d) $\frac{16}{16}$

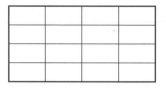

3 Make three copies of this circle.
Shade them to show these fractions:

(a) $\frac{1}{6}$ (b) $\frac{3}{6}$ (c) $\frac{1}{2}$

4 Here is a counting stick with an arrow showing $\frac{7}{10}$:

Draw three more sticks with length 10 cm. Use them to show

(a) $\frac{3}{10}$ (b) $\frac{1}{10}$ (c) $\frac{5}{10}$

8.2 Fractions from words

Sometimes you will need to use fractions to solve problems given in words.

Example 1

John has a collection of 1000 stamps.
113 are British stamps. The others are foreign.

What fraction of John's collection is

(a) British   (b) foreign?

(a) 113 of the 1000 stamps are British.
The fraction is $\frac{113}{1000}$

(b) 1000 − 113 = 887 stamps are foreign.
The fraction is $\frac{887}{1000}$

Exercise 8B

1 There are 28 people on a martial arts course. 13 are female and 15 are male. What fraction of the people are

(a) male   (b) female?

2 28 competitors took part in a surfing competition on a Saturday, and a further 47 took part on Sunday.

(a) How many surfers were there altogether?

(b) What fraction of the surfers competed on Saturday?

(c) What fraction of the surfers competed only on Sunday?

3 A transport company has a fleet of 51 vehicles.
37 are lorries, 10 are vans and 4 are cars.
What fraction of the fleet is

(a) lorries   (b) vans   (c) cars?

4 A plumber's weekly earnings are £317 per week.
£298 is basic pay and £19 is bonus pay.
What fraction of his weekly earnings is

(a) basic pay   (b) bonus pay?

5 In the safari section of the zoo there are 7 zebras, 3 lions,
5 hippos and 1 giraffe.
(a) How many animals are there altogether?
What fraction of the entries are

(b) zebras   (c) lions   (d) hippos   (e) giraffes?

6 An electrical superstore sold 5 CD players, 6 DVD players,
4 refrigerators and 2 freezers.
(a) How many items were sold altogether?
What fraction of the items sold were

(b) CD players   (c) DVD players

(d) refrigerators   (e) freezers?

7 A taxi driver works 11 hours a day.
She spends 6 hours driving, 4 hours waiting for
passengers and 1 hour on paperwork.
What fraction of her working day is spent

(a) driving   (b) waiting   (c) on paperwork?

8.3 Improper fractions and mixed numbers

These fractions are **top heavy**:

$\frac{5}{4}$ is top heavy because 5 is bigger than 4

$\frac{11}{9}$ is top heavy because 11 is bigger than 9

Top heavy fractions are also called **improper fractions**.

An improper fraction can also be written as a **mixed number**
(a mixture of a whole number and a fraction, and a mixed
number can also be written as an improper fraction.

improper fraction —— $\dfrac{11}{9} = \dfrac{9}{9} + \dfrac{2}{9} = 1\dfrac{2}{9}$ —— mixed number

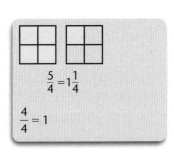

Example 2

Change the mixed number $1\frac{4}{7}$ to an improper fraction.

1 can be written as $\frac{7}{7}$　so　$1\frac{4}{7} = \frac{7}{7} + \frac{4}{7} = \frac{11}{7}$

Example 3

Write $5\frac{3}{7}$ as an improper fraction.

5 can be written as $\frac{5 \times 7}{7} = \frac{35}{7}$　so　$5\frac{3}{7} = \frac{35}{7} + \frac{3}{7} = \frac{38}{7}$

Exercise 8C

1 Change these improper fractions to mixed numbers.

(a) $\frac{5}{2}$　　(b) $\frac{7}{4}$　　(c) $\frac{9}{7}$　　(d) $\frac{11}{8}$

(e) $\frac{9}{8}$　　(f) $\frac{16}{5}$　　(g) $\frac{23}{10}$　　(h) $\frac{24}{5}$

(i) $\frac{16}{7}$　　(j) $\frac{12}{5}$　　(k) $\frac{20}{3}$　　(l) $\frac{16}{9}$

(m) $\frac{39}{4}$　　(n) $\frac{27}{5}$　　(o) $\frac{26}{9}$　　(p) $\frac{17}{10}$

> Divide the bottom number into the top number, e.g. $\frac{7}{2} = 7 \div 2 = 3\frac{1}{2}$

2 Change these mixed numbers to improper fractions.

(a) $1\frac{1}{2}$　　(b) $5\frac{1}{2}$　　(c) $2\frac{3}{4}$　　(d) $1\frac{2}{3}$

(e) $3\frac{1}{4}$　　(f) $4\frac{2}{5}$　　(g) $3\frac{7}{10}$　　(h) $5\frac{1}{5}$

(i) $7\frac{3}{4}$　　(j) $2\frac{1}{4}$　　(k) $1\frac{9}{10}$　　(l) $9\frac{1}{3}$

(m) $2\frac{5}{6}$　　(n) $5\frac{3}{8}$　　(o) $3\frac{5}{8}$　　(p) $1\frac{9}{100}$

8.4 Finding a fraction of a quantity

You need to be able to do calculations like these:

$\frac{3}{4}$ of £60　　　$\frac{5}{8}$ of 160

> $\frac{3}{4} = 3 \div 4$

Example 4

Find $\frac{3}{4}$ of £60.

Multiply the numerator 3 by the quantity 60:　$\frac{3 \times 60}{4} = \frac{180}{4}$

Divide the result 180 by the denominator 4:　$\frac{180}{4} = 45$

So $\frac{3}{4}$ of £60 is £45.

> Another method: one quarter is
> $\frac{60}{4} = 15$
> three quarters is
> $3 \times 15 = 45$

If you are dealing with small numbers then you can use this more practical approach:

Example 5

Find $\frac{5}{6}$ of £48.

You make 6 boxes and count out the 48 pounds between them:

You end up with 8 in each box.

Then count how many there are in 5 of the boxes.

The answer is £40.

Exercise 8D

1 Find

   (a) $\frac{1}{2}$ of 70   (b) $\frac{2}{5}$ of £65   (c) $\frac{3}{10}$ of 80 kg

   (d) $\frac{2}{3}$ of 96   (e) $\frac{3}{8}$ of £56   (f) $\frac{3}{4}$ of 60p

   (g) $\frac{1}{4}$ of £6.80   (h) $\frac{7}{10}$ of 90p   (i) $\frac{7}{8}$ of £3.20

2 Work out

   (a) $\frac{1}{8}$ of 72   (b) $\frac{5}{6}$ of 36

   (c) $\frac{4}{9}$ of 63 litres   (d) $\frac{7}{16}$ of 48 pints

3 Work out

   (a) $\frac{3}{4}$ of 36 lb   (b) $\frac{2}{5}$ of £5.55

   (c) $\frac{11}{12}$ of 720 km   (d) $\frac{4}{7}$ of 490 people

4 A superstore employs 85 people. $\frac{2}{5}$ are men.

   (a) How many men does the store employ?

   (b) How many women does the store employ?

5 A chain store closed $\frac{2}{15}$ of its 345 shops.
How many shops were closed?

6 Out of 186 pupils in Year 10 of Angel High School, $\frac{1}{3}$ have an MP3 player. How many is this?

7 The metal parts of a car weigh 1250 kg. $\frac{3}{10}$ of the metal is recycled. How much does the recycled metal weigh?

8 Stan sold 560 sandwiches today. $\frac{1}{4}$ were ham sandwiches, $\frac{2}{5}$ were salad, $\frac{1}{8}$ were tuna and the rest were cheese. How many of each type did Stan sell?

9 In a survey conducted by a local newspaper, 3500 people were questioned about the construction of a new skate park. $\frac{1}{10}$ were against the project, $\frac{7}{10}$ were in favour and the rest abstained. How many people

(a) were against the project

(b) were in favour of the project

(c) abstained?

10 A department store had 480 customers last Saturday. $\frac{2}{3}$ paid by credit card, $\frac{1}{4}$ paid by cheque and the others paid in cash.
How many customers paid

(a) by credit card

(b) by cheque

(c) in cash?

11 During a 28-week holiday season, $\frac{2}{7}$ of the days were wet. How many dry days were there?

12 Jomo delivers 56 newspapers on his round. On Fridays $\frac{3}{8}$ of the newspapers have a magazine supplement. How many supplements does he deliver?

8.5 Simplifying fractions

Fractions can be **simplified** if the numerator (top) and denominator (bottom) have a common factor.

> Simplifying fractions means writing them in their lowest terms. This is also called cancelling fractions.

For example:

$$\frac{4}{8}$$ 　The numerator will divide by 4
　　　The denominator will divide by 4

4 is a common factor.

$$\frac{4}{8}\ \boxed{\begin{array}{l}4\text{ divided by 4 is 1}\\ 8\text{ divided by 4 is 2}\end{array}}\ \frac{1}{2}\ \text{so }\tfrac{4}{8}\text{ can be simplified to }\tfrac{1}{2}$$

$\frac{4}{8}$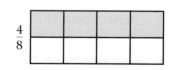

$\frac{4}{8}$ and $\frac{1}{2}$ are **equivalent fractions**. They represent the same value. To simplify a fraction you find an equivalent fraction that has smaller numbers on the top and bottom.

$\frac{1}{2}$

Example 6

Simplify $\frac{9}{15}$ by finding a common factor.

3 is a common factor of 9 and 15. ───

Factors of 9 are: 1, 3, 9
Factors of 15 are: 1, 3, 5, 15

3 is a common factor

$$\frac{9}{15} \quad \boxed{\text{9 divided by 3 is 3}} \quad \frac{3}{5}$$
$$\boxed{\text{15 divided by 3 is 5}}$$

$\frac{9}{15}$ 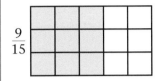 is the same as $\frac{3}{5}$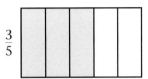

Example 7

Simplify $\frac{24}{30}$ by finding a common factor.

3 is a common factor of 24 and 30.

$$\frac{24}{30} \quad \boxed{\text{24 divided by 3 is 8}} \quad \frac{8}{10}$$
$$\boxed{\text{30 divided by 3 is 10}}$$

$\frac{8}{10}$ can also be simplified. 2 is a common factor of 8 and 10.

$$\frac{8}{10} \quad \boxed{\text{8 divided by 2 is 4}} \quad \frac{4}{5}$$
$$\boxed{\text{10 divided by 2 is 5}}$$

$\frac{4}{5}$ cannot be simplified any more. This fraction is in its **simplest form**.

Exercise 8E

1   Write each fraction in its simplest form.
   (a) $\frac{12}{18}$ (b) $\frac{9}{15}$ (c) $\frac{20}{35}$ (d) $\frac{18}{24}$ (e) $\frac{14}{21}$

2   Write these in their simplest form.
   (a) $\frac{6}{8}$ (b) $\frac{30}{36}$ (c) $\frac{40}{48}$ (d) $\frac{35}{49}$ (e) $\frac{25}{45}$

3   Write these in their simplest form.
   (a) $\frac{20}{32}$ (b) $\frac{48}{64}$ (c) $\frac{21}{27}$ (d) $\frac{24}{60}$ (e) $\frac{48}{72}$

4   Simplify these fractions by finding common factors.
   (a) $\frac{4}{6}$ (b) $\frac{3}{6}$ (c) $\frac{2}{4}$ (d) $\frac{3}{9}$
   (e) $\frac{4}{10}$ (f) $\frac{8}{12}$ (g) $\frac{14}{21}$ (h) $\frac{15}{20}$
   (i) $\frac{14}{22}$ (i) $\frac{24}{28}$ (k) $\frac{27}{36}$ (l) $\frac{25}{30}$

5 Copy these shapes into a table like the one on the right. For each shape use two equivalent fractions to describe how much is shaded. The first shape has been done for you.

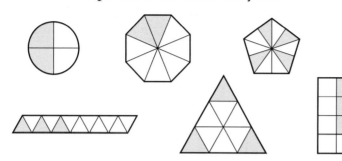

Shape	Fraction	Fraction
	$\frac{2}{4}$	$\frac{1}{2}$

In questions **6**, **7** and **8** write your answers as fractions in their simplest form.

6 A car salesman sold 6 new cars and 15 secondhand cars. What fraction of the cars were

   (a) new   **(b)** secondhand?

7 Siân has collected autographs from 16 pop stars, 28 footballers and 12 athletes. What fraction of her autographs are from

   (a) pop stars   **(b)** footballers

   (c) athletes?

8 Form 11B were surveyed about their favourite type of movies. What fraction chose

   (a) comedy   **(b)** action

   (c) musical   **(d)** other?

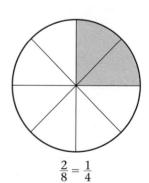

8.6 Equivalent fractions

This circle is divided into 8 parts.

Each part is $\frac{1}{8}$ (or one eighth) of the whole circle.

The shaded area is $\frac{2}{8}$ of the whole circle.

The shaded area is also $\frac{1}{4}$ (or one quarter) of the whole circle.

$\frac{2}{8}$ and $\frac{1}{4}$ represent the same area of the circle. They are called **equivalent fractions**.

$$\frac{2}{8} = \frac{1}{4}$$

   Equivalent fractions are fractions that have the same value.

Example 8

Make a list of fractions equivalent to $\frac{2}{3}$

$$\frac{2}{3} = \frac{4}{6} = \frac{6}{9} = \frac{8}{12} = \frac{10}{15} = \frac{12}{18}\cdots$$

— The top row goes up in the 2 time table.

— The bottom row goes up in the 3 times table.

Example 9

Change $\frac{5}{8}$ to an equivalent fraction with the denominator 48.

$$\frac{5}{8} = \frac{5 \times 6}{8 \times 6} = \frac{30}{48}$$

2 To get an equivalent fraction, multiply the numerator 5 by 6 too.

1 To change the denominator from 8 to 48, multiply 8 by 6.

So $\frac{5}{8}$ and $\frac{30}{48}$ are equivalent fractions.

Exercise 8F

For each of these diagrams write down at least two equivalent fractions that describe the shaded fraction.

1 (a)

(b)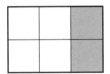

(c)

(d)

(e)

(f)

(g)

(h)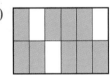

(i)

(j)

Copy and complete each set of equivalent fractions.

2 (a) $\dfrac{3}{4} = \dfrac{}{8} = \dfrac{}{12} = \dfrac{}{16} = \dfrac{}{20} = \dfrac{}{24}$

(b) $\dfrac{2}{7} = \dfrac{}{14} = \dfrac{}{21} = \dfrac{}{28} = \dfrac{}{35} = \dfrac{}{42}$

(c) $\dfrac{4}{5} = \dfrac{}{10} = \dfrac{}{15} = \dfrac{}{20} = \dfrac{}{25} = \dfrac{}{30}$

(d) $\dfrac{1}{3} = \dfrac{}{9} = \dfrac{}{18} = \dfrac{}{27} = \dfrac{}{36} = \dfrac{}{45}$

3 (a) $\dfrac{1}{6} = \dfrac{}{18}$ (b) $\dfrac{3}{7} = \dfrac{}{14}$ (c) $\dfrac{3}{8} = \dfrac{}{48}$ (d) $\dfrac{4}{7} = \dfrac{}{21}$

    (e) $\dfrac{5}{6} = \dfrac{}{36}$ (f) $\dfrac{2}{3} = \dfrac{6}{}$ (g) $\dfrac{4}{9} = \dfrac{24}{}$ (h) $\dfrac{5}{7} = \dfrac{}{56}$

    (i) $\dfrac{9}{10} = \dfrac{90}{}$ (j) $\dfrac{7}{12} = \dfrac{84}{}$ (k) $\dfrac{7}{8} = \dfrac{49}{}$ (l) $\dfrac{2}{9} = \dfrac{}{81}$

4 (a) Find a fraction equivalent to $\frac{1}{2}$ and a fraction equivalent to $\frac{1}{3}$ so that the denominators of the two new fractions are equal.

    (b) Repeat part **(a)** for

       (i) $\frac{2}{5}$ and $\frac{3}{6}$ (ii) $\frac{1}{10}$ and $\frac{1}{7}$ (iii) $\frac{1}{4}$ and $\frac{5}{6}$

       (iv) $\frac{1}{2}$ and $\frac{3}{5}$ (v) $\frac{2}{3}$ and $\frac{1}{8}$ (vi) $\frac{3}{4}$ and $\frac{3}{5}$

8.7 Putting fractions in order of size

Which is larger, $\frac{3}{4}$ or $\frac{3}{5}$? Equivalent fractions can help you decide.

First make lists of equivalent fractions for $\frac{3}{4}$ and $\frac{3}{5}$:

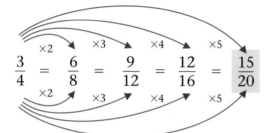 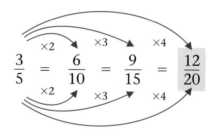

> Compare the lists. Find fractions with the same denominator (bottom).

$\frac{15}{20}$ is larger than $\frac{12}{20}$ (imagine a cake divided into 20 parts and getting either 12 or 15 slices).

As $\frac{15}{20}$ is equivalent to $\frac{3}{4}$ and $\frac{12}{20}$ is equivalent to $\frac{3}{5}$,

$\frac{3}{4}$ must be *larger* than $\frac{3}{5}$

Another way of checking which of two fractions is bigger is to represent them as parts of a rectangle.

For $\frac{2}{3}$ and $\frac{3}{4}$ you need to split a rectangle into 3 and 4 (thirds and quarters).

You split the rectangle in two directions so that you can compare the fractions you have shaded.

8 parts are shaded for $\frac{2}{3}$ and 9 for $\frac{3}{4}$, so $\frac{3}{4}$ is bigger.

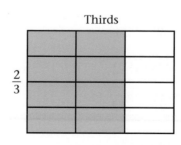 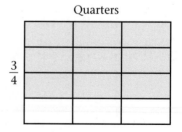

Exercise 8G

1 By shading rectangles show which of each pair of fractions is the larger.

(a) $\frac{3}{4}$ or $\frac{1}{2}$ (b) $\frac{1}{3}$ or $\frac{1}{4}$ (c) $\frac{4}{5}$ or $\frac{3}{4}$ (d) $\frac{5}{6}$ or $\frac{4}{5}$

2 By writing equivalent fractions find the smaller fraction.

(a) $\frac{2}{5}$ or $\frac{1}{4}$ (b) $\frac{3}{4}$ or $\frac{4}{5}$ (c) $\frac{2}{3}$ or $\frac{3}{4}$ (d) $\frac{3}{5}$ or $\frac{7}{10}$

3 Which is larger:

(a) $\frac{2}{5}$ or $\frac{3}{6}$ (b) $\frac{1}{10}$ or $\frac{1}{7}$ (c) $\frac{1}{4}$ or $\frac{5}{6}$

(d) $\frac{1}{2}$ or $\frac{3}{5}$ (e) $\frac{2}{3}$ or $\frac{1}{8}$ (f) $\frac{3}{4}$ or $\frac{3}{5}$?

4 Write these fractions in order of size. Put the smallest one first.

(a) $\frac{1}{2}, \frac{3}{4}, \frac{2}{3}$ (b) $\frac{4}{5}, \frac{5}{6}, \frac{7}{15}$ (c) $\frac{3}{4}, \frac{4}{5}, \frac{1}{2}$ (d) $\frac{3}{7}, \frac{5}{14}, \frac{1}{2}, \frac{4}{7}$

5 Put these fractions in order of size, starting with the largest:

$\frac{2}{5} \quad \frac{1}{2} \quad \frac{7}{8} \quad \frac{3}{4} \quad \frac{2}{10}$

Using fractions in your exam

In your exam, fractions will usually appear in the context of a number problem or in questions on probability, areas or volumes. You need to be able to add, subtract, multiply and divide fractions in such problems. The rest of this chapter shows you how to do this.

8.8 Adding fractions

It is easy to add fractions when the denominators (bottom) are the same:

Easy to add:

$$\frac{1}{4} + \frac{2}{4} = \frac{3}{4}$$

Denominators are the same.

Harder to add:

$$\frac{1}{2} + \frac{2}{3} = ?$$

Denominators are different.

Adding fractions with the same denominator

$$\frac{7}{10} + \frac{2}{10} = \frac{9}{10}$$

Add the numerators (top).

Write them over the **same** denominator (bottom).

Adding fractions with different denominators

$$\frac{1}{2} + \frac{2}{3} = ?$$

First find equivalent fractions to these that have the same denominator (bottom):

Fractions equivalent to $\frac{1}{2}$

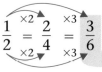

Fractions equivalent to $\frac{2}{3}$

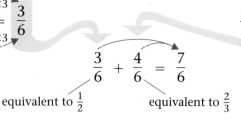

$$\frac{3}{6} + \frac{4}{6} = \frac{7}{6}$$

equivalent to $\frac{1}{2}$ equivalent to $\frac{2}{3}$

These fractions have the same denominator (bottom). Now they are easy to add.

So $\frac{1}{2} + \frac{2}{3} = \frac{7}{6}$

$\frac{7}{6}$ is top heavy. You can write it as a mixed number: $1\frac{1}{6}$

> To **add** fractions, find equivalent fractions that have the same denominator (bottom).

Example 10

Work out $\frac{2}{3} + \frac{7}{12}$

Find equivalent fractions to these that have the same denominator (bottom):

$$\frac{2}{3} + \frac{7}{12} = ?$$

Notice that
$3 \times 4 = 12$

So you only need to change one of the fractions:

$$\frac{2}{3} \quad \overset{\times 4}{\underset{\times 4}{=}} \quad \frac{8}{12}$$

Now both have the same denominator:

$$\frac{8}{12} + \frac{7}{12} = \frac{15}{12}$$

equivalent to $\frac{2}{3}$

So $\frac{8}{12} + \frac{7}{12} = \frac{15}{12}$

$\frac{15}{12}$ is top heavy. It is usually written as a mixed number: $1\frac{3}{12}$

This simplifies to $1\frac{1}{4}$.

Example 11

Work out $\frac{5}{8} + \frac{3}{7}$

Find equivalent fractions to these that have the same denominator (bottom).

$$\frac{5}{8} \xrightarrow[\times 7]{\times 7} \frac{35}{56} \qquad \frac{3}{7} \xrightarrow[\times 8]{\times 8} \frac{24}{56}$$

Notice that $7 \times 8 = 56$
56 is the lowest common multiple of 7 and 8.

$$\frac{35}{56} + \frac{24}{56} = \frac{59}{56}$$

Same denominator – now you can add the numerators.

So $\frac{5}{8} + \frac{3}{7} = \frac{59}{56}$

$\frac{59}{56}$ is top heavy. It is usually written as a mixed number: $1\frac{3}{56}$

Example 12

Work out $2\frac{1}{4} + 3\frac{1}{5}$

These are **mixed numbers**. First add the whole numbers: $2 + 3 = 5$

Then add the fractions:

$$\frac{1}{4} + \frac{1}{5} = ?$$

Change both denominators (bottom) to 20 because $4 \times 5 = 20$:

$$\frac{1}{4} \xrightarrow[\times 5]{\times 5} \frac{5}{20} \qquad \frac{1}{5} \xrightarrow[\times 4]{\times 4} \frac{4}{20}$$

$$\frac{5}{20} + \frac{4}{20} = \frac{9}{20}$$

Same denominator – now you can add the numerators.

Now put the whole numbers and the fractions back together:

5 and $\frac{9}{20}$ is $5\frac{9}{20}$

So $2\frac{1}{4} + 3\frac{1}{5} = 5\frac{9}{20}$

Exercise 8H

1 Work out

(a) $\frac{3}{8} + \frac{4}{8}$ (b) $\frac{2}{9} + \frac{5}{9}$ (c) $\frac{5}{12} + \frac{1}{12}$ (d) $\frac{5}{18} + \frac{11}{18}$

(e) $\frac{1}{2} + \frac{1}{4}$ (f) $\frac{1}{4} + \frac{3}{8}$ (g) $\frac{1}{2} + \frac{7}{8}$ (h) $\frac{2}{3} + \frac{1}{6}$

(i) $\frac{5}{6} + \frac{1}{3}$ (j) $\frac{2}{5} + \frac{3}{10}$ (k) $\frac{7}{12} + \frac{3}{4}$ (l) $\frac{3}{4} + \frac{7}{20}$

(m) $\frac{1}{8} + \frac{3}{8}$ (n) $\frac{2}{7} + \frac{4}{7}$ (o) $\frac{2}{5} + \frac{4}{5}$ (p) $\frac{9}{10} + \frac{7}{10}$

(q) $\frac{7}{9} + 2\frac{4}{9}$ (r) $\frac{5}{6} + 1\frac{5}{6}$ (s) $\frac{3}{4} + \frac{3}{4} + \frac{1}{4}$ (t) $\frac{3}{8} + \frac{5}{8} + \frac{7}{8}$

2 Work out

(a) $\frac{1}{2} + \frac{7}{8}$ (b) $\frac{3}{4} + \frac{1}{10}$ (c) $\frac{4}{9} + \frac{5}{12}$ (d) $\frac{7}{8} + \frac{9}{10}$

(e) $\frac{3}{10} + \frac{4}{15}$ (f) $\frac{5}{6} + \frac{1}{4}$ (g) $\frac{3}{8} + \frac{7}{12}$ (h) $\frac{1}{6} + \frac{8}{9}$

(i) $\frac{5}{8} + \frac{1}{4}$ (j) $1\frac{1}{2} + 2\frac{1}{8}$ (k) $\frac{1}{6} + \frac{5}{8}$ (l) $2\frac{3}{4} + 3\frac{7}{8}$

(m) $1\frac{3}{4} + 2\frac{5}{16}$ (n) $\frac{3}{4} + 3\frac{5}{8}$ (o) $\frac{3}{8} + \frac{11}{16}$ (p) $2\frac{9}{16} + 1\frac{5}{8}$

3 Work out

(a) $\frac{1}{2} + \frac{1}{3}$ (b) $\frac{2}{5} + \frac{1}{6}$ (c) $\frac{5}{8} + \frac{1}{5}$ (d) $\frac{3}{4} + \frac{1}{9}$

(e) $\frac{5}{6} + \frac{3}{7}$ (f) $\frac{9}{10} + \frac{2}{7}$ (g) $\frac{2}{3} + \frac{7}{10}$ (h) $\frac{3}{5} + \frac{3}{4}$

(i) $\frac{1}{5} + \frac{3}{8}$ (j) $\frac{1}{5} + \frac{1}{6}$ (k) $1\frac{3}{10} + 1\frac{2}{3}$ (l) $\frac{2}{3} + \frac{2}{7}$

(m) $3\frac{1}{6} + \frac{2}{7}$ (n) $2\frac{5}{6} + 1\frac{1}{7}$ (o) $3\frac{2}{5} + 2\frac{7}{15}$ (p) $1\frac{2}{3} + 1\frac{2}{9}$

4 Jo cycled $2\frac{3}{4}$ miles to one village and then a further $4\frac{1}{3}$ miles to her home. What is the total distance Jo travelled?

5 Work out

(a) $3\frac{1}{4} + 2\frac{1}{2}$ (b) $2\frac{1}{2} + \frac{2}{3}$ (c) $1\frac{1}{4} + 2\frac{7}{8}$ (d) $3\frac{1}{3} + 5\frac{3}{4}$

(e) $3\frac{5}{16} + 1\frac{7}{8}$ (f) $2\frac{11}{12} + \frac{3}{4}$ (g) $\frac{5}{6} + 6\frac{1}{3}$ (h) $2\frac{2}{3} + 4\frac{3}{5}$

6 In a market garden $\frac{1}{4}$ of the garden is used for potatoes, $\frac{3}{20}$ is used for beans and $\frac{1}{10}$ is used for cabbages. What fraction of the garden is used to grow these vegetables altogether?

7 John gave away his old CD collection to his brother and two sisters. The elder sister received $\frac{3}{10}$ of them and the younger sister $\frac{5}{16}$ of them. The brother received the rest. What fraction of the collection did the sisters receive altogether?

8 Work out the perimeter of this photograph.

9 Two pieces of wood are fixed together. One piece has thickness $2\frac{3}{8}$ inch and the other has thickness $1\frac{5}{16}$ inch. What is the total thickness of the two pieces of wood?

10 In a class, $\frac{1}{6}$ of the students own one pet, and $\frac{2}{5}$ of the students own more than one pet. What total fraction of the students own at least one pet?

11 A bag weighs $\frac{3}{7}$ lb. The contents weigh $1\frac{1}{5}$ lb. What is the total weight of the bag and its contents?

$5\frac{1}{4}$ in

$3\frac{1}{2}$ in

8.9 Subtracting fractions

It is easy to subtract fractions when the denominators (bottom) are the same:

Easy to subtract:

$$\frac{7}{12} - \frac{2}{12} = \frac{5}{12}$$

Denominators are the same.

Harder to subtract:

$$\frac{5}{9} - \frac{1}{4} = ?$$

Denominators are different.

Example 13

Work out $\frac{5}{9} - \frac{1}{4}$

Find equivalent fractions to these that have the same denominator (bottom).

An easy way is to change both denominators to 36 because $9 \times 4 = 36$.

$$\frac{5}{9} \xrightarrow[\times 4]{\times 4} \frac{20}{36} \qquad \frac{1}{4} \xrightarrow[\times 9]{\times 9} \frac{9}{36}$$

$$\frac{20}{36} - \frac{9}{36} = \frac{11}{36} \qquad \text{Same denominator – easy to subtract}$$

equivalent to $\frac{5}{9}$ equivalent to $\frac{1}{4}$

So $\frac{5}{9} - \frac{1}{4} = \frac{11}{36}$

Example 14

Work out $4\frac{1}{2} - 1\frac{5}{11}$

These are **mixed numbers**.

First subtract the whole numbers: $4 - 1 = 3$

$4\frac{1}{2} - 1\frac{5}{11}$ is the same as $3\frac{1}{2} - \frac{5}{11}$

Then find equivalent fractions to $\frac{1}{2}$ and $\frac{5}{11}$ that have the same denominator (bottom).

Change both denominators to 22 because $2 \times 11 = 22$:

$$\frac{1}{2} \xrightarrow[\times 11]{\times 11} \frac{11}{22} \qquad \frac{5}{11} \xrightarrow[\times 2]{\times 2} \frac{10}{22}$$

$$\frac{11}{22} - \frac{10}{22} = \frac{1}{22} \qquad \text{Same denominator – easy to subtract}$$

Now put the whole numbers and fractions back together: 3 and $\frac{1}{22}$ is $3\frac{1}{22}$

So $4\frac{1}{2} - 1\frac{5}{11} = 3\frac{1}{22}$

Example 15

Work out $2\frac{3}{12} - \frac{8}{12}$

$\frac{3}{12}$ is smaller than $\frac{8}{12}$ so you can't just subtract the fractions on their own.

Change the mixed number $2\frac{3}{12}$ into a top heavy (or improper) fraction:

$$2\frac{3}{12} = \frac{24}{12} + \frac{3}{12} = \frac{27}{12}$$

So $\quad 2\frac{3}{12} - \frac{8}{12} = \frac{27}{12} - \frac{8}{12}$

$$= \frac{19}{12}$$

This is usually written as a mixed number: $1\frac{7}{12}$

To **subtract** fractions, find equivalent fractions that have the same denominator (bottom).

Exercise 8I

1 Work out
(a) $\frac{5}{11} - \frac{3}{11}$ (b) $\frac{7}{9} - \frac{5}{9}$ (c) $\frac{7}{8} - \frac{1}{8}$ (d) $\frac{7}{12} - \frac{5}{12}$
(e) $\frac{3}{4} - \frac{1}{4}$ (f) $\frac{5}{8} - \frac{3}{8}$ (g) $\frac{15}{16} - \frac{7}{16}$ (h) $\frac{6}{7} - \frac{3}{7}$

2 Work out
(a) $\frac{1}{2} - \frac{1}{4}$ (b) $\frac{7}{8} - \frac{3}{4}$ (c) $\frac{5}{8} - \frac{1}{2}$ (d) $\frac{3}{4} - \frac{1}{8}$
(e) $\frac{5}{6} - \frac{1}{3}$ (f) $\frac{7}{12} - \frac{1}{3}$ (g) $\frac{9}{10} - \frac{2}{5}$ (h) $\frac{1}{4} - \frac{1}{20}$
(i) $\frac{1}{2} - \frac{3}{8}$ (j) $\frac{7}{8} - \frac{1}{2}$ (k) $\frac{11}{12} - \frac{3}{4}$ (l) $4\frac{5}{8} - 2\frac{1}{4}$

3 Work out
(a) $\frac{2}{3} - \frac{1}{2}$ (b) $\frac{5}{8} - \frac{1}{3}$ (c) $\frac{1}{5} - \frac{1}{6}$ (d) $\frac{3}{5} - \frac{1}{6}$
(e) $\frac{4}{5} - \frac{2}{3}$ (f) $\frac{3}{4} - \frac{3}{5}$ (g) $\frac{7}{10} - \frac{1}{3}$ (h) $\frac{9}{10} - \frac{3}{4}$

4 Work out
(a) $5\frac{1}{4} - \frac{1}{10}$ (b) $7\frac{1}{2} - \frac{1}{3}$ (c) $6\frac{1}{2} - 5\frac{1}{4}$ (d) $9\frac{1}{2} - 7\frac{3}{10}$
(e) $4 - 1\frac{3}{10}$ (f) $4\frac{4}{5} - 3\frac{9}{10}$ (g) $1\frac{2}{3} - \frac{11}{12}$ (h) $5\frac{3}{4} - 2\frac{19}{20}$
(i) $4\frac{7}{8} - 1\frac{2}{3}$ (j) $5\frac{7}{9} - 3\frac{1}{3}$ (k) $3\frac{4}{5} - \frac{3}{8}$ (l) $7\frac{4}{7} - 4\frac{2}{5}$

5 In a school, $\frac{7}{16}$ of the students are girls.
What fraction of the students are boys?

6 $\frac{2}{5}$ of the students at Hay College wear contact lenses.
What fraction of the students do not wear them?

7 The garden of Granny Smith's house measures $1\frac{1}{3}$ acres.
Sharky Estates buy $1\frac{1}{4}$ acres of the garden to build new
homes. How much garden does Granny Smith have left?

8 A box containing tomatoes has a total weight of $5\frac{7}{8}$ kg.
The empty box has a weight of $1\frac{1}{4}$ kg.
What is the weight of the tomatoes?

9 In the first week of its run, the TV drama 'New Heights'
had a respectable $7\frac{1}{2}$ million viewers. Unfortunately after
three weeks $4\frac{3}{8}$ million had deserted.
How many viewers now remained?

10 A plank of wood is $6\frac{1}{2}$ feet long.
A $4\frac{3}{8}$ foot length is cut from one end of the plank.
What length of wood remains?

11 Carol spends $\frac{2}{3}$ of her salary on food. She spends $\frac{1}{4}$ of her
salary on bills. What fraction of her salary is left?

8.10 Multiplying fractions

How to multiply two fractions

To **multiply** two fractions, multiply the numerators together
and multiply the denominators together.

$$\frac{5}{8} \times \frac{7}{10} = \frac{35}{80}$$

Multiply the numerators (top)

Multiply the denominators (bottom)

You can simplify this to $\frac{7}{16}$ (by dividing the top and bottom
of $\frac{35}{80}$ by 5).

Another way of doing this is to simplify the fractions *before*
you multiply them:

$$\frac{5}{8} \times \frac{7}{10} = \frac{5 \times 7}{8 \times 10}$$

5 is a common factor of
5 and 10, so you can
simplify here by dividing
the top and the bottom by 5.

$$\frac{(5 \times 7) \div 5}{(8 \times 10) \div 5} = \frac{7}{8 \times 2} = \frac{7}{16}$$

This method is less obvious
than the first one.

This gives the same answer $\frac{7}{16}$ as the first method.

How to multiply a fraction by a whole number

$$\frac{7}{10} \times 4 = ?$$

You can write 4 as the **top heavy** (or improper) fraction $\frac{4}{1}$

Multiply the numerators (top)

$$\frac{7}{10} \times \frac{4}{1} = \frac{28}{10}$$

Multiply the denominators (bottom)

So $\frac{7}{10} \times 4 = \frac{28}{10}$ This is usually written as a mixed number: $2\frac{8}{10}$

The fraction part of $2\frac{8}{10}$ simplifies (by dividing top and bottom by 2) so $2\frac{8}{10} = 2\frac{4}{5}$

How to multiply two mixed numbers

$$3\frac{1}{4} \times 2\frac{4}{5} = ?$$

Change both mixed numbers to top heavy (or improper) fractions:

$$3\frac{1}{4} = \frac{12}{4} + \frac{1}{4} = \frac{13}{4}$$

$$2\frac{4}{5} = \frac{10}{5} + \frac{4}{5} = \frac{14}{5}$$

Multiply

$$\frac{13}{4} \times \frac{14}{5} = \frac{182}{20}$$

Multiply

So $3\frac{1}{4} \times 2\frac{4}{5} = \frac{182}{20}$ This is usually written as a mixed number: $9\frac{2}{20}$

The fraction part of $9\frac{2}{20}$ simplifies (by dividing top and bottom by 2) so $9\frac{2}{20} = 9\frac{1}{10}$

Exercise 8J

1 Work out

(a) $\frac{1}{2} \times \frac{3}{4}$ (b) $\frac{3}{8} \times \frac{1}{4}$ (c) $\frac{2}{5} \times \frac{4}{5}$ (d) $\frac{3}{8} \times \frac{3}{4}$

(e) $\frac{5}{12} \times \frac{1}{3}$ (f) $\frac{7}{10} \times \frac{3}{4}$ (g) $\frac{3}{10} \times \frac{3}{5}$ (h) $\frac{2}{3} \times \frac{2}{3}$

(i) $\frac{1}{2} \times \frac{3}{8}$ (j) $\frac{4}{5} \times \frac{2}{3}$ (k) $\frac{4}{7} \times \frac{1}{3}$ (l) $\frac{2}{3} \times \frac{2}{5}$

(m) $\frac{2}{7} \times \frac{1}{5}$ (n) $\frac{2}{3} \times \frac{5}{7}$ (o) $\frac{1}{2} \times \frac{3}{4}$ (p) $\frac{3}{5} \times \frac{1}{3}$

2 Work out

(a) $\frac{1}{2} \times \frac{4}{5}$ (b) $\frac{3}{4} \times \frac{4}{5}$ (c) $\frac{5}{6} \times \frac{3}{5}$ (d) $\frac{4}{5} \times \frac{3}{10}$

(e) $\frac{5}{6} \times \frac{3}{4}$ (f) $\frac{7}{12} \times \frac{3}{14}$ (g) $\frac{8}{9} \times \frac{3}{10}$ (h) $\frac{3}{4} \times \frac{16}{21}$

(i) $\frac{1}{3} \times \frac{6}{7}$ (j) $\frac{6}{7} \times \frac{5}{12}$ (k) $\frac{1}{2} \times \frac{4}{5}$ (l) $\frac{2}{3} \times \frac{1}{4}$

(m) $\frac{3}{7} \times \frac{2}{6}$ (n) $\frac{6}{5} \times \frac{1}{3}$ (o) $5 \times \frac{7}{10}$ (p) $\frac{9}{10} \times \frac{13}{18}$

3 Work out

(a) $\frac{1}{2} \times 7$ (b) $\frac{2}{3} \times 5$ (c) $6 \times \frac{4}{5}$ (d) $8 \times \frac{3}{4}$

(e) $\frac{7}{10} \times 20$ (f) $9 \times \frac{2}{3}$ (g) $10 \times \frac{2}{5}$ (h) $\frac{5}{6} \times 12$

(i) $\frac{2}{3} \times 1\frac{1}{3}$ (j) $\frac{2}{5} \times 2\frac{1}{3}$ (k) $1\frac{1}{2} \times \frac{1}{4}$ (l) $1\frac{1}{2} \times 2\frac{1}{2}$

4 Work out

(a) $3\frac{1}{4} \times \frac{1}{2}$ (b) $\frac{2}{3} \times 4\frac{1}{2}$ (c) $\frac{5}{6} \times 1\frac{1}{3}$ (d) $2\frac{1}{2} \times \frac{7}{10}$

(e) $3\frac{1}{2} \times 1\frac{1}{2}$ (f) $2\frac{1}{3} \times 2\frac{3}{8}$ (g) $1\frac{4}{5} \times 2\frac{1}{3}$ (h) $3\frac{3}{4} \times 1\frac{2}{5}$

(i) $2\frac{1}{2} \times \frac{1}{4}$ (j) $1\frac{2}{5} \times 1\frac{1}{3}$ (k) $6 \times 2\frac{2}{3}$ (l) $2\frac{1}{7} \times 1\frac{2}{5}$

5 On Monday to Friday inclusive Jamie spends $2\frac{1}{4}$ hours on his homework but his sister Claire spends only $1\frac{3}{4}$ hours each day on hers.
How long in a week does each one spend on homework?

6 A machine takes $5\frac{1}{2}$ minutes to produce a special type of container. How long would the machine take to produce 15 containers?

7 Calculate the area of a rectangle of length $3\frac{1}{4}$ cm and width $2\frac{1}{4}$ cm.

> Area of rectangle is length × width

8 A melon weighs $2\frac{1}{2}$ lb. Work out the total weight of $8\frac{1}{4}$ melons.

9 Ivor takes $2\frac{1}{4}$ minutes to clean one window. How long will it take him to clean $6\frac{1}{2}$ windows of a similar size?

10 On average it takes Kieran $1\frac{1}{3}$ minutes to complete a lap at the Go Kart Centre.
How long will 15 laps take him?

11 Sharon can paint a garage door in $1\frac{2}{5}$ hours. How long will it take her to paint 7 garage doors?

12 Find the area of
this rectangle.
Leave your answer
as a fraction.

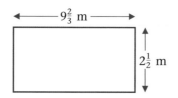

8.11 Dividing fractions

How to divide fractions

To **divide** fractions, invert the dividing fraction (turn it upside
down) and multiply.

$$\frac{1}{4} \div \frac{3}{5} = ?$$

Turn the ÷
sign into
a × sign.

Turn the fraction you are
dividing by upside down.

This is called **inverting**
the fraction.

$$\frac{1}{4} \times \frac{5}{3} = \frac{5}{12}$$

So $\frac{1}{4} \div \frac{3}{5} = \frac{5}{12}$

> **Why inverting works**
> A fraction like $\frac{3}{4}$ is the
> same as:
> $$3 \div 4 \quad \text{or} \quad 3 \times \frac{1}{4}$$
> But $\frac{1}{4}$ is $\frac{4}{1}$ inverted.
> So dividing is the same as
> multiplying by the
> inverted number:
> $$12 \div 3 = 4$$
> $$12 \times \frac{1}{3} = 4 \quad \text{too}$$

How to divide a fraction by a whole number

$$\frac{15}{16} \div 5 = ?$$

Turn ÷
into ×

Invert the dividing
number.

$$\frac{15}{16} \times \frac{1}{5} = \frac{15}{80}$$

So $\frac{15}{16} \div 5 = \frac{15}{80}$
This simplifies to $\frac{3}{16}$ (by dividing top and bottom by 5).

> Remember:
> $5 = \frac{5}{1}$
> so inverting gives
> $\frac{1}{5}$

How to divide mixed numbers:

$$3\frac{1}{2} \div 4\frac{3}{4} = ?$$

Change mixed numbers to top
heavy (or improper) fractions.

$$\frac{7}{2} \div \frac{19}{4}$$

Turn ÷
into ×

Invert the dividing fraction.

$$\frac{7}{2} \times \frac{4}{19} = \frac{28}{38}$$

So $3\frac{1}{2} \div 4\frac{3}{4} = \frac{28}{38}$
This simplifies to $\frac{14}{19}$ (by dividing top and bottom by 2).

Exercice 8K

1 Work out

(a) $\frac{1}{3} \div \frac{1}{4}$ (b) $\frac{1}{4} \div \frac{1}{3}$ (c) $\frac{3}{4} \div \frac{1}{2}$ (d) $\frac{1}{2} \div \frac{7}{10}$

(e) $\frac{2}{3} \div \frac{1}{5}$ (f) $\frac{5}{8} \div \frac{1}{3}$ (g) $\frac{5}{6} \div \frac{3}{4}$ (h) $\frac{7}{10} \div \frac{4}{5}$

(i) $\frac{2}{9} \div \frac{1}{2}$ (j) $\frac{2}{5} \div \frac{3}{4}$ (k) $\frac{3}{8} \div \frac{2}{3}$ (l) $\frac{1}{2} \div \frac{1}{4}$

2 Work out

(a) $2\frac{1}{2} \div \frac{1}{2}$ (b) $3\frac{1}{4} \div 2\frac{1}{2}$ (c) $3\frac{3}{4} \div 2\frac{1}{4}$ (d) $1\frac{5}{8} \div 3\frac{1}{6}$

(e) $3\frac{2}{3} \div 7\frac{1}{3}$ (f) $5\frac{1}{2} \div 2\frac{3}{4}$ (g) $1\frac{7}{10} \div 2\frac{7}{10}$ (h) $\frac{7}{8} \div 1\frac{2}{3}$

3 Work out

(a) $\frac{3}{4} \div 8$ (b) $\frac{5}{6} \div 2$ (c) $\frac{3}{5} \div 6$ (d) $\frac{4}{5} \div 5$

(e) $1\frac{1}{3} \div 4$ (f) $3\frac{1}{4} \div 6$ (g) $2\frac{5}{6} \div 10$ (h) $2\frac{1}{2} \div 15$

(i) $\frac{8}{9} \div 4$ (j) $\frac{2}{3} \div 6$ (k) $4\frac{2}{3} \div 4$ (l) $5\frac{1}{4} \div 3$

4 Work out

(a) $8 \div \frac{1}{2}$ (b) $12 \div \frac{3}{4}$ (c) $6 \div \frac{3}{5}$ (d) $8 \div \frac{7}{8}$

(e) $4 \div \frac{4}{5}$ (f) $1 \div \frac{7}{12}$ (g) $5 \div \frac{1}{3}$ (h) $6 \div \frac{1}{4}$

5 Work out

(a) $1\frac{1}{3} \div 1\frac{1}{2}$ (b) $2\frac{1}{2} \div \frac{1}{3}$ (c) $4\frac{3}{5} \div \frac{2}{3}$ (d) $2\frac{1}{5} \div 1\frac{1}{3}$

(e) $1\frac{1}{3} \div 2\frac{2}{9}$ (f) $2\frac{2}{3} \div 2\frac{2}{5}$ (g) $3\frac{1}{3} \div 7\frac{1}{2}$ (h) $4\frac{4}{5} \div 5\frac{1}{3}$

6 A tin holds $10\frac{2}{3}$ litres of methylated spirit for a lamp. How many times will it fill a lamp holding $\frac{2}{3}$ litre?

7 A newly built swimming pool is $10\frac{4}{5}$ metres long. A tile is $\frac{3}{10}$ metres long. Work out how many tiles are needed for one row along the length of the pool.

8 Tar & Stone Ltd can resurface $2\frac{1}{5}$ km of road in a day. How many days will it take them to resurface a road of length $24\frac{3}{5}$ km?

8.12 Solving problems involving fractions

In this section you are given various problems to solve. Fractions are used in many different situations and these problems introduce you to the types of question that are included in GCSE exams.

Example 16

A bag of flour weighs 2.25 kg. More flour is added, and the weight of the bag of flour is increased by three fifths.

What is the new weight of the bag of flour?

$$\frac{3}{5} \text{ of } 2.25 \text{ kg is } \frac{3}{5} \times 2.25 = \frac{3 \times 2.25}{5} = \frac{6.75}{5} = 1.35 \text{ kg}$$

$\times$ can be read as 'of'

The new weight is 2.25 kg + 1.35 kg = 3.6 kg

Example 17

A 5 litre tin of paint is filled with blue and yellow paint to make a shade of green. The tin contains $1\frac{1}{2}$ litres of blue paint.

What fraction of the paint in the 5 litre tin is blue?

The fraction of paint that is blue is

$$\frac{\text{blue paint}}{\text{whole tin}} = \frac{1\frac{1}{2}}{5} = 1\frac{1}{2} \div \frac{5}{1} = \frac{3}{2} \times \frac{1}{5} = \frac{3}{10}$$

Exercise 8L

1   A loaded lorry has a total weight of 13.2 tonnes.
    This weight is decreased by five eighths when the load is removed.
    Find the weight of the lorry without the load.

2   Last year 204 cars were imported by a garage. This year the number of cars imported has increased by five twelfths.
    How many cars have been imported this year?

3   Of 144 rail passengers surveyed, 32 claimed their train was regularly late.
    What fraction of the total number of passengers was this?

4   There are 225 houses on an estate. Of these houses, 85 have no garage.
    What fraction of houses have no garage?

5   Find the difference between $\frac{3}{5}$ of 36 miles and $\frac{2}{3}$ of 30 miles.

6 A tin contains approximately 440 beans. The manufacturer increases the volume of the tin by three eighths. Approximately how many beans would you expect to find in the larger tin?

7 A newspaper has 14 columns of photographs and 18 columns of advertisements. What fraction of the paper is advertisements?

8 144 men, 80 women and 216 children went on the rollercoaster. What fraction of the total number is made up of children?

8.13 Fractions and decimals

Fractions can be changed into **decimals** by dividing the numerator by the denominator.

___Example 18___

Change $\frac{3}{4}$ into a decimal.

$\frac{3}{4}$ means $3 \div 4$ (numerator ÷ denominator)

$$\begin{array}{r} 0.\,7\,5 \\ 4\overline{)3.^{3}0^{2}0} \end{array}$$ ——— Put two extra '0's here.

$\frac{3}{4} = 0.75$

Some fractions which you often use are shown in this table, along with their decimal equivalents:

Fraction	Decimal
$\frac{3}{10}$	0.3
$\frac{2}{5}$	0.4
$\frac{1}{4}$	0.25
$\frac{1}{2}$	0.5
$\frac{3}{4}$	0.75
$\frac{1}{8}$	0.125
$\frac{1}{3}$	0.3333 ...

Decimals can be changed into **fractions** by using a place value table.

Example 19

Change 0.763 into a fraction.

The place value table shows that 0.763 is 7 tenths,
6 hundredths and 3 thousandths. This is
the same as 763 thousandths, so you can
write the decimal as a fraction like this:

$$\frac{763}{1000}$$

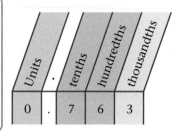

Example 20

Write as a fraction　　(a) 0.7　　(b) 0.59　　(c) 0.071

Using the place value table:

(a) 7 tenths $= \frac{7}{10}$

(b) 59 hundredths $= \frac{59}{100}$

(c) 71 thousandths $= \frac{71}{1000}$

Exercise 8M

1　Change these fractions to decimals. Show your working.

(a) $\frac{3}{5}$　　　(b) $\frac{1}{2}$　　　(c) $\frac{7}{10}$　　　(d) $\frac{7}{20}$

(e) $\frac{4}{25}$　　　(f) $\frac{3}{50}$　　　(g) $\frac{7}{8}$　　　(h) $\frac{9}{20}$

(i) $\frac{19}{25}$　　　(j) $\frac{5}{16}$　　　(k) $\frac{1}{8}$　　　(l) $\frac{27}{50}$

(m) $\frac{9}{100}$　　(n) $\frac{13}{200}$　　(o) $\frac{2}{3}$　　　(p) $\frac{19}{20}$

2　Change these decimals to fractions.

(a) 0.3　　　(b) 0.37　　　(c) 0.93　　　(d) 0.137

(e) 0.293　　(f) 0.07　　　(g) 0.59　　　(h) 0.003

(i) 0.000 03　(j) 0.0013　　(k) 0.77　　　(l) 0.077

(m) 0.39　　(n) 0.0041　　(o) 0.019　　(p) 0.031

3　Write as decimals:

(a) $\frac{4}{5}$　　　(b) $\frac{3}{4}$　　　(c) $1\frac{1}{8}$　　　(d) $\frac{19}{100}$

(e) $3\frac{3}{5}$　　　(f) $\frac{13}{25}$　　　(g) $\frac{5}{8}$　　　(h) $3\frac{17}{40}$

(i) $\frac{7}{50}$　　　(j) $4\frac{3}{16}$　　　(k) $3\frac{3}{20}$　　　(l) $4\frac{5}{16}$

(m) $\frac{7}{1000}$　　(n) $1\frac{7}{25}$　　　(o) $15\frac{15}{16}$　　(p) $2\frac{7}{20}$

4　Write as fractions in their simplest form:

(a) 0.48　　(b) 0.25　　　(c) 1.7　　　(d) 3.406

(e) 4.003　　(f) 2.025　　(g) 0.049　　(h) 4.875

(i) 3.75　　(j) 10.101　　(k) 0.625　　(l) 2.512

(m) 0.8125　(n) 14.14　　(o) 9.1875　　(p) 60.065

8.14 Recurring decimals

Not all fractions have an exact equivalent decimal.

The fraction $\frac{2}{3}$ is $2 \div 3 = 0.666\,666\,6...$ This is called a *recurring* decimal since one of the digits recurs (repeats).

You usually put a dot over the digits that repeat:

$\frac{2}{3} = 0.6666666... = 0.\dot{6}$ $\qquad \frac{5}{12} = 0.4166666... = 0.41\dot{6}$

$\frac{1}{3} = 0.3333333... = 0.\dot{3}$ $\qquad \frac{3}{11} = 0.2727272... = 0.\dot{2}\dot{7}$

$\frac{7}{9} = 0.7777777... = 0.\dot{7}$

$\frac{1}{7} = 0.142\,857\,142\,857\,142\,857... = 0.\dot{1}4285\dot{7}$

If you work out $2 \div 3$ or $\frac{2}{3}$ on a calculator the result on the display could be 0.6666667. The result has been corrected to 7 s.f. by the calculator.

You need two dots here since both the 2 and the 7 repeat.

The two dots show that this group of digits repeats.

Recurring decimal notation:
$0.\dot{3}$ means 0.3333333... recurring and
$0.\dot{1}\dot{7}$ means 0.17171717... recurring.

Example 21

Write these fractions as recurring decimals.

(a) $\frac{6}{11}$ $\qquad$ (b) $3\frac{8}{9}$

Write your answers
(i) as shown on the calculator display
(ii) using recurring decimal notation.

(a) (i) $\frac{6}{11} = 6 \div 11 = 0.545454\,5$ (ii) $0.\dot{5}\dot{4}$

(b) (i) $3\frac{8}{9} = 3 + (8 \div 9) = 3.8888888$ (or 3.8888889)
$\quad$ (ii) $3.\dot{8}$

Your calculator may round 3.8888888 to 3.8888889

Exercise 8N

Write the fractions in questions 1–10 as recurring decimals.

Write your answers
(i) as shown on the calculator display
(ii) using recurring decimal notation.

1 $\frac{5}{6}$ $\qquad$ **2** $1\frac{2}{9}$ $\qquad$ **3** $3\frac{1}{6}$ $\qquad$ **4** $\frac{11}{12}$ $\qquad$ **5** $5\frac{5}{9}$

6 $4\frac{9}{11}$ $\qquad$ **7** $\frac{3}{44}$ $\qquad$ **8** $2\frac{7}{11}$ $\qquad$ **9** $9\frac{21}{22}$ $\qquad$ **10** $\frac{25}{30}$

11 Write these fractions as recurring decimals:
$\frac{1}{7}, \frac{2}{7}, \frac{3}{7}, \frac{4}{7}, \frac{5}{7}, \frac{6}{7}$ $\qquad$ What do you notice?

12 Write these fractions as recurring decimals:
$\frac{1}{9}, \frac{2}{9}, \frac{3}{9}, \frac{4}{9}, \frac{5}{9}, \frac{6}{9}, \frac{7}{9}, \frac{8}{9}$ $\qquad$ What do you notice?

8.15 Reciprocals

The **reciprocal** of a number is made dividing the number into 1.

Reciprocal of $5 = 1 \div 5 = \frac{1}{5}$

Example 22

(a) The reciprocal of 2 is $\frac{1}{2}$ or a half or 0.5

(b) The reciprocal of 3 is $\frac{1}{3}$ or a third or 0.3333333...

(c) The reciprocal of $\frac{2}{3}$ is $\frac{3}{2}$

(d) The reciprocal of $\frac{1}{2}$ is $\frac{2}{1}$ or 2

You can use the reciprocal function on your calculator.
On some calculators it is shown as $\boxed{1/x}$ or $\boxed{x^{-1}}$.

Exercise 80

1 Find the reciprocals of these numbers without using a calculator.

(a) 5   (b) 4   (c) 6   (d) 8   (e) 10

(f) $\frac{1}{4}$ (g) $\frac{1}{8}$ (h) $\frac{3}{5}$ (i) $\frac{5}{6}$ (j) $\frac{5}{3}$

2 Use your calculator to find the reciprocals of these numbers.

(a) 25   (b) 50   (c) 3   (d) 7   (e) 9

(f) 75   (g) 100   (h) $\frac{1}{40}$ (i) 0.125   (j) 0.05

(k) 0.001   (l) 0.003   (m) 0.0002   (n) $\frac{2}{7}$ (o) $\frac{7}{5}$

Mixed exercise 8

1 (a) Write down the fraction of this shape that is shaded.
Write your fraction in its simplest form.

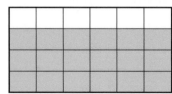

(b) Copy the shape. Shade $\frac{2}{3}$ of this shape.

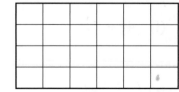

[E]

2 Here are two fractions: $\frac{3}{5}$ and $\frac{2}{3}$.

Explain which is the larger fraction.
You may use grids like these to help with your explanation.

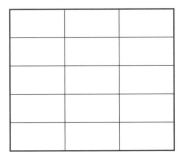 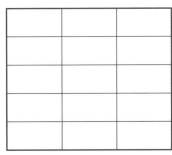

[E]

3 Write these fractions in order of size: $\frac{1}{2}$, $\frac{2}{3}$, $\frac{2}{5}$, $\frac{3}{4}$ [E]

4 Write down a fraction that is greater than a half and less than two thirds.

5 Ted spent $\frac{1}{4}$ of his pocket money on a new computer game.
He spent $\frac{2}{5}$ of his pocket money on a ticket for a football match.
Work out the fraction of his pocket money that he had left.

6 Work out
(a) $\frac{2}{5} + \frac{2}{3}$ (b) $4\frac{3}{4} - 1\frac{2}{3}$ (c) $5\frac{2}{3} - 1\frac{3}{4}$
(d) $\frac{11}{14} - \frac{5}{7}$ (e) $1\frac{2}{3} + 3\frac{1}{2}$ (f) $4\frac{3}{5} + 1\frac{1}{4}$

7 One glass of Summer Spring water holds $\frac{1}{6}$ of a whole bottle. How many bottles are needed for 54 glasses of Summer Spring?

8 Write the following improper fractions as mixed numbers.
(a) $\frac{16}{3}$ (b) $\frac{35}{4}$ (c) $\frac{11}{2}$ (d) $\frac{19}{3}$ (e) $\frac{55}{13}$

9 Write the following mixed numbers as improper fractions.
(a) $1\frac{9}{11}$ (b) $3\frac{1}{6}$ (c) $4\frac{16}{25}$ (d) $3\frac{3}{4}$ (e) $10\frac{1}{10}$

10 Work out
(a) $\frac{2}{5} \times \frac{2}{3}$ (b) $3\frac{3}{4} \div 1\frac{2}{3}$ (c) $5\frac{1}{3} \times 1\frac{3}{4}$
(d) $\frac{11}{14} \div \frac{5}{7}$ (e) $1\frac{2}{7} \times 3\frac{1}{2}$ (f) $4\frac{4}{5} \div 1\frac{1}{5}$

11 Work out
(a) $\frac{3}{4}$ of £60   (b) $\frac{5}{6}$ of 54 km   (c) $\frac{2}{3}$ of 48 kg

12 Here is part of a map.

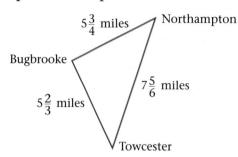

Fran drives from Bugbrooke to Northampton via Towcester.
Rea drives from Bugbrooke to Northampton directly.

How many miles further does Fran drive than Rea?

13 Seamus buys petrol from his local garage.
On Monday he filled up his petrol tank.

On Tuesday his tank was $\frac{4}{5}$ full.

(a) What fraction of a full tank had he used?

(b) Write $\frac{4}{5}$ as a decimal.

(c) Write $\frac{4}{5}$ as a percentage.

14 Change these fractions into decimals.

(a) $\frac{1}{2}$ (b) $\frac{1}{4}$ (c) $\frac{3}{4}$ (d) a third

(e) $\frac{3}{5}$ (f) $\frac{3}{7}$ (g) $\frac{2}{9}$

15 Change these decimals into fractions.

(a) 0.2   (b) 0.35   (c) 0.075   (d) 0.125

16 Work out the reciprocals of these numbers.

(a) $\frac{1}{2}$ (b) $\frac{3}{4}$ (c) 5   (d) 0.125

(e) 500   (f) 0.05   (g) 0.2   (h) 25

17 Find two equivalent fractions for each of the following:

(a) $\frac{6}{9}$ (b) $\frac{13}{25}$ (c) $\frac{1}{3}$ (d) $\frac{5}{17}$

18 Express the following fractions in their simplest form.

(a) $\frac{9}{12}$ (b) $\frac{15}{25}$ (c) $\frac{98}{100}$ (d) $\frac{35}{49}$

19 Write these fractions as recurring decimals. Write your answers

(i) as shown on the calculator display

(ii) using recurring decimal notation.

(a) $\frac{4}{9}$ (b) $\frac{3}{7}$ (c) $2\frac{1}{7}$ (d) $5\frac{6}{11}$ (e) $4\frac{16}{26}$

Summary of key points

1　Top heavy fractions, e.g. $\frac{11}{9}$, are also called **improper fractions**.

2　An improper fraction can also be written as a **mixed number** (a mixture of a whole number and a fraction), and a mixed number can also be written as an improper fraction.

$$\text{improper fraction} \quad \frac{11}{9} = \frac{9}{9} + \frac{2}{9} = 1\frac{2}{9} \quad \text{mixed number}$$

3　Fractions can be **simplified** if the numerator (top) and denominator (bottom) have a common factor.

$$\frac{8}{12} \quad \text{simplifies to} \quad \overset{\div 4}{\underset{\div 4}{\longrightarrow}} \quad \frac{2}{3} \qquad \text{The common factor is 4}$$

4　**Equivalent fractions** are fractions that have the same value.

$$\frac{8}{12} = \frac{4}{6} = \frac{2}{3}$$

5　To **add** fractions, find equivalent fractions that have the same denominator (bottom).

$$\overset{\times 3}{\underset{\times 3}{\frac{1}{2}}} + \frac{4}{6} = \frac{3}{6} + \frac{4}{6} = \frac{7}{6}$$

6　To **subtract** fractions, find equivalent fractions that have the same denominator (bottom).

$$\overset{\times 3}{\underset{\times 3}{\frac{4}{6}}} - \frac{1}{2} = \frac{4}{6} - \frac{3}{6} = \frac{1}{6}$$

7　To **multiply** two fractions, multiply the numerators together and multiply the denominators together.

Multiply the numerators (top)

$$\frac{3}{4} \times \frac{4}{7} = \frac{12}{28}$$

Multiply the denominators (bottom)

8 To **divide** fractions, invert the dividing fraction (turn it upside down) and multiply.

Turn ÷ into ×

$$\frac{1}{4} \div \frac{2}{5} = \frac{1}{4} \times \frac{5}{2} = \frac{5}{8}$$

Invert (turn upside down)

9 Fractions can be changed into **decimals** by dividing the numerator by the denominator.

10 Decimals can be changed into **fractions** by using a place value table.

11 A **recurring decimal** is one where a group of digits after the decimal place continually repeat themselves.

Recurring decimal notation:
$0.\dot{3}$ means 0.3333333... recurring
$0.\dot{1}\dot{7}$ means 0.1717171717... recurring.

12 The **reciprocal** of a number is made by dividing the number into 1.
For example, the reciprocal of 2 is $1 \div 2 = \frac{1}{2}$ and the reciprocal of $\frac{1}{3}$ is $1 \div \frac{1}{3} = 3$.

⑨ Estimating and using measures

9.1 Estimating

In real life people estimate all the time. How long will it take me to walk to the shops? Have I got time for a cup of tea? Is there enough milk in the fridge for the rest of the week?

Here are some measures that you have to estimate in real life:

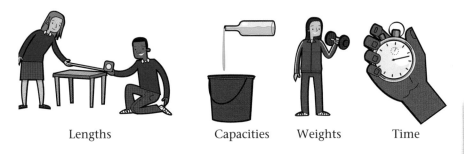

Lengths   Capacities   Weights   Time

Some imperial measures
12 inches = 1 foot
3 feet = 1 yard
1760 yards = 1 mile
8 pints = 1 gallon

You need to be able to estimate measurements in metric units and in imperial units such as gallons, miles and pounds.

9.2 Estimating lengths

Lengths and **distances** are measured in these metric and imperial units:

metric: kilometres (km), metres (m), centimetres (cm), millimetres (mm)

imperial: miles, yards, feet, inches

Example 1 shows some estimates of distances in real life.

Example 1

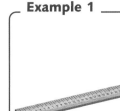   

A 30 cm ruler is about 1 foot long.

A door is 2 m high or about $6\frac{1}{2}$ feet.

A long stride is 1 m long or about 3 feet.

$2\frac{1}{2}$ times around the track is 1 km or about $\frac{5}{8}$ mile.

Exercise 9A

Look at this picture, then write down an estimate for each of the following in real life.

1 The height of the (a) man (b) girl (c) bus (d) car.
2 The length of the (a) car (b) bus.
3 The height of the (a) house (b) tree.
4 The width of the (a) drive (b) garage (c) house.

9.3 Estimating capacities

Capacity is a measure of the amount a container can hold.
It is measured in these units:

metric: litres (*l*), centilitres (*cl*), millilitres (*ml*)
imperial: gallons, pints, fluid ounces

20 fluid ounces = 1 pint
8 pints = 1 gallon

Example 2

This milk carton holds
1 pint or about 570 ml.

This petrol can holds
1 gallon or about 4.5 litres.

A mug and a can of cola hold
about ½ pint or about 300 ml.

Exercise 9B

Look at this picture, then copy and complete the table with your estimates for each of the following in real life.

	Amount of	Metric	Imperial
1	milk in a full carton		
2	cola in a full can		
3	lemonade in the bottle		
4	lemonade in the glass		
5	coffee in the jug		
6	water in a full bucket		
7	water in a full paddling pool		

9.4 Estimating weights (masses)

Weight is measured in these units:

    metric: tonnes (t), kilograms (kg),
                      grams (g), milligrams (mg)
    imperial: tons, hundredweight,
                      stones, pounds (lb), ounces (oz)

> 16 ounces = 1 pound
> 14 pounds = 1 stone
> 8 stones = 1 hundredweight
> 20 hundredweights = 1 ton

Example 3

A 125g packet of tea weighs about $\frac{1}{4}$ pound.

A 1 kg bag of sugar weighs about 2.2 pounds.

A 50 kg bag of cement weighs about 110 pounds.

> You are really dealing with the *mass* of these quantities. However, in everyday life we talk about the *weight* of a quantity so that word is used here.

Exercise 9C

Look at this picture, then copy and complete the table with your estimates for the items in real life.

	Weight of the	Metric	Imperial
1	bag of potatoes		
2	block of butter		
3	bag of apples		
4	packet of coffee		
5	loaf of bread		
6	packet of cereal		
7	bottle of squash		
8	packet of biscuits		
9	packet of crisps		
10	box of soap powder		

9.5 Choosing appropriate units of measure

When you want to measure something you have to choose the most appropriate units to use. For example, to measure how long it takes to run 100 m you use seconds. But to measure how long it takes to run a 26 mile marathon you would need to use hours, minutes and seconds.

> Should I use hours, minutes or seconds to time the 400 metre race?

Exercise 9D

Copy and complete this table with appropriate units for each measurement.

		Metric	Imperial
1	The length of your classroom		
2	The width of this book		
3	The distance from Edinburgh to London		
4	The length of a double decker bus		
5	The weight of a sack of potatoes		
6	The weight of a packet of sweets		
7	The weight of a lorry full of sand		
8	The amount of petrol in a car's petrol tank		
9	The amount of liquid in a full cup of tea		
10	The amount of medicine in a medicine spoon		
11	The amount of water in a raindrop		
12	The amount of water in a reservoir		
13	The time it takes to boil an egg		
14	The time it takes to run 400 metres		
15	The time it takes to walk 20 miles		
16	The time it takes to sail from Southampton to New York		
17	The length of a ballpoint pen		
18	The thickness of a page in this book		
19	The weight of 30 of these books		
20	The time it takes to travel from the Earth to Mars		

Sensible estimates

Example 4

Julie says 'My car is 20 m long.' Is this estimate sensible?

This is not a sensible statement because it means the car would be over 20 paces long, or about as long as an articulated lorry.

A sensible answer would be about 4 or 5 m.

Exercise 9E

For each of these statements say whether the measurement is sensible or not. If the statement is not sensible then give a reasonable estimate for the measurement.

1 (a) My teacher is 20 m tall.
   (b) My father is 20 cm tall.
   (c) The classroom measures 2 m by 3 m.
   (d) I bought 2 g of potatoes at the supermarket.
   (e) A can of cola holds 3 *l* of liquid.
   (f) A house is 10 m high.

2 (a) The tallest boy in school is 2 m tall.
   (b) John can just lift 50 kg.
   (c) Jane has to walk 1 km to school each day.
   (d) A cup full of tea contains 2 *l* of liquid.
   (e) The river Thames is 20 km long.
   (f) A 50p piece weighs 0.5 kg.

3 (a) A box of chocolates weighs 500 g.
   (b) A pint glass will hold 1 *l* of liquid.
   (c) The capacity of the petrol tank in my car is 5 *l*.

4 (a) The Eiffel Tower in Paris is more than 200 m high.
   (b) The capacity of the petrol tank in my car is 50 gallons.
   (c) A packet of tea weighs 50 g.
   (d) A kilogram bag of sugar weighs 2 pounds.

9.6 Measuring time

You need to be able to
- read the time using digital and analogue clocks
- use 12-hour and 24-hour clock times and convert from one type to the other.

Digital clocks have a number display:

Analogue clocks have hands:

Reading the time from an analogue clock

When you *say* the time you can use phrases such as 'half past four' and 'ten to five'.

This clock shows the key phrases you need to know:

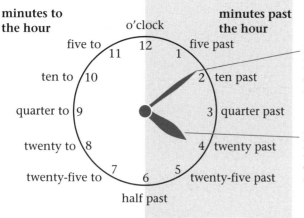

For the long 'minute' hand the journey from one number to the next takes 5 minutes.

For the short 'hour' hand the journey from one number to the next takes 1 hour.

Remember: 60 minutes = 1 hour

Two of the four clock faces of Big Ben, illuminated at night.

Exercise 9F

1   Write down in words the times shown by these clocks as you would say them.

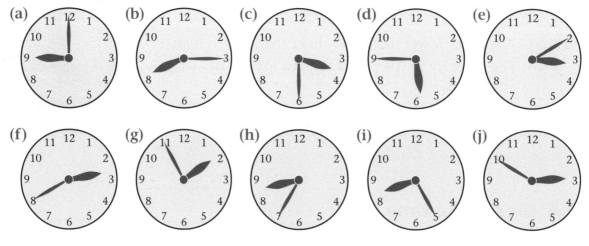

2   Draw six clock faces and mark these times on them.

   (a) seven o'clock

   (b) ten past eight

   (c) quarter to five

   (d) twenty to three

   (e) quarter past nine

   (f) twenty-five past four

Reading the time from a digital clock

Example 5

Write these times as you would say them, in two different ways.

09:20 — The colon keeps the hours and minutes apart.

09:40   40 minutes past 9 = 20 minutes to 10.

20 minutes past 9 or nine twenty   20 minutes to 10 or nine forty.

Exercise 9G

1 Write these times as you would *say* them, in two different ways.
   (a) 08 30   (b) 10 10   (c) 11 05   (d) 04 45   (e) 03 55

2 Draw five digital watches and show the following times on them:
   (a) quarter past 9   (b) half past 3   (c) twenty to 5
   (d) quarter to 7   (e) five o'clock

12-hour and 24-hour clock times

You need to be able to tell the difference between times such as 2 o'clock in the morning and 2 o'clock in the afternoon. There are two ways of doing this.

12-hour clock times use **am** or **pm** to show whether a time is before or after midday:

12 midnight yesterday	3 am	ante meridiem before midday am	midday or noon today	3 pm	post meridiem after midday pm	12 midnight today

12 1 2 3 4 5 6 7 8 9 10 11 12 1 2 3 4 5 6 7 8 9 10 11 12

24-hour clock times number the hours from **1** to **24**:

3 o'clock in the morning   3 o'clock in the afternoon

00:00 01:00 02:00 03:00 04:00 05:00 06:00 07:00 08:00 09:00 10:00 11:00 12:00 13:00 14:00 15:00 16:00 17:00 18:00 19:00 20:00 21:00 22:00 23:00 24:00

Example 6

Write down the times shown.

Morning

09:25

The time shown by these clocks is 9:25 am or 09 25

Afternoon

13:35

The time shown by these clocks is 1:35 pm or 13 35

Changing 12-hour clock times to 24-hour clock times

Up to 12 noon the times are the same:

12-hour → 24-hour

9:35 am → 09 35

A 24-hour digital clock shows a zero here.

After 12 noon add 12 to the hour number:

12-hour → 24-hour

1:45 pm → 13 45

+12

Exercise 9H

1 Change these times from 12-hour clock times (am and pm) to 24-hour clock times.

   (a) 10:00 am   (b) 10:00 pm   (c) 9:30 am   (d) 9:30 pm

   (e) 8:20 pm   (f) 8:20 am   (g) 7 am   (h) 8 pm

   (i) 3:30 pm   (j) 4:40 am   (k) 1:08 am   (l) 1:08 pm

  (m) 5:50 pm   (n) 5:50 am   (o) 11 pm   (p) 8 am

   (q) quarter past 8 in the morning

   (r) quarter to 9 in the evening

   (s) five to three in the afternoon

   (t) twenty to seven in the morning

2 Change these times from 24-hour clock times to 12-hour clock times (am or pm).

   (a) 08:00   (b) 09:20   (c) 21:30   (d) 13:10

   (e) 12:10   (f) 00:20   (g) 01:40   (h) 08:00

   (i) 15:45   (j) 18:00   (k) 16:30   (l) 21:10

  (m) 23:55   (n) 14:02   (o) 06:25   (p) 00:00

   (q) 24:00   (r) 12:00   (s) 10:55   (t) 20:55

9.7 Reading scales

You need to be able to read these types of scales:

• a ruler to measure lengths   • weighing scales   • a measuring cylinder to measure amounts of liquid.

Example 7

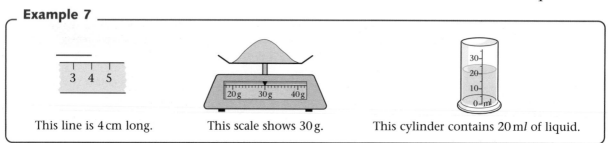

This line is 4 cm long.   This scale shows 30 g.   This cylinder contains 20 ml of liquid.

Exercise 9I

1 Write down the readings on these scales.

(a)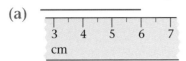

(b)

(c) 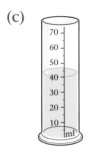 (d)

(e)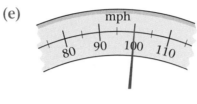

(f)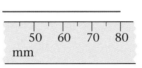

2 Draw diagrams to show these readings on a scale.

(a) 5 cm   (b) 20 ml   (c) 50 g

(d) 3 cm   (e) 25 ml   (f) 250 g

Using the marks on a scale

Example 8

Write down the measurements shown on these scales.

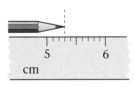 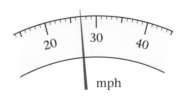 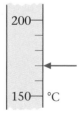

This pencil ends between the 5 and the 6.

There are 10 spaces between the 5 and the 6 so each mark shows $\frac{1}{10}$ or 0.1

As the pencil ends on the third mark it must be 0.3 or $\frac{3}{10}$ more than 5.

The pencil is 5.3 cm long.

This pointer is between 20 and 30.

There are 10 spaces between 20 and 30 so each mark shows 1 unit.

As the pointer is on the seventh mark it must be 7 more than 20.

The reading is 27 mph.

This reading is between 150 and 200.

There are 5 spaces marked between 150 and 200 so each mark shows 10 units.

As the pointer is on the second mark it must be 20 more than 150.

The reading is 170 °C.

Exercise 9J

Write down the readings on these scales.

1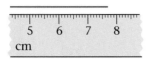

2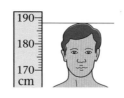

3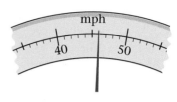

4

5

6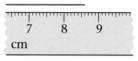

Estimating from a scale

Some scales have no helpful marks on them so you have to estimate a reading.

Example 9

Estimate the reading shown.

The middle mark on this scale is halfway between 4 and 5 at 4.5.

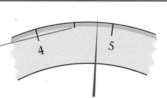

The pointer is a little more than halfway between 4.5 and 5. So a good estimate is 4.8 units.

Exercise 9K

Estimate the measurements on these scales.

1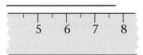

2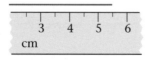

3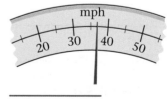

4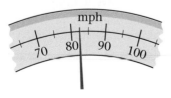

5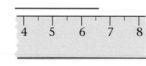

6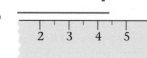

Measuring lines accurately

When you measure the length of a line, remember to start measuring from the 0 on the scale you are using, *not the end of the ruler.*

Example 10

Write down the length of this line in cm.

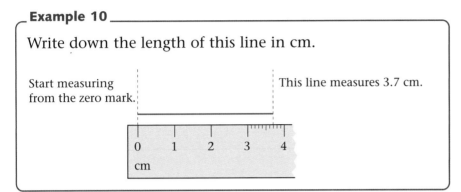

Start measuring from the zero mark.

This line measures 3.7 cm.

Exercise 9L

1 Measure and write down the lengths of these lines in centimetres.

(a) ————

(b) ——————

(c) ————————

(d) ————————————

(f)

(g) ————

(e)

(h) ——————————

2 Draw and label lines with lengths

(a) 4 cm   (b) 6 cm   (c) 2.5 cm

(d) 5.7 cm   (e) 4.8 cm   (f) 3.2 cm

(g) 8.3 cm   (h) 10.2 cm   (i) 4.6 cm

(j) 3.9 cm   (k) 6.4 cm   (l) 7.2 cm

3 Draw and label lines with lengths

(a) 20 mm   (b) 35 mm   (c) 55 mm

(d) 100 mm   (e) 74 mm   (f) 8 mm

(g) 18 mm   (h) 68 mm

Marking part way along a line

Sometimes you will have to measure or draw a line and mark a point that is half, a third or a quarter of the way along your line.

___Example 11___

Draw a line 8 cm long and mark the point halfway along it. Divide 8 cm by 2, 8 cm ÷ 2 = 4 cm. Measure 4 cm from one end and put a cross to show halfway.

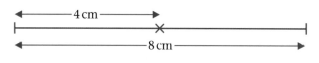

Exercise 9M

1 Copy these lines. Mark the halfway point of each.

   (a) _____

   (b) _____

   (c) _____

   (d) _____

2 Copy these lines. On each mark the point a quarter of the way along the line.

   (a) _____

   (b) _____

   (c) _____

3 Draw two lines that are 6 cm long.

   (a) Mark a point one third of the way along the first line.

   (b) Mark a point two thirds of the way along the second line.

4 Draw two lines that are 12 cm long.

   (a) Mark a point one quarter of the way along the first line.

   (b) Mark a point three quarters of the way along the second line.

5 Draw four lines that are 10 cm long.

   (a) Mark a point one tenth of the way along the first line.

   (b) Mark a point three tenths of the way along the second line.

   (c) Mark a point seven tenths of the way along the third line.

   (d) Mark a point nine tenths of the way along the fourth line.

Mixed exercise 9

1 Copy and complete this table.
   Write a sensible unit for each measurement.

	Metric	Imperial
The weight of a turkey		pounds
The volume of water in a swimming pool		gallons
The width of this page	centimetres	

[E]

2 A petrol station has a diagram for converting gallons to litres.

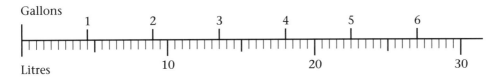

Use the diagram to convert

(a) 4 gallons to litres   (b) 3 gallons to litres

(c) 27 litres to gallons   (d) 20 litres to gallons.

3 (a) Draw a line *AB* with length 10 cm.

   (b) Mark a point *P* halfway along the line.

4 (a) What metric unit of length would you use to measure the length of a large coach?

   (b) Using the unit in part (a) estimate the length of a large coach.

5 It takes a world-class athlete about 10 seconds to run 100 metres.

   (a) Estimate the time an average 16 year old would take to run 100 metres.

   (b) Estimate the time your maths teacher would take to run 100 metres.

6 Draw clock faces to show these times:

   (a) 7 pm   (b) 08 30   (c) a quarter to 4

7 The scale diagram shows a man and a dinosaur called a *Tyrannosaurus rex*.

The man is 6 ft or approximately 2 metres tall.
Estimate the height of the *Tyrannosaurus rex*:

(a) in feet

(b) in metres.

Tyrannosaurus rex   Man (to scale)

Summary of key points

1 **Lengths** and **distances** are measured in these metric and imperial units:

    metric: kilometres (km), metres (m), centimetres (cm), millimetres (mm)

    imperial: miles, yards, feet, inches

2 **Capacity** is a measure of the amount a container can hold. It is measured in these units:

    metric: litres (*l*), centilitres (c*l*), millilitres (m*l*)

    imperial: gallons, pints, fluid ounces

3 **Weight** is measured in these units:

    metric: tonnes (t), kilograms (kg), grams (g), milligrams (mg)

    imperial: tons, hundredweight, stones, pounds (lb), ounces (oz)

4 **Digital** clocks have a number display:

5 **Analogue** clocks have hands:

6 Up to 12 noon the times are the same: After 12 noon add 12 to the hour number:

12-hour → 24-hour
9:35 am → 09 35

A 24-hour digital clock shows a zero here.

12-hour → 24-hour
1:45 pm → 13 45

+12

⑩ Collecting and recording data

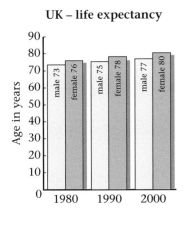

UK – life expectancy

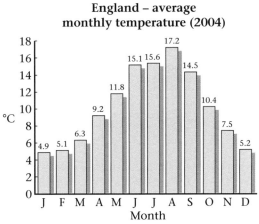

England – average monthly temperature (2004)

2012 Olympics – First round voting

You often see charts and tables like this in the press and on TV. They give you information or **data** as it is usually called. Sometimes you can use this data to make forecasts and plan for the future.

For example, the number of babies born this year helps councils to plan the number of school places needed in five years' time.

Statistics is the branch of mathematics concerned with

- **collecting** and **recording** data
- **sorting** and **tabulating** that data
- presenting data visually in **charts** and **diagrams**
- making **calculations**
- **interpreting** results.

This chapter shows you how to start collecting and recording data.

There were four rounds of voting before London was chosen to host the 2012 Olympic Games.
One city was eliminated in each round.

10.1 Ways of collecting data

You can collect data

- by using a questionnaire
- by making observations and recording the results
- by carrying out an experiment
- from records or a database
- from the internet.

You must be careful how you collect data. If you want to find out what people think about marriage, for example, it is not sensible just to ask people at a wedding. They are interested in marriage and you might be led to the wrong conclusions!

10.2 Designing questions to collect data

When you are writing questions for a **questionnaire**:
- be clear what you want to find out, and what data you need
- ask short, simple questions
- provide tick boxes with possible answers.

Here are some good examples:

Are you:

Male ☐ —————— This has a clear choice of two answers.

Female ☐

What age are you?

Under 17 ☐

17–20 ☐

21–30 ☐

Over 30 ☐

Which of these styles of music do you like?
(Tick as many boxes as you want)

Metal ☐

House ☐

Grunge ☐

Pop ☐

These both offer four choices.

Avoid questions which are too vague, too personal, or which may influence the answer.

How often do you go swimming?

Sometimes ☐   Occasionally ☐   Often ☐

Sometimes, occasionally and *often* may mean different things to different people.

Have you ever stolen anything from a shop?

Yes ☐   No ☐

Even a hardened criminal is unlikely to answer this question honestly!

Do you agree that the UK should have the euro?

Yes ☐   No ☐

This question suggests that the right answer is Yes. It is **biased**.

Test your questionnaire on a few people first to see if it works or needs to be improved. This is called a **pilot survey**.

Exercise 10A

1   Look at these pairs of questions. Decide whether Question X
    or Question Y is better to do the job in the *To find out* column.

	To find out:	Question X	Question Y
(a)	if people like the Labour party	Do you like the Labour party? Yes/No	Do you agree that New Labour is the best party? Yes/No
(b)	which age group a person is in	How old are you?	Are you under 21, 21 to 40, 41 to 60, over 60?
(c)	the most popular soap on TV	Do you watch Eastenders? Yes/No	Do you watch Eastenders/ Coronation Street/ Emmerdale/Hollyoaks/ Other?
(d)	if they watched the film	Did you see the film *War of the Worlds*? Yes/No	Do you like Steven Spielberg?
(e)	if someone is short sighted	How good is your eyesight?	Can you read that sign without glasses? Yes/No
(f)	if people give money to charity	Do you give money to charity? Yes/No	Everyone gives money to charity, don't they? Yes/No
(g)	if the hotel was satisfactory	Was everything all right? Yes/No	Did you enjoy your stay? Yes/No
(h)	if newspapers should be censored	Newspapers should be censored: Agree/Disagree/Don't know	What do you think about censoring newspapers?

Example 1

Decide if the following question is suitable for use in a questionnaire.
If it is not, give a reason and rewrite the question to improve it.

How much pocket money do you get?

a little ☐   some ☐   a lot ☐

A little to some people may be *a lot* to others. Also the word *some* means different
amounts to different people. It would be better to be more precise. A better
question would be:

How much pocket money do you get each month?

0–£14.99 ☐   £15–£24.99 ☐   £25–£34.99 ☐   over £35 ☐

Exercise 10B

1 Here are some questions that are not suitable for a questionnaire. For each one, say why and write a more suitable question.

(a) Do you agree that the UK should have a monarchy?

Yes ☐   No ☐   Don't know ☐

(b) What was the weather like on your holiday?

Terrible ☐   Quite good ☐   OK ☐

(c) Most people approve of corporal punishment. Do you?

Yes ☐   No ☐

(d) Do you still play football?

Yes ☐   No ☐

(e) How many hours of television do you watch?

1 ☐   2 ☐   3 ☐

(f) Does your local library have wheelchair access?

2 Finn wants to find out about people's mobile phones. He has designed the following questionnaire for his web page.

Questionnaire: Mobile phones

1 Do you have a mobile phone?

Yes ☐   No ☐

2 Who is your service provider?

Mobile P ☐ H_4 ☐   Five ☐

Fonavode ☐   Pineapple ☐   Other ☐

3 Do you: Pay monthly   ☐
                 Pay-As-You-Go   ☐

4 How much do you spend on your phone each month?

£5 ☐   £10 ☐   £15 ☐   £20 ☐

(a) How could you improve part **4** of the questionnaire?

(b) Finn also wants to write a question about how people buy their call time. Design a question he could use. Include tick boxes for a response.

Activity – Holidays

- Design a questionnaire to find out about the kind of holidays people had last year.
- Test your questions by asking some of your friends.

10.3 Collecting data by sampling

If you carry out a survey in a mixed school, but only question the first five students on each form register, you could end up asking all boys or all girls.

Ideally you should ask everyone in the school – but this is usually not practical. Instead you ask a limited number of students – a **sample**.

You need to make sure each student in the school has an equal chance of being picked to be part of the sample. You might question six students from each class, drawing their names out of a hat. This is called a **random sample**. Then questioning your sample should give a similar result to questioning the whole school.

If your sample is not random your answers may be **biased**. In a survey to find out which sports a typical teenager watches, choosing a sample from teenagers at a football match will **bias** your answers – there will be more football lovers than in a random sample.

A **random sample** helps this market researcher find out what a typical person thinks without asking them all. For a fair survey you may need to ask people of different ages, genders, jobs, nationalities, and so on.

> When you carry out a survey, select a **random sample** to avoid **bias**.

Exercise 10C

For each question, select the most appropriate group of people to ask, **A**, **B** or **C**.

	Data needed	Who to ask
1	How people get to work	A Every fifth person near a bus stop B A group of people arriving together C A group of people during a tea break
2	If people think Coldplay is a good group	A People in a library B People going to a Coldplay concert C People in your class
3	If people think private healthcare is a good idea	A Unemployed people B Doctors C People in a town centre
4	If people are in favour of a new pedestrian crossing	A Car drivers using the road B Local residents C Pedestrians crossing the road
5	If people want harsher prison sentences for criminals	A The police B People in a shopping centre C Prisoners

10.4 Collecting data by observation

You could do a traffic survey by counting vehicles and recording what type they are as they pass you.

You would have to decide where, how and for how long to carry out your survey.

For example, if you did your survey during rush hour the results would be different from a survey early one Sunday morning.

Here is a **data capture sheet** from a traffic survey:

Traffic survey by H. Short on 5/6/05 at Main Street, Ash 9.00–9.30 am.

Type of vehicle	Tally	How many
Bus	ЖЖ ЖЖ II	12
Car	ЖЖ ЖЖ ЖЖ ЖЖ II	22
Lorry	ЖЖ II	7
Van	ЖЖ ЖЖ	10
Motorcycle	ЖЖ ЖЖ ЖЖ I	16

Remember to record 5 in a tally chart like this:
ЖЖ

Exercise 10D

1   Prepare data capture sheets for surveys to find out two of the following by observation

(a)   the make of people's MP3 players

(b)   the colour of people's eyes

(c)   the CPU speed and hard disk space on people's computers

(d)   the age and sex of people entering a supermarket.

10.5 Collecting data by experiment

When you carry out an experiment you can use a **data capture sheet** to record your results.

Example 2

Greta has a six-sided dice. She throws it 60 times and records her results in a data capture sheet.

Score	Tally	Frequency
1	卌 IIII	9
2	卌 卌 I	11
3	卌 卌 II	12
4	卌 IIII	9
5	卌 卌	10
6	卌 IIII	9

From Greta's data, do you think the dice is fair?
The dice seems to be fair as the results for each score are about the same.

Exercise 10E

Carry out the following experiments.

1 Find out how accurate people are at estimating.
   Ask people to estimate
   (a) the length in centimetres of a piece of wood
   (b) the number of sweets in a jar
   (c) the weight in grams of a piece of metal.

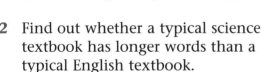

2 Find out whether a typical science textbook has longer words than a typical English textbook.
   ● Choose two passages of about 50 words from each book.
   ● For each passage make a data collection table like the one on the right and complete it.
   ● Compare the results.

Number of letters in a word	Tally	Frequency
1		
2		
3		
4		

3 Find two newspapers, one 'serious' and one 'lightweight'. Find an article in each paper about the same story. Carry out an experiment to find out which paper has the greater average word length by counting the length of the first 100 words in each article in each paper.

10.6 Secondary data

Data you collect is called **primary data**. Data that has been collected by other people is called **secondary data**.

The National Census is carried out every 10 years and provides information about people in the UK. The National Statistics Office publishes monthly and annual figures on a wide range of subjects.

Example 3

Here is an extract from a table in the 1991 Census which shows information about residents in some London boroughs. The figures are percentages.

	Bexley	Brent	Bromley	Camden	Croydon	Newham	Greenwich	Average London
Retired	17.4	14.3	19.6	17.3	16.1	14.2	17.6	16.8
Birth rate	13.8	17.0	12.8	13.5	15.1	20.2	15.9	15.4
Unemployment	38.1	41.6	35.5	40.6	40.2	43.6	44.6	40.8
2-car families	26.1	16.0	28.9	9.4	24.6	8.8	14.8	18.2
No-car families	26.7	43.4	25.6	55.8	30.5	53.5	43.6	40.7

(a) Which borough has the highest percentage
    (i) birth rate   (ii) unemployment?
(b) What percentage of families have two cars in
    (i) Bromley   (ii) Brent?
(c) Use information from the table to suggest a reason why Camden has a large percentage of families with no car.
(d) Which boroughs have a higher percentage of families with two cars than the average figure for all of London?

(a) (i) Newham   (ii) Greenwich
(b) (i) 28.9   (ii) 16.0
(c) High unemployment
(d) Bexley, Bromley and Croydon

Exercise 10F

1   The table shows the percentage unemployment figures for August.

Year	1999	2000	2001	2002	2003	2004	2005
Male	5.2	4.7	4.0	3.6	3.7	3.4	3.3
Female	4.7	4.1	3.8	3.0	3.0	2.7	2.5

(a) What was the female unemployment rate in 2004?

(b) Which year had the
 (i) highest (ii) lowest percentage total unemployment?

(c) Between which two years did male unemployment
 fall the most?

2 This table shows the money spent or collected, in pounds per
person, in different London boroughs:

	Camden	Barnet	Haringey	Islington	Lambeth	Redbridge	Richmond	Southwark
Average weekly rent	106	102	112	100	82	122	96	88
Management	36	26	28	32	32	32	24	46
Repairs	18	22	20	26	28	40	24	28
Bad debts	8	0.08	6	1.54	0.96	0.46	0.28	3.52
Rent rebates	64	62	82	62	48	86	54	26

(a) Which borough has
 (i) the highest (ii) the lowest average weekly rent?

(b) Which borough has a bad debts figure of 0.28?

(c) Which borough has
 (i) the highest (ii) the lowest repairs figure?

(d) What is the rent rebate per person in Richmond?

10.7 Obtaining data from a database

A **database** is an organised collection of information.
It can be stored on paper or on a computer.

Here is a spreadsheet showing part of a database stored on a
computer:

	A	B	C	D	E	F	G	H
1	Year group	Surname	Years	Months	Gender	Sport	Height (m)	Weight (kg)
2	10	Abejurouge	15	3	Male	Rugby	1.63	60
3	10	Aberdeen	15	0	Male	Rounders	1.75	45
4	11	Ableson	16	6	Female	Table Tennis	1.83	60
5	11	Acton	16	3	Female	Basketball	1.67	52
6	10	Adam	15	1	Male	Judo	1.80	49
7	10	Agha	15	7	Male	Cricket	1.66	70

A computer database allows you to obtain information quickly
and in a variety of forms, for example:
- in alphabetical order   • in numerical order
- girls' results only   • males over a certain height.

Activity – Mayfield School database (Go to www.heinemann.co.uk/hotlinks, insert the express code 4084P and click on this activity.)

Use the Mayfield School database to answer these questions:

(a) How tall is David Hazelwood (Year 9)?

(b) How many KS4 pupils were born in April?

(c) How many KS3 pupils said their favourite TV programme was The Simpsons? Which one of these said their favourite sport was running?

(d) How many of the KS3 pupils are right handed and have dark brown eyes? Which of these said their favourite TV programme was Eastenders?

(e) Which female KS4 pupil has 5 pets and said her favourite subject was PE?

Exercise 10G

1 This database contains details of some second-hand cars.

Make	Model	Colour	Insurance group	Number of doors	Year	Price (£)
BMW	3 series	Blue	11	3	2001	8845
Suzuki	Alto	Red	5	5	2003	2695
Porsche	Cayenne	Red	20	5	2003	30 795
Proton	Persona	Green	8	4	1999	1995
Citroën	C8	Silver	11	5	2002	10 295
Daewoo	Matiz	Blue	2	5	2000	1895
Volkswagen	Passat	Red	9	4	1997	3145
Seat	Ibiza	Yellow	2	3	2002	4145
Nissan	Primera	Black	9	4	2002	6345
Vauxhall	Corsa	Silver	2	3	1998	1645

Use the database to answer the following questions.
- **(a)** Which is the oldest car?
- **(b)** Which is the most expensive car?
- **(c)** Which car has the highest insurance group?
- **(d)** How many cars have 5 doors?
- **(e)** Karen has £3000. Which cars could she buy?
- **(f)** Which is the cheapest 5-door red car?
- **(g)** List the models of car in order of price, most expensive first.

2   This database contains information about some African
    countries.

	A	B	C	D	E	F	G
1	Country	Religion	Currency	Population 2004 (millions)	Urban population	Fertility rate (births/woman)	Population 2015 (est.) (millions)
2	Algeria	Islam	Dinar	32.1	59%	2.0	38
3	Angola	Christianity	New Kwanza	11	36%	6.3	20.8
4	Botswana	Indigenous beliefs	Pula	1.5	52%	3.2	1.7
5	Benin	Indigenous beliefs	Franc	7.3	45%	6.0	9.4
6	Burundi	Christianity	Franc	6.2	10%	5.9	9.8
7	Chad	Islam and Christianity	Franc	9.5	25%	6.4	12.4

(a) Use the database to find out
    (i) which country has both Islam and Christianity
       as major religions
    (ii) which country has the lowest fertility rate
   (iii) which country had the highest population in
       2004
    (iv) what is the estimated population of Angola for
       2015.

(b) Compare the urban population of Burundi with
    those of other countries in the database.

(c) Write a question of your own using at least two
    pieces of data from the database.

3   Give an example of a database used in your school.
    Who uses it? What information does it contain?

10.8 Obtaining data from the internet

The internet can be a very useful source of data. But remember
that data collected from the internet may be inaccurate or out
of date.

When you collect data from the internet make sure that:
- the data comes from a reliable source
- the data is accurate – check against other sources.

Activity – Internet search

Use the internet to find the following information.
Give two reliable sources for each answer.

(a) The members of the European Union.

(b) The heights of the five highest mountains in the world.

(c) The average life expectancy of people in the UK.

(d) The number of gold, silver and bronze metals won by Great Britain in the Paralympic Games in 2004.

10.9 Using mileage charts

In books of roadmaps you often see tables that give the distances between towns.

Here is an example of how one of these tables can be built up.

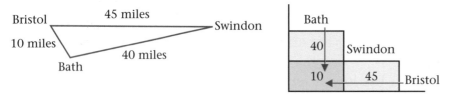

To use the mileage chart to find the distance between Bath and Bristol you follow the arrows from Bath and Bristol, and find where they meet. In this case it is 10. The distance is 10 miles.

Exercise 10H

1 Here is a mileage chart:

York				
71	Manchester			
24	44	Leeds		
91	74	110	Kendal	
211	204	201	268	London

The distance from Manchester to Kendal is 74 miles.
Use this mileage chart to find the distance between these places:

(a) London and Manchester   (b) York and Kendal

(c) Leeds and York   (d) Leeds and London

(e) Manchester and Leeds   (f) London and York.

2 Here is a mileage chart:

Use this mileage chart to find the shortest distance between these places:

(a) London and Bristol

(b) Cardiff and Salisbury

(c) Oxford and Bristol

(d) Oxford and London

(e) Cardiff and London

(f) Bristol and Salisbury.

Bristol				
44	Cardiff			
73	107	Oxford		
52	98	70	Salisbury	
120	153	56	169	London

3 Here is a mileage chart:

Use this mileage chart to find the distance between these places:

(a) London and Glasgow

(b) Edinburgh and Glasgow

(c) Stranraer and Edinburgh

(d) Edinburgh and London

(e) Inverness and Glasgow

(f) London and Inverness.

Glasgow				
47	Edinburgh			
176	157	Inverness		
86	132	261	Stranraer	
410	413	574	420	London

4 The diagram shows the shortest distances between these four cities:

Use the distances to make up a mileage chart to show the shortest distances between these cities.

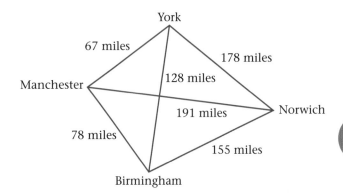

5 Here is a table showing the journey times between places.

Use the table to find the times for these journeys:

(a) London to Manchester

(b) York to Kendal

(c) Leeds to York

(d) Leeds to London

(e) Manchester to Leeds

(f) London to York.

York				
1h 22 min	Manchester			
40 min	54 min	Leeds		
2h 09 min	1h 25 min	1h 58 min	Kendal	
3h 52 min	3h 52 min	3h 38 min	4h 48 min	London

Mixed exercise 10

1 Tony decides to collect information on how people were going to vote in an election. He uses the question 'What do you think of the Government?'
Explain what is wrong with Tony's question.

2 Catherine wants to find out what types of DVDs her friends own.
Draw a suitable data collection sheet she could use.

3 Daisy and Don want to know what type of music their friends listen to.
Draw a suitable data collection sheet they could use.

4 Joe plans to carry out a traffic survey of the types of vehicles that pass the school gate at the end of a school day.
Draw a suitable data collection sheet he could use.

5 Shaun plans to carry out a survey into the television viewing habits of his tutor group.
One of his questions is 'How much television do you watch?'
Amy tells him that this is not a very good question.
Write down an improved question that Shaun could use.

6 Lewis is going to use this data collection sheet to carry out a survey of the age of cars in the school car park.

Age of car	Tally	Frequency
0–1		
1–2		
2–3		
4–5		
Over 5		
Over 10		

Explain two faults on Lewis's data collection sheet.

7 The headteacher in a school wants to carry out a survey of what students think of the school. Explain how she could select a random sample of students to use in the survey.

8 Mr Beeton is going to open a restaurant.
He wants to know what type of restaurant people like.
He designs a questionnaire.
(a) Design a suitable question he could use to find out
what type of restaurant people like.
He asks his family 'Do you agree that pizza is better than
pasta?'
This is **not** a good way to find out what people who
might use his restaurant like to eat.
(b) Write down **two** reasons why this is **not** a good way
to find out what people who might use his
restaurant like to eat.   [E]

9 (a) Explain why each of these ways of sampling is not
random:
   (i) Standing outside the school tuck shop when you
   want to find out where students buy snacks.
   (ii) Telephoning people on a Friday night when you
   want to find out how often they go to the
   cinema on a Friday night.
   (iii) Asking people who are shopping in an out-of-
   town shopping mall if they have a car.
   (iv) Asking people travelling on a train, on a snowy day,
   what they think about the punctuality of trains.
(b) What would be a suitable sampling method to find
out how London office workers get to work?

10 Here is a mileage chart:

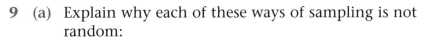

Cardiff					
232	Dover				
393	490	Edinburgh			
201	295	224	Liverpool		
152	78	403	210	London	
318	365	108	172	292	Newcastle

Use the mileage chart to find the distance between these
places:
(a) London and Dover   (b) Cardiff and Liverpool
(c) Newcastle and Edinburgh   (d) Liverpool and London
(e) Cardiff and Edinburgh   (f) Newcastle and London.

Summary of key points

1 When you are writing questions for a **questionnaire**:
   - be clear what you want to find out and what data you need
   - ask short, simple questions
   - provide tick boxes with possible answers
   - avoid questions which are too vague, too personal, or which may influence the answer.

2 When you carry out a survey, select a **random sample** to avoid **bias**.
   In a random sample everyone has an equal chance of being chosen.

3 When you carry out an experiment you can use a **data capture sheet** to record your results.

4 Data you collect is called **primary data**. Data that has been collected by other people is called **secondary data**.

5 A **database** is an organised collection of information.
   It can be stored on paper or on a computer.

6 When you collect data from the internet make sure that:
   - the data comes from a reliable source
   - the data is accurate – check against other sources.

⑪ Linear equations

11.1 Simple equations

In algebra letters are used to represent numbers.

$a + 3 = 7$ The letter a must equal 4 because 4 add 3 equals 7.
    $a = 4$

$a - 3 = 2$ a must equal 5 because 5 take away 3 equals 2.
    $a = 5$

These are examples of **equations**.

Equations are used to solve real-life problems. For example, the value of t in the equation $20 = 5 + 10t$ tells a sky diver how long it takes to go from a speed of 5 metres per second to 20 metres per second.

Exercise 11A

Find the value of the letter in these equations.

1 $a + 2 = 5$	**2** $b + 1 = 4$	**3** $c + 2 = 9$
4 $w + 5 = 7$	**5** $m + 3 = 4$	**6** $y + 5 = 5$
7 $x - 2 = 3$	**8** $k - 4 = 1$	**9** $n - 3 = 3$
10 $h - 5 = 3$	**11** $g - 2 = 2$	**12** $f - 5 = 4$
13 $d + 2 = 7$	**14** $2 + e = 5$	**15** $4 + y = 7$
16 $10 + x = 14$	**17** $7 - m = 3$	**18** $5 - d = 2$
19 $k + 6 = 15$	**20** $12 = y + 2$	**21** $15 - t = 5$
22 $z - 2 = 2$	**23** $z + 2 = 2$	**24** $n - 5 = 0$

The balance method

In Exercise 11A you probably spotted the answers and then wrote them down. There is another way of looking at equations.

> An equation is a balancing act!

Example 1 shows a way of working out the value of the letter in an equation that does not rely on guessing the answer.

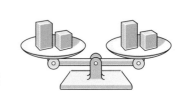

Example 1

To find a from $a + 6 = 9$:

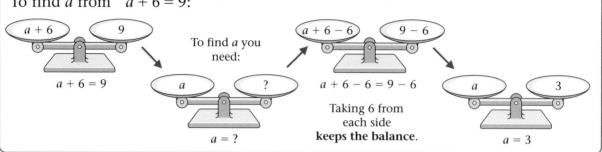

Example 2

To find k from $k - 7 = 13$:

$k - 7 \qquad = 13$

$k - 7 + 7 = 13 + 7$ ——————— Adding 7 to each side keeps

$k \qquad\quad = 20$ the balance.

Exercise 11B

Find the value of the letter in these equations. Use the balancing method to help you.

1 $a + 6 = 7$	**2** $y + 3 = 5$	**3** $h + 2 = 9$
4 $p - 5 = 4$	**5** $q - 3 = 7$	**6** $d - 6 = 2$
7 $x + 3 = 3$	**8** $t - 4 = 0$	**9** $r + 7 = 10$
10 $k + 2 = 3$	**11** $n + 1 = 2$	**12** $x - 2 = 3$
13 $m + 7 = 12$	**14** $y - 7 = 9$	**15** $w + 5 = 5$
16 $q - 10 = 2$	**17** $5 + p = 7$	**18** $6 + t = 6$
19 $a + 19 = 31$	**20** $21 + x = 21$	**21** $p - 15 = 23$
22 $7 = a + 3$	**23** $6 = b + 5$	**24** $10 = y + 10$

Wot, no letter z?

Exercise 11C

Find the value of the letter in these equations.

1 $a + 5 = 10$	**2** $p - 4 = 7$	**3** $q - 3 = 5$
4 $x + 7 = 15$	**5** $y + 4 = 17$	**6** $s + 12 = 15$

7 $x - 7 = 15$ **8** $y - 4 = 17$ **9** $s - 12 = 15$

10 $a + 5 = 6$ **11** $p - 5 = 6$ **12** $c + 17 = 21$

13 $5 + a = 6$ **14** $11 + p = 16$ **15** $12 + q = 12$

16 $4 = a + 2$ **17** $5 = b + 3$ **18** $12 = c - 3$

19 $10 = p + 5$ **20** $11 = y - 10$ **21** $15 = t + 10$

22 $12 = p + 12$ **23** $12 = p - 12$ **24** $p + 12 = 12$

Example 3 shows how to find the value of the letter when the letter is multiplied by a number.

Example 3

$3a = 12$

This means $a \times 3 = 12$

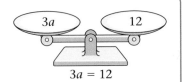

Remember:
$3a$ means 3 lots of a or $3 \times a$

To work out $a = ?$ you need to keep the balance in the equation.

To keep the equation balanced you must do the same to each side.

Try: $3a \div 3 = 12 \div 3$

$a = 4$

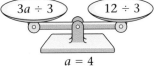

The inverse of $\times 3$ is $\div 3$.

To keep an **equation** balanced you must do the same to each side.

Exercise 11D

Find the value of the letter in these equations.

1 $3a = 6$ **2** $4p = 8$ **3** $5p = 15$

4 $6s = 18$ **5** $2k = 10$ **6** $7u = 28$

7 $2g = 14$ **8** $5k = 35$ **9** $6j = 12$

10 $8f = 32$ **11** $3r = 27$ **12** $5v = 45$

13 $2t = 42$ **14** $4d = 48$ **15** $7t = 63$

Example 4

$$\frac{w}{3} = 5$$

This means $w \div 3 = 5$

$$\frac{w}{3} \times 3 = 5 \times 3 \quad\rule{2cm}{0.4pt}\quad \text{Multiply each side of the equation by 3.}$$

$$w = 15$$

> Look for the opposite (or inverse) operation.
> The inverse of $\div 3$ is $\times 3$.

Exercise 11E

Find the value of the letter in these equations.

1 $\dfrac{a}{2} = 5$ **2** $\dfrac{b}{5} = 4$ **3** $\dfrac{s}{4} = 3$

4 $\dfrac{c}{6} = 5$ **5** $\dfrac{t}{4} = 6$ **6** $\dfrac{s}{8} = 9$

7 $\dfrac{h}{6} = 12$ **8** $\dfrac{f}{4} = 7$ **9** $\dfrac{d}{3} = 15$

10 $\dfrac{a}{3} = 15$ **11** $\dfrac{b}{5} = 8$ **12** $\dfrac{r}{4} = 13$

13 $\dfrac{a}{12} = 5$ **14** $\dfrac{b}{2} = 16$ **15** $\dfrac{k}{3} = 16$

Exercise 11F

Solve these equations.

1 $a + 4 = 5$ **2** $b + 3 = 6$ **3** $c + 4 = 9$

4 $p - 3 = 6$ **5** $q - 2 = 2$ **6** $d - 6 = 2$

7 $2p = 6$ **8** $4r = 8$ **9** $5t = 20$

10 $\dfrac{a}{2} = 6$ **11** $\dfrac{b}{5} = 12$ **12** $\dfrac{s}{4} = 5$

13 $4 + r = 7$ **14** $6 + e = 7$ **15** $7 + p = 7$

> Solve means 'find the value of the letter'. So for question 1, find the value of a.

11.2 Equations combining operations

You have dealt with equations where you added or subtracted numbers and where you multiplied or divided by numbers. You are now going to look at what happens when these are combined into one equation.

> In a combined equation, deal with the $+$ or $-$ first.

Example 5

$$2a + 3 = 11$$
$$2a + 3 - 3 = 11 - 3 \quad\text{———— Take 3 from each side.}$$
$$2a = 8$$
$$2a \div 2 = 8 \div 2 \quad\text{———— Divide each side by 2.}$$
$$a = 4$$

> First try to get letters only on one side.

Example 6

$$5p - 3 = 7$$
$$5p - 3 + 3 = 7 + 3 \quad\text{———— Add 3 to each side.}$$
$$5p = 10$$
$$5p \div 5 = 10 \div 5 \quad\text{———— Divide each side by 5.}$$
$$p = 2$$

Example 7

$$\frac{m}{4} + 3 = 8$$
$$\frac{m}{4} + 3 - 3 = 8 - 3 \quad\text{———— Take 3 from each side.}$$
$$\frac{m}{4} = 5$$
$$\frac{m}{4} \times 4 = 5 \times 4 \quad\text{———— Multiply each side by 4.}$$
$$m = 20$$

Exercise 11G

Find the value of the letter in these equations.

1 $2a + 1 = 5$　　　**2** $2a - 1 = 5$　　　**3** $3a + 2 = 8$

4 $3a - 5 = 4$　　　**5** $3p + 7 = 7$　　　**6** $3p + 7 = 13$

7 $4q + 5 = 17$　　　**8** $5r - 6 = 4$　　　**9** $6t - 12 = 18$

10 $7f - 12 = 9$　　　**11** $2r - 11 = 15$　　　**12** $10a - 5 = 5$

13 $10a + 5 = 5$　　　**14** $4d + 7 = 19$　　　**15** $5c - 2 = 18$

16 $\dfrac{a}{3} + 2 = 3$　　　**17** $\dfrac{z}{5} + 1 = 2$　　　**18** $\dfrac{r}{6} + 4 = 7$

19 $\dfrac{s}{4} + 6 = 9$　　　**20** $\dfrac{b}{3} + 7 = 13$　　　**21** $\dfrac{c}{4} - 2 = 4$

22 $\dfrac{f}{3} - 6 = 3$　　　**23** $\dfrac{h}{2} - 4 = -2$　　　**24** $\dfrac{x}{5} - 1 = 2$

All the equations dealt with so far have had solutions that are whole numbers. Look at the following examples. You can see that solutions can be fractions or decimals as well.

Example 8

$$4p + 7 = 16$$
$$4p + 7 - 7 = 16 - 7 \quad\text{———— Take 7 from each side.}$$
$$4p = 9$$
$$4p \div 4 = 9 \div 4 \quad\text{———— Divide each side by 4.}$$
$$p = 2\tfrac{1}{4}$$

Example 9

$$5q - 8 = 3$$
$$5q - 8 + 8 = 3 + 8 \quad\text{———— Add 8 to each side.}$$
$$5q = 11$$
$$5q \div 5 = 11 \div 5 \quad\text{———— Divide each side by 5.}$$
$$q = 2.2$$

Exercise 11H

Find the value of the letter in these equations.

1	$2a + 3 = 6$	**2**	$2a - 4 = 3$	**3**	$3a + 7 = 15$
4	$3a - 6 = 7$	**5**	$5p + 7 = 15$	**6**	$5p - 7 = 15$
7	$5e + 3 = 3$	**8**	$4t + 3 = 9$	**9**	$8j - 7 = 5$
10	$7c - 4 = 7$	**11**	$8k + 3 = 5$	**12**	$3d - 7 = 3$
13	$9u + 7 = 9$	**14**	$4q - 4 = 5$	**15**	$7y + 6 = 15$

So far all the solutions to the equations you have looked at have been positive. Example 10 shows how to deal with equations when the solutions are negative.

Example 10

$$2a + 7 = 1$$
$$2a + 7 - 7 = 1 - 7 \quad\text{———— Take 7 from each side.}$$
$$2a = -6$$
$$2a \div 2 = -6 \div 2 \quad\text{———— Divide each side by 2.}$$
$$a = -3$$

Exercise 11I

Find the value of the letter in these equations.

1 $2a + 3 = 1$ **2** $2a + 5 = 1$ **3** $2a + 9 = 1$

4 $3a + 8 = 5$ **5** $3a + 7 = 1$ **6** $5p + 12 = 2$

7 $2s + 7 = -3$ **8** $5p - 2 = -12$ **9** $4k - 5 = -9$

10 $8h + 10 = 2$ **11** $4y + 12 = -8$ **12** $3e + 47 = 20$

13 $6t - 12 = -12$ **14** $3w + 4 = 1$ **15** $2c + 15 = 11$

16 $13a + 9 = 9$

Exercise 11J

Find the value of the letter in these equations.

1 $2s + 4 = 10$ **2** $5d + 3 = 18$ **3** $8m - 7 = 33$

4 $4h - 2 = 14$ **5** $4k + 7 = 43$ **6** $3y + 7 = 13$

7 $5p + 2 = 9$ **8** $4f + 4 = 17$ **9** $3s - 6 = 5$

10 $-7g - 4 = 12$ **11** $4f - 5 = 12$ **12** $5k - 12 = 6$

13 $-3s - 15 = 2$ **14** $6j - 3 = 19$ **15** $9b + 7 = 2$

16 $-2r + 12 = 5$ **17** $5t + 15 = -12$ **18** $7y - 15 = -21$

19 $3e - 5 = -6$ **20** $-4f - 7 = -2$ **21** $5g + 17 = 15$

22 $4h + 4 = 0$ **23** $-3c - 5 = 0$ **24** $8s + 9 = 4$

25 $\dfrac{z}{2} + 2 = 4$ **26** $\dfrac{x}{5} - 3 = 2$ **27** $\dfrac{p}{2} - 5 = -3$

28 $\dfrac{c}{3} + 4 = -2$ **29** $\dfrac{a}{8} - 1 = 5$ **30** $-\dfrac{e}{3} + 2 = 10$

11.3 Equations with brackets

Chapter 3 dealt with quite complicated algebraic expressions. You can use what you learned there to solve quite complicated equations.

Example 11

Find the value of p for

$$3(2p + 3) = 5$$
$$3 \times 2p + 3 \times 3 = 5$$
$$6p + 9 = 5$$
$$6p + 9 - 9 = 5 - 9$$
$$6p = -4$$
$$6p \div 6 = -4 \div 6$$
$$p = -\tfrac{4}{6} \text{ or } -\tfrac{2}{3}$$

Remember to deal with brackets first. Multiply each term inside the brackets by 3.

$$3(2p + 3)$$
$$3 \times 2p + 3 \times 3$$

In an equation with brackets, expand the brackets first.

Exercise 11K

Find the value of the letter in these equations.

1 $2(p + 4) = 10$ **2** $3(d - 2) = 9$ **3** $2(c + 5) = 16$

4 $3(b - 2) = 1$ **5** $3(g + 2) = 15$ **6** $5(g - 2) = 15$

7 $2(v + 3) = 2$ **8** $4(4 + s) = 20$ **9** $2(3d + 3) = 4$

10 $3(t - 5) = 2$ **11** $4(h - 3) = 0$ **12** $2(3h - 7) = 10$

13 $2(2s + 5) = 22$ **14** $4(2y - 3) = 16$ **15** $4(4r - 12) = 32$

Exercise 11L

Solve these equations.

1 $2(a + 2) = 6$ **2** $3(h - 4) = 12$ **3** $4(g + 5) = 8$

4 $6(f - 3) = 18$ **5** $5(q + 7) = 35$ **6** $9(k - 2) = 18$

7 $5(4 + g) = 25$ **8** $4(5 + h) = 12$ **9** $3(d + 2) = 3$

10 $2(v + 7) = 3$ **11** $3(s + 7) = 4$ **12** $5(2n - 3) = 20$

13 $4(4f + 5) = 6$ **14** $6(7d - 12) = 30$ **15** $2(5m + 11) = 0$

Equations with letters on both sides

If there are letters on both sides of an equation you have to deal with the problem slightly differently. It is a good idea always to keep the letter on the side with the most; in Example 12 this is the side with $5p$.

Example 12

Find the value of p in the equation

$$5p - 2 = 3p + 6$$
$$5p - 3p - 2 = 3p - 3p + 6 \quad\text{———— Take } 3p \text{ from both sides.}$$
$$2p - 2 = 6$$
$$2p = 6 + 2 \quad\text{———— Add 2 to both sides.}$$
$$2p = 8$$
$$p = 4 \quad\text{———— Divide by 2.}$$

Exercise 11M

Find the value of the letter in these equations.

1 $2k - 3 = k + 2$ **2** $5s - 4 = 3s + 3$

3 $4p + 2 = 3p + 6$ **4** $5g + 4 = 3g + 2$

5 $7t - 4 = 4t + 7$ **6** $2k + 6 = 3k - 3$

7 $4d + 9 = 5d + 2$ **8** $5c + 8 = 7c + 2$

9 $5z + 6 = 3z + 4$ **10** $7b + 12 = 3b - 6$

11 $9p + 8 = 3p - 2$ **12** $4g + 9 = 3g + 17$

Exercise 11N

Solve these equations.

1 $5h - 5 = 4h + 7$ **2** $7t + 11 = 6t + 3$

3 $5d + 3 = 3d + 1$ **4** $6f + 9 = 4f + 3$

5 $3s + 5 = 4s - 2$ **6** $4d + 13 = 5d + 7$

7 $2a + 7 = 4a - 2$ **8** $3q + 9 = 6q - 3$

9 $4y + 4 = 7y + 6$ **10** $2e + 6 = 5e + 9$

11 $12s + 6 = 6s - 4$ **12** $5u + 9 = 3u - 2$

13 $5t - 5 = 2t - 9$ **14** $6s + 9 = 2s + 2$

15 $3q + 6 = 7q - 5$ **16** $2w + 3 = 7w + 9$

17 $8h + 4 = 3h - 4$ **18** $3s + 4 = 2s - 3$

19 $r + 2 = 5r + 6$ **20** $5a - 7 = 2a + 4$

Equations with brackets

The most complicated equations you will be asked to solve
will have letters on both sides and perhaps brackets as well.

Example 13

$$4(2x - 3) = 2(x + 3)$$
$$8x - 12 = 2x + 6$$
$$8x - 2x - 12 = 2x - 2x + 6$$
$$6x - 12 = 6$$
$$6x - 12 + 12 = 6 + 12$$
$$6x = 18$$
$$x = 3$$

The first step is to expand
the brackets. Then sort
out the equation in the
usual way.

Exercise 11O

Find the value of the letters in these equations.

1 $4(2p + 3) = 2(p + 8)$ **2** $5(2h - 9) = 3(3h + 7)$

3 $6(5r - 7) = 4(3r + 7)$ **4** $7(2t + 6) = 3(5t + 7)$

5 $4(3g + 5) = 2(5g + 7)$ **6** $5(4d + 9) = 6(3d + 5)$

7 $8(2k - 6) = 5(3k - 7)$ **8** $7(2m + 3) = 4(5m - 3)$

9 $7(9d - 5) = 12(5d - 6)$ **10** $5(3j + 7) = 4(4j + 3)$

11 $4(8y + 3) = 6(7y + 5)$ **12** $3(6t + 7) = 5(4t + 7)$

Mixed exercise 11

Solve these equations.

1 $x + 8 = 13$ **2** $14 = 20 - x$

3 $5t + 7 = 3t + 10$ **5** $4g + 7 = 3g + 9$

5 $6s - 6 = 4s + 2$ **7** $5q - 5 = 3q + 7$

7 $2d + 4 = 5d - 6$ **8** $6k - 3 = 2k + 7$

9 $2(a + 3) = 7$ **10** $5(2k - 4) = 15$

11 $5 = 2(2d + 7)$ **12** $8 = 4(7p - 3)$

13 $2(3p + 2) = 5p - 7$ **14** $3(5r + 2) = 12r - 7$

15 $2(6t + 2) = 3(5t - 6)$ **16** $6(g + 7) = 3(4g + 2)$

17 $5(2a + 1) + 3(3a - 4) = 4(3a - 6)$ **18** $\dfrac{x}{4} - 2 = 3$

Summary of key points

1 In algebra letters are used to represent numbers. For example $a = 5$.

2 To keep an **equation** balanced you must do the same to each side.

$$a + 4 = 7 \quad \rightarrow \quad a + 4 - 4 = 7 - 4 \quad \rightarrow \quad a = 3$$

$$a - 3 = 1 \quad \rightarrow \quad a - 3 + 3 = 1 + 3 \quad \rightarrow \quad a = 4$$

$$5a = 30 \quad \rightarrow \quad 5a \div 5 = 30 \div 5 \rightarrow \quad a = 6$$

$$\frac{a}{2} = 7 \quad \rightarrow \quad \frac{a}{2} \times 2 = 7 \times 2 \quad \rightarrow \quad a = 14$$

3 In a combined equation, deal with the $+$ and $-$ first.

$$3a + 7 = 1 \quad \rightarrow \quad 3a + 7 - 7 = 1 - 7$$

$$3a = -6$$

$$a = -2$$

4 In an equation with brackets, expand the brackets first.

$$3(x + 1) = 4 \quad \rightarrow \quad 3x + 3 = 4$$

12 Sorting and presenting data

12.1 Some ways of presenting data

In a survey, 60 pupils were asked how many text messages they got last Saturday. Here are the results:

3 6 2 5 4 7 7 6 7 9 5 7 8 6 6 5 7 8 6 3 7 7 6 9 8 4 5 5 4 7
6 4 8 3 5 7 3 7 6 8 7 5 8 4 8 7 1 9 7 6 8 2 6 5 4 5 8 6 7 9

To see this information more clearly you can draw up a **tally chart**:

Number of messages	Tally	Frequency
0		0
1	|	1
2	||	2
3	||||	4
4	JHT |	6
5	JHT ||||	9
6	JHT JHT |	11
7	JHT JHT ||||	14
8	JHT ||||	9
9	||||	4

This tally chart, or frequency table, shows the frequencies of the different numbers of messages (how often each number occurred). Tally marks are grouped in fives to make them easier to count:

JHT JHT JHT \|\|\|

is easier to count than

\|\|\|\|\|\|\|\|\|\|\|\|\|\|\|\|\|\|

Another way to show up any pattern in data is to draw a **bar chart**.

This bar chart shows the data from the text message survey.

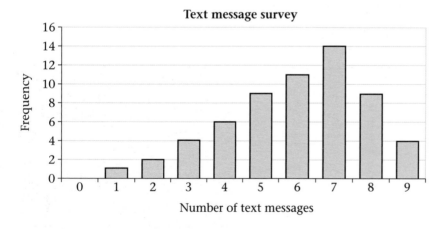

When drawing a bar chart you must make sure that
- the horizontal and vertical axes are clearly labelled
- the chart has a title
- the scale is designed so that the bar chart is a sensible size.

Activity – Text messages

Collect data for the number of text messages received by the students in your class yesterday. Draw a bar chart to show this information.

It is important always to check the scale on a bar chart carefully.

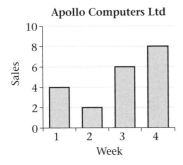

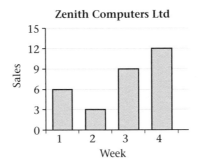

These computer sales figures look the same until you look at the scales on the vertical axes.

For Apollo Computers Ltd the number of computers sold in the four weeks was $4 + 2 + 6 + 8 = 20$

For Zenith Computers Ltd the number sold was $6 + 3 + 9 + 12 = 30$

Tally charts and **bar charts** are two ways of displaying data that can be counted.

You must leave a gap between the bars when you draw bar charts of data that can be counted.

Here is a bar chart showing what sports people watch on TV.

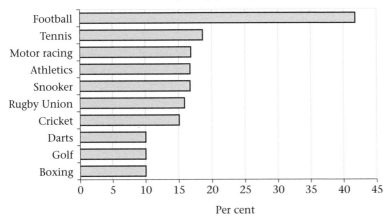

It shows that football is the most popular sport that people watch on TV.

Exercise 12A

For each of the following sets of data recorded at an island weather station, display the information in

(a) a tally chart   (b) a bar chart.

1 Hours of sunshine

5	6	0	1	3	1	4	7	5	6	6	2
4	3	1	0	7	10	9	11	5	4	7	6
9	9	11	12	12	7	9	10	11	10	9	7
8	4	6	5	7	8	10	8	6	3	6	8
3	3	4	1	10	9	11	7	2	6	10	7

2 Force of wind measured on the Beaufort scale

3	1	4	4	3	5	2	6	4	2	2	2
0	1	4	2	5	3	3	4	4	3	6	7
5	4	0	1	2	3	1	5	4	3	2	2
8	10	9	7	7	8	6	5	4	3	5	2
6	7	5	5	1	2	6	4	3	4	6	5

3 Maximum temperature in degrees Celsius

18	19	19	21	19	21	18	18	19	18	16	18
17	18	18	17	19	18	17	16	21	22	21	21
20	22	22	23	21	18	23	21	21	22	22	17
19	17	19	21	19	19	17	19	19	16	19	17
20	22	21	20	23	21	21	22	21	21	20	20

12.2 Grouping data

When there are lots of different data values, it is useful to group the data.

Here are the numbers of cars photographed by a speed camera on each of 60 days:

17	39	36	22	16	43	25	43	55	26	67	13
38	37	37	18	30	11	5	54	23	24	43	0
32	43	4	30	22	23	55	26	21	24	36	23
43	26	46	47	17	3	36	38	11	57	12	32
8	58	27	34	15	24	43	25	61	25	64	15

First group the number of photographs per day in tens and make a frequency table.

Photographs	Tally	Frequency
0–9	卌	5
10–19	卌 卌	10
20–29	卌 卌 卌	16
30–39	卌 卌 |||	13
40–49	卌 |||	8
50–59	卌	5
60–69	|||	3
70+		0

The **modal class** is 20–29 because this group has the highest frequency.

The intervals 0–9, 10–19, ... are called **class intervals**.

The **modal class** is the group which has the highest frequency.

Next draw a bar chart to illustrate the data.

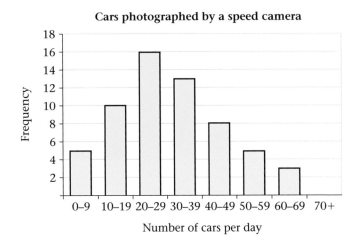

Cars photographed by a speed camera

Exercise 12B

1 In a music contest the marks awarded were:

```
15  21  13  18  22  17   9  12   7  19
24  16  11   8  14  28  17  15  18   7
 5  17  10  26   7  16  23  14  11  20
12   6  26  16  10  19  13  29  17   8
```

(a) Using class intervals 0–4, 5–9, ..., draw up a frequency table.

(b) Draw a bar chart to represent your frequency table.

2 The number of people logged on at an internet café was recorded every hour over a 48-hour period.
Here are the results:

$$14 \quad 14 \quad 24 \quad 9 \quad 25 \quad 18 \quad 22 \quad 5$$
$$13 \quad 7 \quad 11 \quad 14 \quad 4 \quad 16 \quad 11 \quad 27$$
$$17 \quad 19 \quad 13 \quad 15 \quad 34 \quad 15 \quad 14 \quad 9$$
$$25 \quad 7 \quad 28 \quad 3 \quad 15 \quad 12 \quad 20 \quad 13$$
$$1 \quad 16 \quad 10 \quad 24 \quad 6 \quad 29 \quad 7 \quad 22$$
$$20 \quad 14 \quad 29 \quad 12 \quad 24 \quad 8 \quad 16 \quad 10$$

(a) Draw up a frequency table, using class intervals 0–5, 6–10, 11–15, ...

(b) Draw a bar chart of the data.

(c) What is the modal class?

3 Bowling shoes may be hired at Bronx Bowling Alley.
Here are the sizes of the shoes at the alley:

$$3\tfrac{1}{2} \quad 4 \quad 5 \quad 1 \quad 5 \quad 9\tfrac{1}{2} \quad 2\tfrac{1}{2} \quad 4 \quad 5 \quad 4$$
$$5 \quad 2 \quad 7\tfrac{1}{2} \quad 3 \quad 6 \quad 4 \quad 7 \quad 6\tfrac{1}{2} \quad 3 \quad 7$$
$$4 \quad 7 \quad 5 \quad 9 \quad 3\tfrac{1}{2} \quad 10 \quad 5 \quad 2\tfrac{1}{2} \quad 4\tfrac{1}{2} \quad 7\tfrac{1}{2}$$
$$5\tfrac{1}{2} \quad 3 \quad 6\tfrac{1}{2} \quad 5 \quad 7 \quad 5 \quad 6 \quad 6\tfrac{1}{2} \quad 8 \quad 6$$
$$2 \quad 6 \quad 4\tfrac{1}{2} \quad 7 \quad 5 \quad 3 \quad 3 \quad 5\tfrac{1}{2} \quad 7\tfrac{1}{2} \quad 2$$

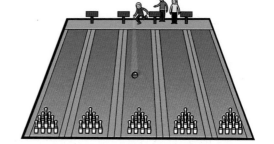

(a) Draw up a frequency table for the data. Choose classes with equal intervals.

(b) Draw a bar chart of the data.

(c) Comment on your findings.

12.3 Comparing data

You can use bar charts to compare different sets of data.

The numbers of patients who attended morning and evening surgeries in a doctor's practice one week are shown in the table and the following bar chart.

	Mon	Tue	Wed	Thu	Fri	Sat
Morning	145	120	96	116	125	28
Evening	81	65	43	55	64	–

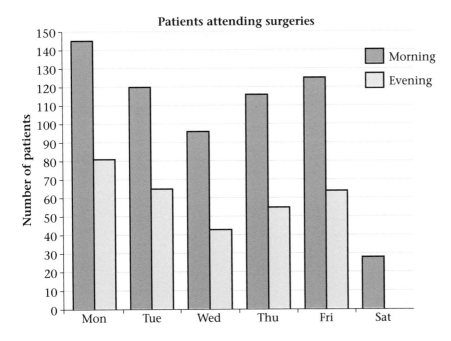

This type of graph is called a **dual bar chart** because it compares **two** sets of data. Often it is easier to see a pattern by looking at the chart rather than the table.

A **dual bar chart** is used to compare two sets of data.

Example 1

Use the table and bar chart to answer the following questions.
(a) On which day did most patients attend?
(b) On which day did fewest patients attend?
(c) On which day was there no evening surgery?
(d) On which day did 171 patients attend?
(e) How many more patients attended on Tuesday morning than on Tuesday evening?

(a) Monday —— This is clear from the bar chart
(b) Saturday —— This is clear from the bar chart
(c) Saturday —— Use the table or the bar chart
(d) Thursday —— Use the table for exact numbers
(e) 55 —— Use the table

Activity – Homework time

Record the times you and a friend spend doing homework on each day during a week. Enter the results in a table and draw a dual bar chart of the data.

Example 2

Here is a bar chart showing information about applications for asylum in the UK in 2003.

Use the bar chart to answer these questions:

(a) Which is the most common age group for asylum-seekers?

(b) Which age group(s) had the same percentage of males as of females?

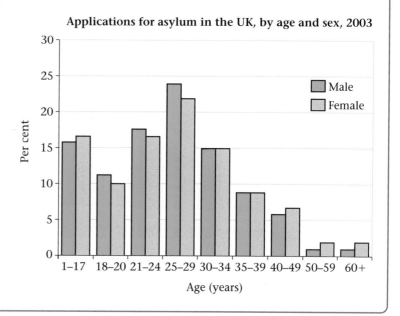

Applications for asylum in the UK, by age and sex, 2003

(a) 25–29
(b) 30–34 and 35–39

Exercise 12C

1 The average daily temperatures, in °F, in London and Majorca are recorded in the table.

	Oct	Nov	Dec	Jan	Feb	Mar	Apr
London	58	50	45	42	43	50	58
Majorca	71	65	58	52	58	62	68

(a) Draw a dual bar chart to illustrate the data.
(b) Write down three things you notice from your chart.

2 The prices of holiday accommodation in Majorca per person, in £ sterling per week, are given in the table.

	Oct	Nov	Dec	Jan	Feb	Mar	Apr
Hotel	260	290	270	280	295	315	330
Self catering	190	150	140	110	125	150	180

(a) Draw a dual bar chart to illustrate the data.
(b) Which months have the greatest difference in price between hotel and self catering?
(c) Write down three things you notice from your chart.

> Think carefully about the vertical scale you choose.

3 The amounts of money, in euros, spent by Norma and
   Adrian buying presents were:

	Mon	Tue	Wed	Thu	Fri	Sat
Norma	7.60	0	12.30	2.00	25.40	6.00
Adrian	5.50	7.10	2.40	20.80	6.00	4.00

(a) Represent this data by drawing a dual bar chart.
(b) Write down three statements about Norma's and
     Adrian's spending.

12.4 Pictograms

A **pictogram** is a quick, visual way of showing information by
using a symbol to represent a quantity.

For example, a primary teacher recorded the number of
students in his class who got a merit one week and drew a
pictogram for classroom display:

Rashid went round a factory car park and made a note of the
colours of the cars. His findings were:

Black	35	White	20
Red	10	Grey	15
Silver	15	Beige	2
Green	5	Other	14

He decided to use the symbol to represent 5 cars and drew this pictogram.

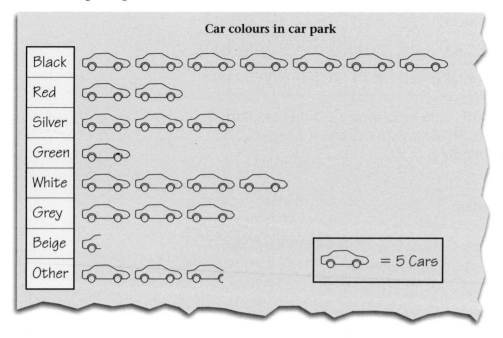

Exercise 12D

1   Draw a pictogram to illustrate each set of data. First decide what symbol you will use and what it will represent.

(a)   This table shows the numbers of different types of housing in a village.

	Flats	Bungalows	Detached	Semi-detached
Number	50	80	40	60

(b)   This table shows the numbers of telephone calls to an answering service between midnight and 7:00 am during a certain week.

	Mon	Tue	Wed	Thu	Fri	Sat	Sun
Calls	24	20	32	48	28	32	12

(c)   This table shows the numbers of members in the European parliament for certain countries in 2004.

	Belgium	France	Germany	Ireland	Spain	UK
Members	24	78	99	13	54	78

2 The pictograms show how many drinks were sold from two machines.

Drinks machine sales

Dining room

Coffee	
Tea	
Hot chocolate	
Soup	
Hot blackcurrant	

Staff room

Coffee	
Tea	
Hot chocolate	
Soup	
Hot blackcurrant	

Key: 🥤 10 drinks sold
🥤 5 drinks sold

(a) (i) Which drink was the most popular in the dining room?
　(ii) How many hot blackcurrants were sold in the dining room?
　(iii) How many hot chocolates were sold in the staff room?

(b) The staff room machine also sold 45 teas.
Copy and complete the pictogram.

(c) Work out the total number of drinks sold in the dining room.

(d) 64 people used the machine in the dining room.
Find the average number of drinks sold per person.

(e) Comment on the differences in sales from the two machines. [E]

12.5 Discrete and continuous data, and line graphs

It is important, when drawing graphs, to know if the data is discrete or continuous.

Data which can be counted is called **discrete data**.

For example, George has three sisters.
Southampton beat Liverpool 2–1.
There are ten coins in my pocket.

Data which is measured is called **continuous data**.

For example, Mike is 1.79 m tall.
The athlete ran 100 m in 10.3 seconds.
The weight of a bag of sugar is 1 kg.

Line graphs can be used to show continuous data.

The table shows the temperature in Leeds at midday during the first week in May.

May	1	2	3	4	5	6	7
Temperature (°C)	12	16	14	11	12	15	13

You could show this data on a **line graph**.
Here are two ways of doing this.

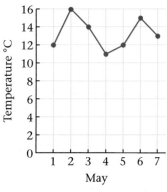

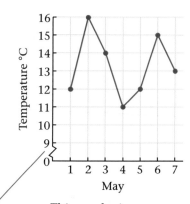

The temperature scale on this graph starts at 0 °C.

The break in the axis shows that the scale goes straight from 0 to 9.

This graph gives more space on the *y*-axis to values between 10 and 16 °C. This shows the pattern in the data more clearly.

The data is *continuous* so you can join the points.

This table shows the number of passengers that got off a train at each stop on a line in South-East London.

Station	London Bridge (B)	Hither Green (G)	Lee (L)	Mottingham (M)
Passengers	30	19	28	24

If you drew a graph like the one on the right, it might give the impression that people got off the train between stations!

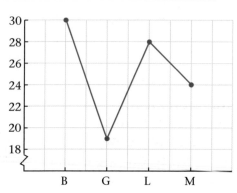

The data is *discrete* so you should not join the points.

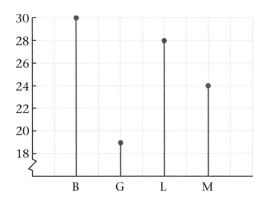

This is called a **vertical line graph** or **bar-line graph**. It is similar to a bar chart, and is used to display data that can be counted.

Activity – Sweets

Count the numbers of different colours of sweets in a packet and record the data in a suitable diagram.

Compare your findings with those from a packet of the same brand of sweet.

Example 3

Here is a line graph showing the percentage of household waste recycled in England.

Use the graph to answer these questions:

(a) What percentage of waste was recycled in England in 1998?

(b) In which year was 11.2% of waste recycled?

(c) Make a comment about what the graph shows.

(a) 9.0%

(b) 2000

(c) The percentage of waste that was recycled rose every year from 1996 to 2002 – the graph shows an increasing trend.

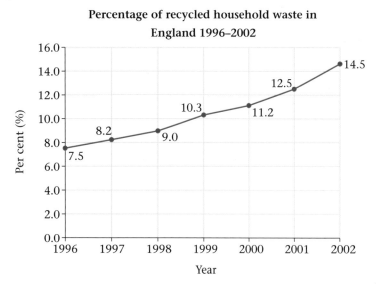

Exercise 12E

1 Which of the following are discrete data and which are continuous?

(a) the number of pages in a book
(b) the weight of a bag of sweets
(c) the temperature of a bottle of milk
(d) the number of sweets in a tube of Tasties
(e) the Third World debt
(f) the number of countries in the EU
(g) the distance to the Moon
(h) the number of people living in France
(i) the number of questions you get right
(j) the time it takes you to do this exercise.

2 Draw suitable graphs to represent each of the following sets of data.

(a) The number of letters delivered to an office one week

	Sat	Sun	Mon	Tue	Wed	Thu	Fri
Letters	20	0	12	25	15	19	23

(b) The noon temperature in Weymouth for certain days in August

August	1	2	3	4	5	6	7
Temperature (°F)	73	69	65	70	75	79	76

(c) The lengths of some of the longest rivers in the British Isles, in km to the nearest 10 km

River	Severn	Wye	Shannon	Tay	Thames
Length	340	210	390	190	340

3 The graphs show the sales of bikes from January to May.

(a) (i) Look quickly at the graphs. Which shop appears
to sell more bikes?

(ii) Look at the scales carefully.

Which shop sells more bikes?

(b) How many bikes did Cycleshop sell in March?

(c) How many bikes were sold altogether by

(i) Cycleshop   (ii) Bikeshop?

(d) In which month did both shops sell the same number
of bikes?

4   The graphs show the numbers of vehicles coming for
petrol at two garages during a week.

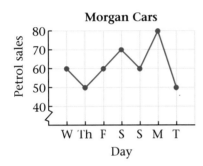
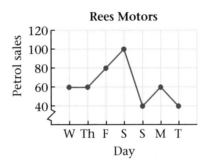

(a) Copy and complete the table below.

Petrol Sales	Wed	Thu	Fri	Sat	Sun	Mon	Tue
Morgan Cars							
Rees Motors							

(b) Draw a dual bar chart for this information.

(c) Use your chart to make three comments about the
sales.

12.6 Time series

A line graph used to illustrate data collected at intervals in time
(e.g. hourly, daily, weekly, …) is called a **time series** graph.

By observing results over time, you can predict what may
happen in the future.

Example 4

This graph shows the temperature, in degrees Celsius, at noon during the first ten days of June in Llangrannog.

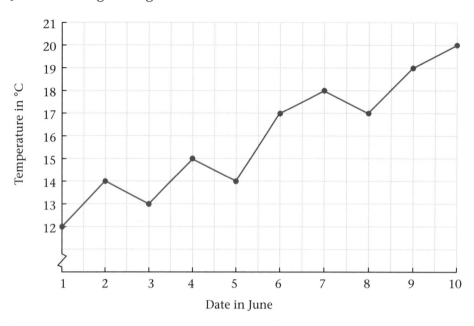

(a) What was the highest temperature recorded?

(b) What do you think the temperature might be over the next few days?

(c) Give a reason why your prediction might be wrong.

(a) 20 °C   (b) 20–21 °C

(c) The weather may change very suddenly.

Exercise 12F

1   This table shows the numbers of anglers fishing in Richmond Pond each year from 1998 to 2005.

Year	1998	1999	2000	2001	2002	2003	2004	2005
Number	279	268	272	240	228	212	209	195

(a) Draw a time series graph to represent this data.

(b) Comment on your graph. •—————

(c) Make a prediction for the number of anglers in 2006.

Hint: You could say what the highest and lowest values were, whether the graph has gone up or down, or if there is a repeating pattern in the data.

2 This table shows the values, in pence, of shares in two companies on the last day of each month last year.

	Jan	Feb	Mar	Apr	May	Jun	Jul	Aug	Sep
UXP	74	75	74	72	70	68	69	67	66
HCOR	35	36	40	41	39	42	41	43	44

(a) Using the same axes, draw a time series graph for each of these companies.

(b) What do you think the value of each share might be in October? Give a reason for your answer.

3 This table shows the quarterly sales of cars at Autobuy Garages.

Year	1998				1999				2000			
Quarter	1	2	3	4	1	2	3	4	1	2	3	4
Sales	90	86	82	77	94	92	88	85	100	95	92	

(a) Draw a time series graph to represent this data.

(b) Comment on your graph.

(c) Make a prediction of sales for the last quarter of 2000. Give a reason for your answer.

> This is a frequency distribution. It shows the number of cars sold every quarter.

12.7 Histograms

You usually draw bar charts or bar-line graphs to represent frequency distributions. These diagrams use the heights of bars or lines to represent the frequency. If the data is continuous and is grouped you can use a **histogram**.

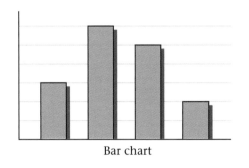

Bar chart

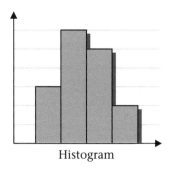

Histogram

> This histogram, with equal bar width and group size, is a special case. Most histograms do not have equal bar width.

You will notice that a histogram looks much like a bar chart except that there are no gaps between the bars in a histogram.

A **histogram** is used to display grouped data that is continuous.

Activity – Hand-spans

(a) Measure the hand-span of each person in your class.

(b) Record the data in a frequency table using class intervals of equal width.

(c) Draw a histogram to display your data.

12.8 Frequency polygons

Another useful way of displaying data is a **frequency polygon** in which the values at the midpoints of the class intervals are joined by straight lines.

The table shows the frequency distribution of the ages of members of a swimming club in 2001 and 2002.

Age	0–9	10–19	20–29	30–39	40–49	50–
2001	5	15	21	30	19	15
2002	10	24	28	22	10	6

You can draw histograms and join the midpoints to get a frequency polygon for each of the years.

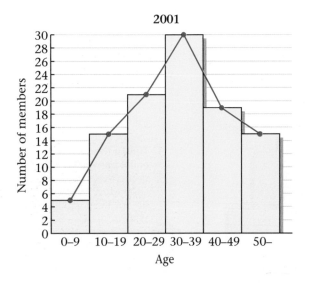

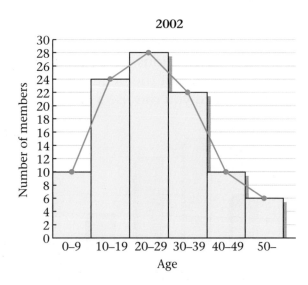

A **frequency polygon** can show the general pattern of data represented by a histogram.

It is often easier to compare data like this by placing one polygon on top of the other:

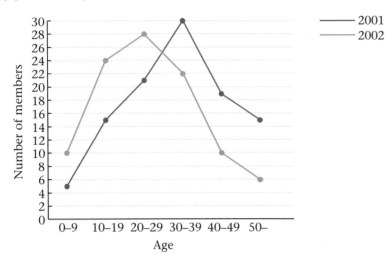

Exercise 12G

1 The numbers of students late for school in a two-week period are given in this table.

	Mon	Tue	Wed	Thu	Fri
Week 1	6	8	14	10	12
Week 2	9	13	8	6	10

(a) Draw bar charts of this data.

(b) Join the midpoints to make frequency polygons.

(c) Use the frequency polygons to compare the two weeks and write down three observations.

> You can use a bar chart to help you draw a frequency polygon.

2 The table shows the results of 75 students in a fitness programme with assessments in September, January and May.

Mark	0–4	5–9	10–14	15–19	20–24
Sept	10	12	22	16	15
Jan	6	15	26	18	10
May	2	8	25	27	13

(a) Draw frequency polygons for each set of results.

(b) Make a tracing of the January polygon. Put it on the same axes as the May polygon.
Comment on the changes you find.

3 This table gives information on the sales of petrol and diesel in a garage during one week.

Day	Number of litres of petrol sold	Number of litres of diesel sold
Monday	400	400
Tuesday	600	200
Wednesday	700	300
Thursday	450	700
Friday	200	900
Saturday	700	800
Sunday	600	700

Draw two frequency polygons on the same axes to represent this data.

4 Mr North measured the times it took for his students to run around a track. Here are the results:

Time in seconds	Frequency
41–45	1
46–50	5
51–55	8
56–60	4
61–65	7
66–70	4

Draw a frequency polygon to show these results.

Mixed exercise 12

1 Helen collected 20 leaves and wrote down their lengths in centimetres. Here are her results:

4   8   4   3   4   2   6   7   5   4

7   6   4   3   5   7   6   4   8   5

(a) Copy and complete the following frequency table to show Helen's results.

Length of leaf in cm	Tally	Frequency
2		
3		
4		
5		
6		
7		
8		

(b) Draw a bar chart of Helen's results.

2 Martin weighed 20 bags of crisps in grams. Here are his results:

31 35 39 28 38 32 39 43 33 40
34 36 25 22 39 42 36 27 26 30

(a) Copy and complete the grouped frequency table for Martin's results.

Weight of crisps (grams)	Tally	Frequency
20–24		
25–29		
30–34		
35–39		
40–44		

(b) Write down the modal class.

(c) Copy and complete this graph to show these results.

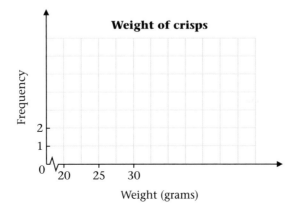

3 Here is a graph of the average temperatures last year in Manchester:

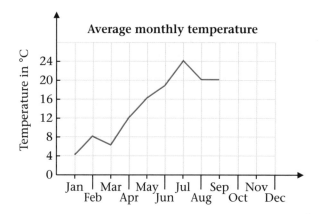

(a) Which month had the highest average temperature?

(b) Which month had the lowest average temperature?

The average temperatures in the remaining three months were:

     October   16 °C

     November 10 °C

     December 6 °C

(c) Copy and complete the line graph to show this information.

4 Here is a pictogram. It shows the number of boxes of chocolates sold last week from 'Chocs 4 U'.

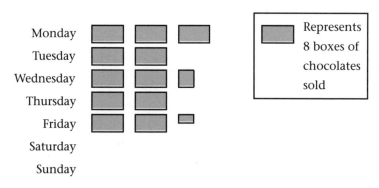

(a) Write down the number of boxes of chocolates sold on

     (i) Monday,   (ii) Tuesday,   (iii) Wednesday.

On Saturday, 32 boxes of chocolates were sold.

(b) Copy and complete the pictogram to show this information.

On Sunday, 11 boxes of chocolates were sold.

(c) Add this to the pictogram.

5 Mr North measured the times it took for his Year 7 class and his Year 10 class to run around a running track. Here are his results:

Time in seconds	Frequency Year 7	Frequency Year 10
41–45	1	2
46–50	3	7
51–55	5	8
56–60	8	4
61–65	5	3
66–70	2	1

(a) Draw two frequency polygons, on the same grid, to show the results for Mr North's two classes.

(b) What do your frequency polygons tell you about Mr North's classes?

6 The amount of petrol (in litres) in the storage tank at a garage was measured every hour between 7 am and 7 pm on one day. This is the shape of the line graph showing the results:

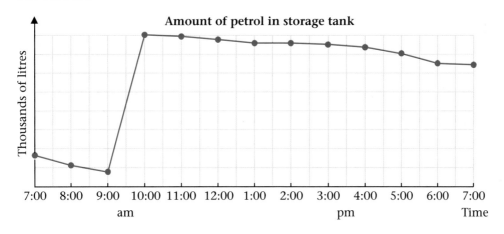

(a) When was the amount of petrol in the tank at its lowest?

(b) What do you think happened between 9 am and 10 am?

(c) What were the sales like between 1 pm and 4 pm?

(d) Give a reason for your answer to part (c).

7 Muriel recorded the maximum and minimum
   temperatures over a period of ten days. Her results are
   given in this table.

April 2006	4th	5th	6th	7th	8th	9th	10th	11th	12th	13th
Max (°C)	12	9	10	10	13	17	15	19	16	18
Min (°C)	5	2	4	5	6	7	5	8	6	7

(a) Draw a graph to illustrate both sets of temperatures
     on the same axes.
(b) Write a comment about each set of data.

Summary of key points

1 **Tally charts** and **bar charts** are two ways of displaying data that can be counted.
   You must leave a gap between the bars when you draw bar charts of data that can
   be counted.

2 The **modal class** is the group which has the highest frequency.

3 A **dual bar chart** is used to compare two sets of data.

4 A **pictogram** is a quick, visual way of showing information by using a symbol to
   represent a quantity.

5 Data which can be counted is called **discrete data**.

6 Data which is measured is called **continuous data**.

7 **Line graphs** can be used to show continuous data.

8 A line graph used to illustrate data collected at intervals in time (e.g. hourly, daily,
   weekly, ...) is called a **time series** graph.

9 A **histogram** is used to display grouped data that is continuous.

10 A **frequency polygon** can show the general pattern of data represented by a
    histogram.

13 3-D shapes

All the boxes and packets shown on the supermarket shelves in the picture are 3-dimensional or 3-D. They have height, width and depth. This chapter is all about 3-D shapes.

13.1 Horizontal and vertical surfaces

In the picture above the shelves are horizontal surfaces. (The floor and ceiling would also be horizontal surfaces.)

The sides of the boxes are vertical surfaces. (The walls would also be vertical surfaces.)

A flat surface is called a **plane**. The roof of this block of flats is a horizontal plane. The end wall is a vertical plane.

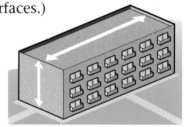

Exercise 13A

1   Identify and list 5 horizontal and 5 vertical surfaces in your classroom. You can include the floor and the walls as part of your answer.

2   Identify and list 5 horizontal and 5 vertical surfaces in this picture:

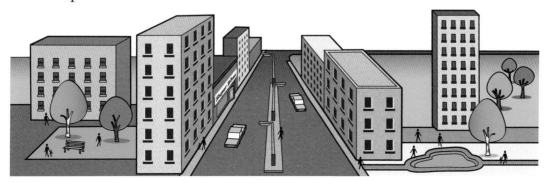

13.2 Faces, edges and vertices

Flat surfaces of 3-D shapes are called **faces**.

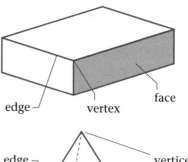

The shaded surface on the box is called a face.
The box has 6 faces.

The line where two faces meet is called an **edge**.

The box has 12 edges.

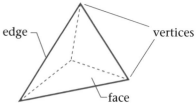

The point where three edges meet is called a **vertex**.

The box has 8 vertices.

> Broken lines show edges that you can't see.

Exercise 13B

1   Here are some 3-D shapes. Count the faces, edges and
    vertices of each shape and write them in a copy of the
    table below.

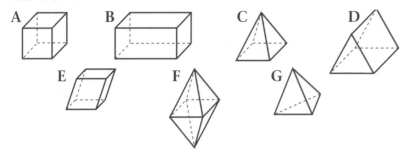

Shape	Number of faces	Number of vertices	Number of edges

2   There is a rule which connects the number of faces and
    the number of vertices with the number of edges. Use
    your results from question 1 to find this rule.

13.3 Looking at shapes

A **sketch** is a drawing which does not pretend to be exact. But it should be good enough not to be misleading.

The chart below shows pictures, sketches, names and some of the properties of some 3-D shapes.

> In sketches parallel lines are drawn parallel. Vertical lines always look vertical. Horizontal lines may be drawn in any direction.

Name and properties	Picture	Sketch
Cube 6 square faces		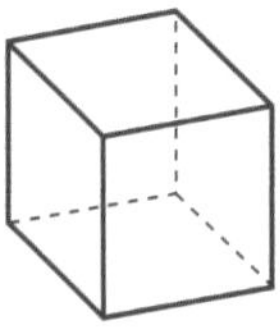
Cuboid 6 rectangular faces		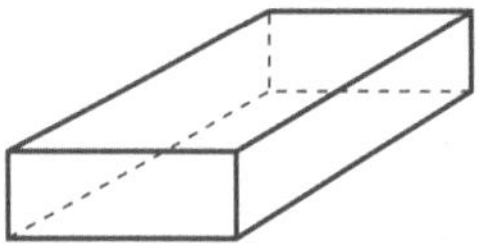
Sphere		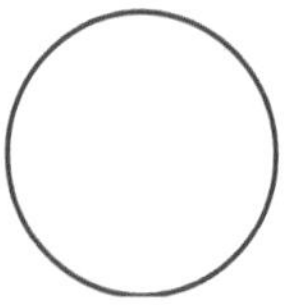
Square-based pyramid Square base, 4 triangular faces	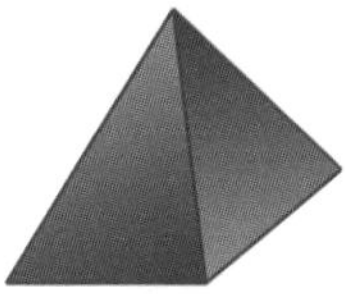	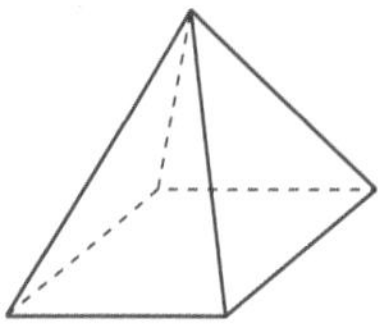
Triangular-based pyramid (tetrahedron) 4 triangular faces	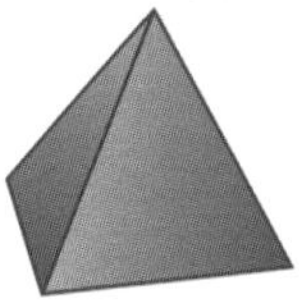	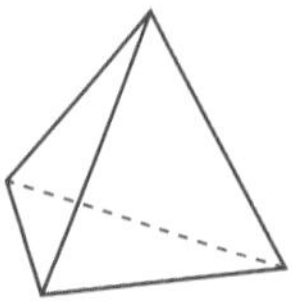
Cone A special pyramid with a circular base		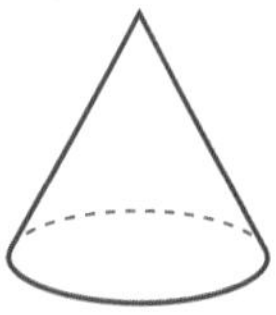
Cylinder 2 circular faces		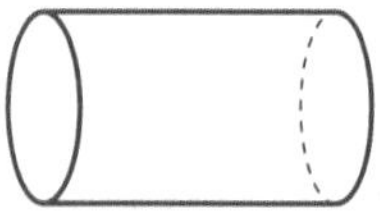

Example 1

Sketch a cube.

Step 1 Draw a square.

Step 2 Draw another square the same size, slightly to the right and slightly above the original square.

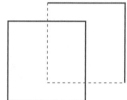

Step 3 Join the corners of the squares.

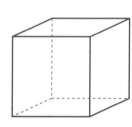

Example 2

Sketch a square-based pyramid:

Step 1 Draw the base.

Step 2 The top is above the middle of the base.

Step 3 Join the top to the other corners.

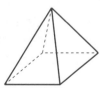

Exercise 13C

1 Look at the picture below and make a list of as many 3-D
shapes as you can. For example, the football is a sphere.

> There are at least 12 3-D shapes.

2 Sketch

(a) a triangular-based pyramid   (b) a cuboid

(c) a cube   (d) a cylinder

(e) a square-based pyramid.

13.4 Prisms

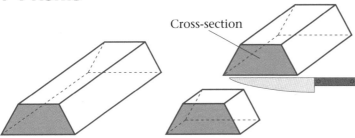

Cross-section

The faces at either end of this shape are identical and parallel.
The cross-section is identical to the end faces. A shape that has
a uniform cross-section like this is called a **prism**.

> Parallel means the faces are the same distance from each other at all points.

A **prism** is a shape which has a uniform cross-section.

A **cross-section** is a slice through the shape, parallel to the
end faces.

Some other prisms are drawn below. Where the shape of the cross-section is a known 2-D shape then it is used to describe the type of prism.

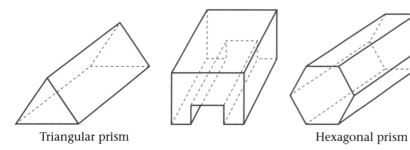

Triangular prism   Hexagonal prism

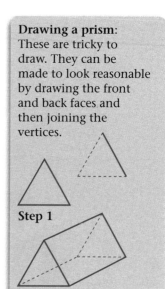

Exercise 13D

1 Which of the following shapes are prisms?

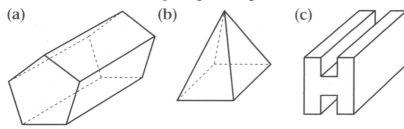

(a)   (b)   (c)

2 What name is usually given to a circular prism?

3 Write down the names of two other 3-D shapes that are also prisms.

4 Write down 5 things in your classroom which are prisms.

13.5 Nets

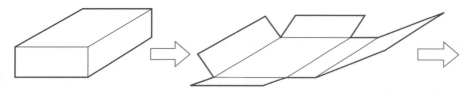

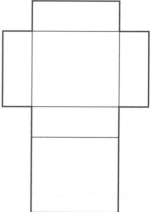

The box (cuboid) in the diagram has been opened out to make a 2-D shape. This 2-D shape is called the **net** of the box.

A **net** is a 2-D shape that can be folded into a 3-D shape.

Example 3

Draw the net of this triangular prism.

The prism has three rectangular faces
measuring 6 cm by 3 cm which are
joined along their long sides.
These faces can be drawn as:

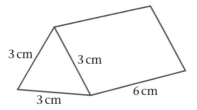

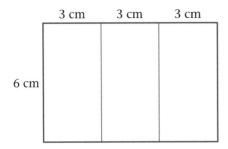

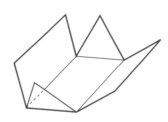

The faces at either end of the prism are equilateral triangles with 3 cm sides. These
must join to the short side of one of the rectangles. This makes the complete net.

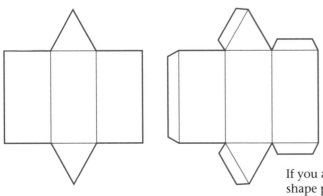

You need to be able to
construct accurate
drawings of 2-D shapes
if your nets are to fold
together to make good
solids. For more on
accurate constructions
see Chapter 7.

If you are going to make the
shape put a tab on alternate sides.
You can start with any side.

Exercise 13E

You need a ruler, pencil and pair of compasses for some of the
questions in this exercise.

1 Sketch the nets of these solids:

 (a) 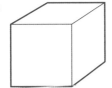 **(b)**

(a regular
tetrahedron)

(c)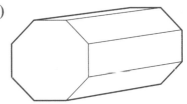

2 These nets will form a 3-D solid.
Draw a sketch of each solid.

(a)

(b)

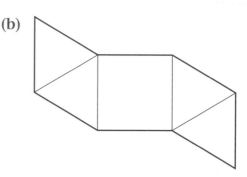

3 Which of the following are nets of a cube?

(a)   **(b)**   **(c)**

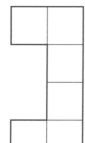 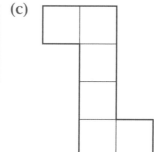

4 Which of the following are nets of a tetrahedron (triangular-based pyramid with base and all sides equilateral triangles)?

(a)   **(b)**   **(c)**

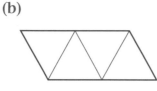

5 Draw accurate nets for these shapes:

(a)   **(b)**   **(c)**

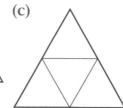

(a) 5 cm, 5 cm, 5 cm, 4 cm, 5 cm

(b) 2 cm, 8 cm, 5 cm

(c) 8 cm, 8 cm, 5 cm, 5 cm

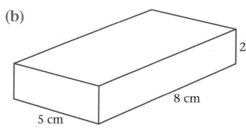 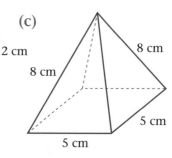

6 Draw an accurate net for each of the following shapes:

(a) a cube with sides of 5 cm

(b) a regular tetrahedron with sides of 4 cm.

> You could do this on card and make the shapes (remember to add tabs).

7   Here is a net of a cube:

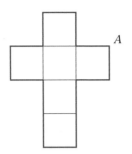

The net is folded to make the cube.
Copy the diagram.
Two other vertices of the net meet at *A*.
Mark each of them with the letter *A*.   [E]

8   Sketch the following solids and their nets:
   (a) cuboid   (b) cylinder
   (c) cone   (d) tetrahedron
   (e) hexagonal prism.

9   Sketch the solids that these nets form.
   Mark the measurements on your sketches.
   (a)   (b)

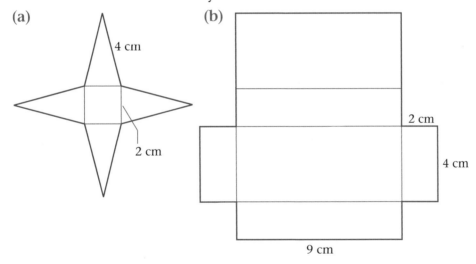

10 Draw an accurate net for each of these solids.
   (a)   (b)

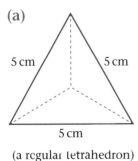
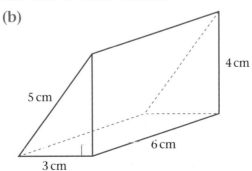

13.6 Plan and elevation

Architects and designers often represent 3-D objects with 2-D drawings.

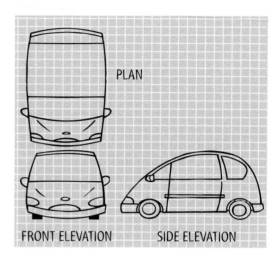

PLAN

FRONT ELEVATION   SIDE ELEVATION

The **plan** of a solid is the view when seen from above.

The **front elevation** is the view when seen from the front.

The **side elevation** is the view when seen from the side.

Example 4

Draw the plan and elevations of this shape.

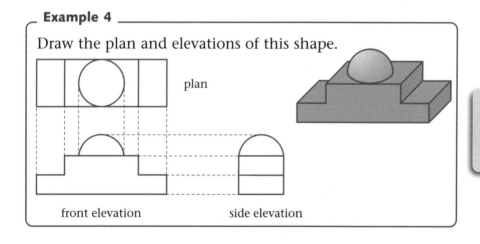

plan

front elevation   side elevation

> You should draw plans and elevations using dotted lines to show how the different drawings match up.

Exercise 13F

1 Sketch the plan and elevations of each of these shapes:

(a)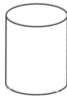

(b)

(c)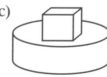

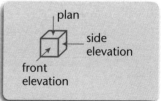

plan

side elevation

front elevation

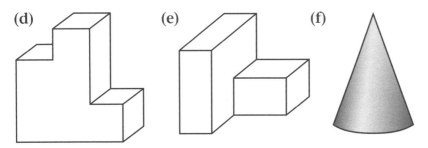

(d) (e) (f)

2 Use multilink cubes to construct these solids.
   Sketch each one.

(a)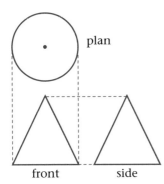

(b)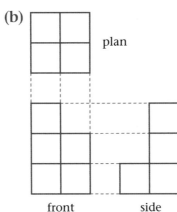

(c)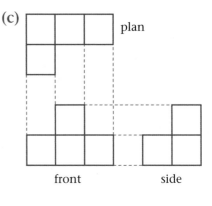

3 Describe the solids with these plans and elevations:

(a) (b)

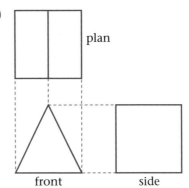

(c) Draw your own set of three shapes. Try to describe a
     solid which has your shapes as its plan, front
     elevation and side elevation.

4 Here are the plan and front
   elevation of a prism.
   The cross-section of the
   shape is represented by the
   front elevation.

   (a) On squared paper draw
        a side elevation.

   (b) Draw a 3-D sketch
        of the shape.

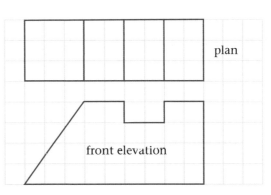

[E]

13.7 Symmetry in 3-D shapes

A 3-D shape has a **plane of symmetry** if the plane divides the shape into two halves and one half is the mirror image of the other half.

plane of symmetry

Example 5

Draw diagrams to show the planes of symmetry of a cuboid.

A cuboid has 3 planes of symmetry. To show the planes of symmetry clearly, draw a diagram for each plane:

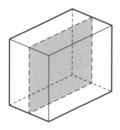 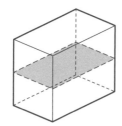 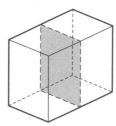

Exercise 13G

You may want to use tracing paper in this exercise.

1 Write down the number of planes of symmetry for each of the following shapes.

(a) 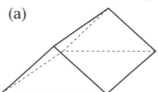   (b) 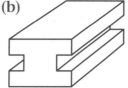   (c)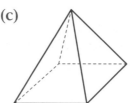

(d) 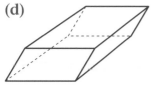   (e) 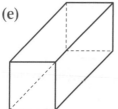   (f)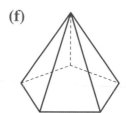

2 Copy or trace the following shapes and clearly mark any
planes of symmetry on your drawings.

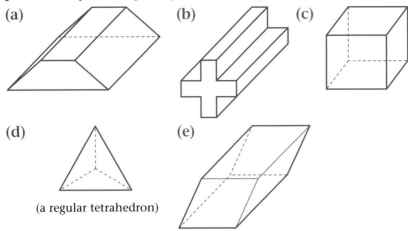

(a) (b) (c)

(d) (e)

(a regular tetrahedron)

3 Copy these shapes that represent 3-D objects and draw
all their planes of symmetry on separate diagrams.

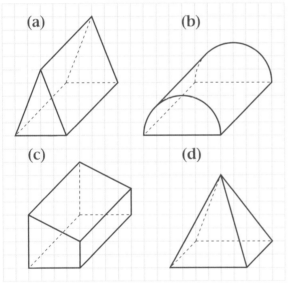

(a) (b)

(c) (d)

4 The drawings below each show half of a 3-D solid.
Copy and complete each solid so that the shaded face
forms a plane of symmetry.

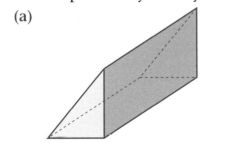

(a)

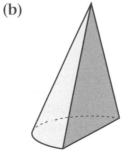

(b)

Mixed exercise 13

1   For each shape in this question write down
     (i) the name
    (ii) the number of edges
   (iii) the number of faces
   (iv) the number of vertices.

(a) 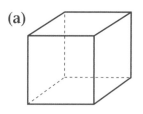   (b) 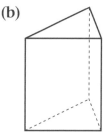   (c)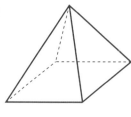

2   The base of each shape in question 1 is horizontal.
    (i) Write down the number of horizontal edges each
         shape has.
    (ii) Write down the number of vertical edges each shape
         has.

3   Which of these shapes are prisms?
    (a)   (b)   (c)

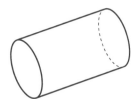   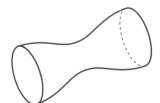   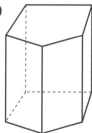

4   Here is the net of a 3-D shape.

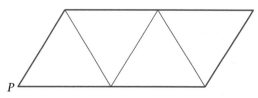

    (a) Write down the name of the 3-D shape.

    (b) Copy the net. When the net is folded to make the
         3-D shape one vertex on the net meets vertex P.
         Mark that vertex with the letter P.

5 (a) For this shape write down the number of
     (i) edges
     (ii) vertices
     (iii) faces.
  (b) Make a sketch of the solid.
     (i) Mark a vertical face.
     (ii) Mark a horizontal face.

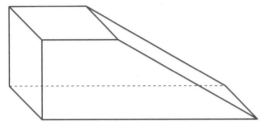

6 A, B, C, D and E are five 3-D shapes.
P, Q, R, S and T are five nets.
Match the shapes to the nets.

  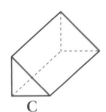 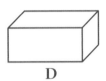

A   B   C   D   E

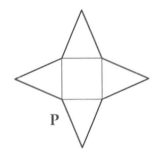 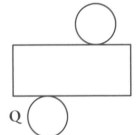 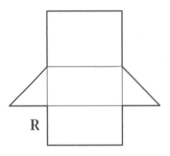

P   Q   R

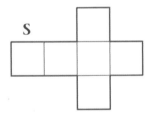 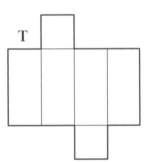

S   T

7 Write down the names of these shapes.

(a) 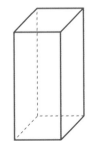   (b)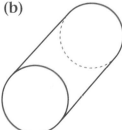

8 The diagram shows part of net for a cuboid.

One face of the cuboid is missing.

The cuboid is 2 cm by 3 cm by 4 cm.

(a) Write down the size of the missing face.

(b) Draw an accurate version of the net, including the missing face.

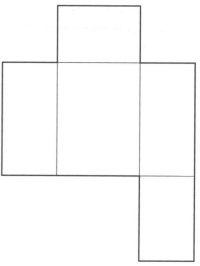

9 Draw an accurate net for each of the following shapes:

(a)

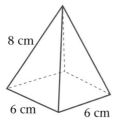

(b) a regular tetrahedron with sides of 4 cm.

10 Draw a sketch of a

(a) cube   (b) cuboid   (c) cylinder

(d) square-based pyramid   (e) triangular prism.

11 Here is a sketch of a 3-D shape.

Draw a sketch of the plan, front and side elevations of the shape.

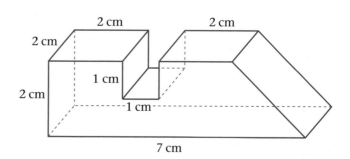

12 Make two copies of this 3-D shape.

Draw in one plane of symmetry of the shape on each copy.

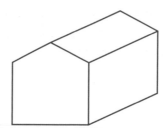

13 Here are the plan and front elevation of a prism.
The cross-section of the shape is represented by the front
elevation.

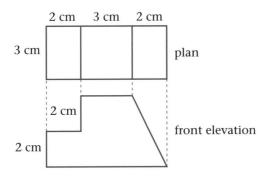

(a) Make an accurate drawing of the side elevation.

(b) Draw a sketch of the 3-D shape.

Summary of key points

1 A flat surface is called a **plane**.

2 Flat surfaces of 3-D shapes are called **faces**.

3 The line where two faces meet is called an **edge**.

4 The point where three edges meet is called a **vertex**.

5 A **prism** is a shape which has a uniform cross-section.
A **cross-section** is a slice through the shape, parallel to the end face

6 A **net** is a 2-D shape that can be folded into a 3-D shape.

7 The **plan** of a solid is the view when seen from
above.

8 The **front elevation** is the view when seen
from the front.

9 The **side elevation** is the view when seen
from the side.

10 A 3-D shape has a **plane of symmetry** if the plane
divides the shape into two halves and one half is
the mirror image of the other half.

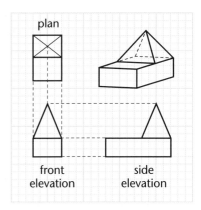

14 Units of measure

14.1 Changing metric units

Before you tackle this section you will need to be able to multiply and divide whole numbers and decimals by 10, 100 and 1000.

Check Chapters 1 and 5 if you need to remind yourself.

You need to know that:

Length	Weight	Capacity
10 mm = 1 cm 100 cm = 1 m 1000 mm = 1 m 1000 m = 1 km	1000 mg = 1 g 1000 g = 1 kg 1000 kg = 1 tonne	100 cl = 1 litre 1000 ml = 1 litre 1000 l = 1 cubic metre

You need to remember:

When you change from small units to large units you divide.

When you change from large units to small units you multiply.

Example 1

(a) Change 2 kilometres to metres.

(b) Change 250 mm to cm.

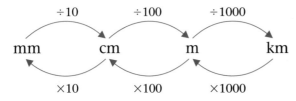

(a) Kilometres are larger units than metres so you multiply by the number of metres in a kilometre, which is 1000:

$$2 \times 1000 = 2000 \text{ m}$$

(b) Millimetres are smaller units than centimetres so you divide by the number of millimetres in a centimetre, which is 10:

$$250 \div 10 = 25 \text{ cm}$$

Exercise 14A

1 Change these lengths to centimetres.
(a) 3 m   (b) 30 mm   (c) 6 m
(d) 12 m   (e) 100 mm

2 Change these lengths to millimetres.
(a) 2 cm   (b) 5 cm   (c) 12 cm
(d) 20 cm   (e) 100 cm

3 Change these lengths to metres.
(a) 5 km   (b) 300 cm   (c) 10 km
(d) 2000 cm   (e) 60 km

4 Change these weights to grams.
(a) 5 kg   (b) 40 kg   (c) 100 kg
(d) 250 kg   (e) 1000 kg

5 Change these capacities to litres.
(a) 3000 m*l*   (b) 8000 m*l*
(c) 50 000 m*l* (d) 75 000 m*l*

6 Change these volumes to millilitres.
(a) 6 *l*   (b) 40 *l*   (c) 100 *l*
(d) 350 *l*   (e) 25 *l*

7 Change these lengths to kilometres.
(a) 3000 m   (b) 7000 m
(c) 40 000 m   (d) 45 000 m

8 Change these weights to tonnes.
(a) 4000 kg   (b) 7000 kg
(c) 30 000 kg   (d) 55 000 kg

9 Change these weights to kilograms.
(a) 2000 g   (b) 3 tonnes   (c) 50 000 g
(d) 12 tonnes   (e) 100 000 g

10 How many millimetres equal 1 metre?

11 Jeremy walks 10 kilometres. How many centimetres is this?

12 Jim's lorry weighs 8 tonnes. How many grams is this?

13 Work out the number of centimetres in 1 kilometre.

14 Pritti has an average pace length of 75 cm.
When she walks 3 km how many paces does she take?

15 Work out the number of millimetres in 1 kilometre.

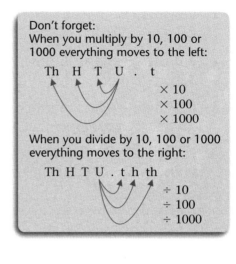

Don't forget:
When you multiply by 10, 100 or 1000 everything moves to the left:

Th   H   T   U . t
                        × 10
                        × 100
                        × 1000

When you divide by 10, 100 or 1000 everything moves to the right:

Th H T U . t h th
                        ÷ 10
                        ÷ 100
                        ÷ 1000

75 cm

Exercise 14B

1 Put these weights in order, largest first.

   250 g   25 g   2 kg   250 kg   3000 g

> Change them all into the same units.

2 Put these lengths in order, smallest first.

   3 m   5 mm   20 cm   3 km   50 mm

3 Put these lengths in order, smallest first.

   75 cm   3000 mm   2 m   4000 m   4 cm

4 Put these capacities in order, smallest first.

   200 ml   5 l   600 ml   2000 ml   1 l

So far all of the answers in this section have been whole numbers.
In the following exercises you will find it easier if you use your
calculator *but* don't forget to **check if your answer is sensible.**

Example 2

(a) Change 450 g to kg.   (b) Change 2.4 l to ml.

(a) $450 \div 1000 = 0.45$ kg
(b) $2.4 \times 1000 = 2400$ ml

> Changing small units to larger units so divide:
> 1000 g in 1 kg so ÷ 1000

> Changing large units to smaller units so multiply:
> 1000 ml in 1 l so × 1000

Exercise 14C

1 Change these lengths to metres.
   (a) 250 cm   (b) 50 cm   (c) 3.6 km
   (d) 75 cm   (e) 0.005 km   (f) 35 cm
   (g) 475 cm   (h) 0.6 km   (i) 0.04 km
   (j) 5 mm

2 Change these weights to grams.
   (a) 4.5 kg   (b) 0.4 kg   (c) 10.3 kg
   (d) 0.03 kg   (e) 0.005 kg

3 Change these lengths to centimetres.
   (a) 350 mm   (b) 2.5 m   (c) 5.4 m
   (d) 5 mm   (e) 0.08 m   (f) 0.8 m
   (g) 35 mm   (h) 50 mm   (i) 85 mm
   (j) 275 mm

125 cm or 1.25 m

4 Change these capacities to millilitres.
   (a) 3.5 l   (b) 0.5 l   (c) 15.4 l
   (d) 0.05 l   (e) 0.003 l

5   Change these lengths to millimetres.
  (a) 3.5 cm   (b) 0.7 cm   (c) 0.08 cm
  (d) 12.5 cm   (e) 0.005 m

6   Write these lengths in kilometres.
  (a) 300 m   (b) 50 m   (c) 1250 m
  (d) 75 m   (e) 375 m

7   Change these capacities to litres.
  (a) 250 ml   (b) 100 ml   (c) 50 ml
  (d) 3500 ml   (e) 1 ml

8   Change these weights to kilograms.
  (a) 500 g   (b) 0.3 tonnes   (c) 50 g
  (d) 5.5 tonnes   (e) 0.006 tonnes

9   Write these weights in tonnes.
  (a) 3500 kg   (b) 450 kg   (c) 50 kg
  (d) 3000 g   (e) 75 kg

10 How many 75 ml glasses can be filled from a bottle
    holding 1.5 l of cola?

11 How many 50 mm pieces of wood can be cut from a
    piece of wood of length 3 m, assuming there is no waste?

12 It takes 150 g of flour to make a batch of rock cakes.
    How many batches of rock cakes can be made from
    1.2 kg of flour?

Exercise 14D

1   Write these lengths in order, smallest first.
  (a) 25 mm, 3 cm, 2.4 cm, 50 mm, 6 cm, 57 mm
  (b) 30 cm, 0.4 m, 270 mm, 1.2 m, 500 mm, 45 cm
  (c) 2 m, 340 cm, 4000 mm, 4 m, 370 cm, 3500 mm
  (d) 5 cm, 45 mm, 36 cm, 0.3 m, 55 mm, 0.2 cm, 4 mm
  (e) 50 cm, 0.4 m, 560 mm, 0.45 m, 34 cm

2   Write these weights in order, smallest first.
  (a) 250 g, 0.3 kg, 500 g, 0.05 kg
  (b) 500 g, 350 g, 0.4 kg, 0.52 kg
  (c) 5000 g, 3000 g, 4 kg, 4.5 kg, 0.5 tonnes, 400 kg

3   Write these capacities in order, smallest first.
  (a) 300 ml, 0.4 l, 500 ml, 250 ml, 0.3 l
  (b) 500 ml, 450 ml, 0.4 l, 360 ml, 0.05 l, 45 ml

14.2 Metric and imperial conversions

You may need to change from metric units to imperial units (the old style units) and vice versa. To do this it helps to memorise these facts:

Metric	Imperial
8 km	5 miles
1 kg	2.2 pounds
25 g	1 ounce
1 l	1$\frac{3}{4}$ pints
4.5 l	1 gallon
1 m	39 inches
30 cm	1 foot
2.5 cm	1 inch

These conversions are only approximate.

Some petrol pumps have a conversion table to show how many litres or gallons you are buying.

Example 3

Change 10 km to miles.

Using 8 km = 5 miles

First find 1 km.

$$1 \text{ km} = 5 \div 8 = 0.625 \text{ miles}$$
$$\text{So } 10 \text{ km} = 0.625 \times 10 = 6.25 \text{ miles}$$

Multiply by 10 to find 10 km.

 Exercise 14E

The Evans family are going on holiday to Scotland. The family consists of Mr and Mrs Evans and their three children, Glenys, Eira and Gareth.

1 Mr Evans works out the distance from their home in London to Scotland. He makes it 400 miles. Approximately what is this distance in kilometres?

2 Mrs Evans packs a 3 litre bottle of water for the trip. About how many pints is 3 litres?

3 The petrol tank of the family's car holds 15 gallons. About how many litres is this?

4 Glenys estimates the weight of all the luggage as 100 kg. About how many pounds is that?

5 Gareth puts 1 pint of water in the car's radiator.
About how many litres is that?

6 Mr Evans puts 30 litres of petrol in the car.
About how many gallons is that?

7 Mrs Evans puts 0.5 *l* of oil in the engine.
About how many pints is that?

8 The family stop at a service station 150 km from home.
About how many miles is that?

9 Eira buys 800 g of chocolate.
About how many pounds is that?

10 When they get to Scotland there is half a bottle of water
left. About how many pints is that?

Exercise 14F

Class 11E are taking part in their school's Inter Generation
Day. They invite local older people for a coffee morning.

1 Sybil brings ten 2 *l* cartons of milk to make hot
chocolate. About how many gallons is this?

2 Henri brings 20 packets of biscuits.
Each packet weighs 1 pound.
About how many kilograms is this altogether?

3 Jonathan makes plates that are 6 inches across.
About how many centimetres is this?

4 The trays the class use are 24 inches long and
15 inches across.
Change these measurements to centimetres.

5 The tables the class use are 48 inches long. Will
tablecloths with a length of 1.2 m fit the tables?

6 Nilmini makes sandwiches and uses 5 kg of bread and
500 g of spread.
Change these weights to pounds.

7 At the end of the coffee morning there are 5 pints of
milk left. About how many litres is this?

8 Claire cooks some rock cakes. She makes 72 cakes and
uses 24 ounces of fat, 40 ounces of flour and 32 ounces
of dried fruit. She only has a metric set of scales.
Approximately how many grams of each ingredient
should she use?

9 In the 'guess the weight of the cake' competition the correct answer was 5 pounds. Robin said the weight was 5.1 pounds and Hazel said 2.3 kilograms.
Which of these two answers was nearer the correct weight?

10 The visitors ate 3.5 kilograms of Claire's cakes.
About how many pounds is that?

14.3 Calculating time

You need to know that:

$$60 \text{ seconds} = 1 \text{ minute}$$
$$60 \text{ minutes} = 1 \text{ hour}$$
$$24 \text{ hours} = 1 \text{ day}$$
$$365 \text{ days} = 1 \text{ year}$$
$$366 \text{ days} = 1 \text{ leap year}$$
$$3 \text{ months} = 1 \text{ quarter}$$
$$12 \text{ months} = 1 \text{ year}$$

Many people make mistakes when they are calculating with time because they forget that there are 60 minutes in an hour and not 100.

> Why does 30 minutes and 45 minutes give 1 hour and 15 minutes?
>
> You can't use an ordinary calculator to add times.

Example 4

(a) How many minutes are there in 3 hours?

(b) How many hours are there in 135 minutes?

(a) $3 \times 60 = 180$ minutes

(b) $135 \div 60 = 2.25$ hours
Some people might write this as 2 hours 25 minutes but they would be *wrong*. To change the 0.25 hours to minutes you must multiply 0.25 by 60.

$$0.25 \times 60 = 15$$

So 135 minutes is 2 hours 15 minutes.

Example 5

(a) Change 2.4 hours into hours and minutes.

(b) Change 5 hours 48 minutes into hours.

(a) **Step 1** Keep the 2 hours.
Step 2 Multiply the 0.4 hours by 60 (the number of minutes in an hour).
Step 3 Put the numbers together.

2 hours and $0.4 \times 60 = 2$ hours and 24 minutes

(b) **Step 1** Keep the 5 hours.
   Step 2 Divide the 48 minutes by 60 (the number of
          minutes in an hour).
   Step 3 Put the numbers together.

   5 hours and 48 ÷ 60 = 5 hours and 0.8 hours = 5.8 hours

Exercise 14G

1 Change these times into minutes.
   (a) 2 hours
   (b) 5 hours
   (c) 2 hours 30 minutes
   (d) $5\frac{1}{2}$ hours
   (e) $6\frac{1}{4}$ hours
   (f) 5 hours 15 minutes

2 Change these times into hours.
   (a) 180 minutes
   (b) 240 minutes
   (c) 75 minutes
   (d) 260 minutes
   (e) 325 minutes
   (f) 90 minutes
   (g) 3 days
   (h) $5\frac{1}{2}$ days
   (i) 500 minutes

3 How many seconds are there in 1 hour?

4 How many minutes are there in 1 day?

5 How many seconds are there in
   (a) a year
   (b) a leap year?

6 Change these times into hours and minutes.
   (a) 2.5 hours
   (b) 3.6 hours
   (c) $5\frac{1}{2}$ hours
   (d) $3\frac{3}{4}$ hours
   (e) 4.1 hours
   (f) 3.25 hours
   (g) 1.125 hours
   (h) 2.7 hours

7 Change these times into decimals of an hour.
   (a) 2 hours 30 minutes
   (b) 5 hours 15 minutes
   (c) 3 hours 36 minutes
   (d) 4 hours 12 minutes
   (e) 6 hours 20 minutes
   (f) 3 hours 18 minutes
   (g) 12 hours 45 minutes
   (h) 8 hours 3 minutes

8 Sam worked out his time for a journey using the formula
   $$\text{time} = \frac{\text{distance}}{\text{speed}}$$
   Sam travelled a distance of 90 miles at a speed of
   40 miles per hour. He said that the journey took 2 hours
   and 25 minutes. Explain why Sam was wrong.

Time calculations

When you come to make calculations involving times you have to be careful when it comes to dealing with the carry digit.

___ **Example 6** _____

(a) Add $2\frac{1}{2}$ hours to the time of 10:40.

(b) Take 3 hours 15 minutes away from 11:10.

(a) 10:40
     $\underline{\quad 2:30}$
     13:10   Not 70 because 70 minutes make 1 hour 10 minutes.
     $\scriptstyle 1$

(b) 11:10   You have to carry 60 minutes so 70 – 15 gives 55.
     $\underline{-\quad 3:15}$
     $\quad$7:55

It might help to write 11:10 as 10:70:

$\qquad$ 11:10 $\qquad\qquad\qquad$ 10:70
$\quad -\ \underline{\ 3:15}\qquad$ is $\qquad -\ \underline{\ 3:15}$
$\qquad\ \underline{\ 7:55}\qquad\qquad\qquad \underline{\ 7:55}$

> Don't forget:
> 60 minutes make 1 hour

Exercise 14H

1 Add 15 minutes to each of these times.
   (a) 10:30   (b) 09:45   (c) 11:40   (d) 09:55

2 Add 50 minutes to each of these times.
   (a) 09:00   (b) 10:30   (c) 11:40   (d) 08:05

3 Add 2 hours 40 minutes to each of these times.
   (a) 09:40   (b) 10:45   (c) 11:50   (d) 06:10

4 Add 12 hours 45 minutes to each of these times.
   (a) 02:30   (b) 07:15   (c) 12:50   (d) 16:45

5 Subtract 15 minutes from each of these times.
   (a) 09:55   (b) 11:40   (c) 08:10   (d) 09:05

6 Subtract 50 minutes from each of these times.
   (a) 08:55   (b) 11:40   (c) 10:30   (d) 09:00

7 Subtract 2 hours 30 minutes from each of these times.
   (a) 09:55   (b) 11:40   (c) 08:10   (d) 09:05

8 Subtract 12 hours 45 minutes from each of these times.
   (a) 14:50   (b) 17:30   (c) 12:00   (d) 08:30

9 Jack's friend Dorota is taking the train from Oxford to Southampton. She is due to leave Oxford at 15:30 and arrive in Southampton 1 hours 25 minutes later. That day she phones Jack to tell him that the train is delayed by 45 minutes. What time will Dorota arrive in Southampton?

14.4 Dealing with dates

You will often need to add days onto dates.

This traditional rhyme can help:

30 days hath September,
April, June and November.
All the rest have 31
except for February alone
which has just 28 days clear
and 29 in each leap year.

___ **Example 7** _____

Jane agreed to go out with John in 10 days' time.
Today is Tuesday 23rd April. When is their date?

	April					May				
Monday	1	8	15	22	29		6	13	20	27
Tuesday	2	9	16	23	30		7	14	21	28
Wednesday	3	10	17	24		1	8	15	22	29
Thursday	4	11	18	25		2	9	16	23	30
Friday	5	12	19	26		3	10	17	24	31
Saturday	6	13	20	27		4	11	18	25	
Sunday	7	14	21	28		5	12	19	26	

Start at 23rd April and count on 10 days.
You get to Friday 3rd May.

> Remember that April has only 30 days.

Exercise 14I

1 Count on 10 days from the following dates.
   (a) 1st January   (b) 2nd March   (c) 3rd June
   (d) 5th July   (e) 10th September (f) 20th May
   (g) 25th June   (h) 27th August

2 Count on 14 days from the following dates.
   (a) 2nd February   (b) 3rd March
   (c) 3rd April   (d) 7th December
   (e) 15th November   (f) 18th September
   (g) 23rd March   (h) 25th November

3   Count on 30 days from the following dates.

(a) 5th April   (b) 6th June   (c) 17th May
(d) 1st September   (e) 7th June   (f) 20th May
(g) 30th November   (h) 5th December

Use the calendar in Example 7 to answer the following questions.

4   What day of the week and date is 5 days after 5th April?

5   Which day and date is 5 days after 27th April?

6   Which day and date is 7 days before 20th May?

7   What is the day and date 10 days before 5th May?

8   Write down the day and date two weeks after 19th April.

14.5 Timetables

Bus and train timetables are often used to test your knowledge of time in GCSE exams.

On the timetable in Example 8 each train's times start at the top and then go down the page. The time it should leave a stopping place can then be read off opposite the place name.

Example 8

Find how long it takes for the 08 15 train from Swindon to get to London (Paddington).

07 10 train from Bristol arrives in London at 08 40

You first have to find the 08 15 train from Swindon. It is in the third column along. Follow that column down to the bottom to find the arrival time in London, 09 10.

Bristol	07 10	07 25	07 40	07 55
Bath	07 30	07 45	08 00	08 10
Swindon	07 45	08 00	08 15	08 25
Didcot	08 05	08 20	08 35	08 45
Reading	08 15	08 30	08 45	08 55
London (Paddington)	08 40	08 55	09 10	09 20

08 15 train from Swindon

Arrives in London at 09 10

You could subtract 08 15 from 09 10 by doing a subtraction and carrying a 60. Here is another way of dealing with the problem that you may find easier:

15 minutes   30 minutes   10 minutes

08 15 to 08 30 is   08 30 to 09 00 is   09 00 to 09 10 is
15 minutes   30 minutes   10 minutes

Total time is   15   +   30   +   10   = 55 minutes

Exercise 14J

Use these timetables to answer the following questions.

Bus timetable			
Coate	07 05	07 35	08 05
Piper's Way	07 10	07 40	08 10
Old Town	07 20	07 50	08 20
Drove Road	07 25	07 55	08 25
New Town	07 30	08 00	08 30
Bus Station	07 35	08 05	08 35

Train timetable				
Bristol	07 10	07 25	07 40	07 55
Bath	07 30	07 45	08 00	08 15
Swindon	07 45	08 00	08 15	08 30
Didcot	08 05	08 20	08 35	08 50
Reading	08 15	08 30	08 45	09 00
London (Paddington)	08 40	08 55	09 10	09 25

1 At what time should the 07 35 bus from Coate be at Drove Road?

2 At what time should the 07 40 train from Bristol be at Didcot?

3 At what time should the 08 30 train from Reading leave from Bristol?

4 At what time should the 08 00 bus from New Town be at Piper's Way?

5 Buses from Coate leave every half hour.
Continue the bus timetable for the next three buses. You can assume that each bus takes the same amount of time between stops as the previous ones.

6 Rashmi arrives at the train station in Bath at 07 35.
What time is the next train he could catch to London?

7 Claude arrives at the train station in Didcot at 08 25.
What time is the next train he could catch to London?

8 Trains from Bristol leave every quarter of an hour.

(a) Continue the train timetable for the next three trains. You can assume that each train takes the same amount of time between stations as the previous ones.

(b) Cecille arrives at the train station in Swindon at 09 10. What time is the next train she could catch to Reading?

(c) Sophia arrives at the train station in Bristol at 08 00. What time is the next train she could catch to Bath?

9 How long should it take to travel by bus from Coate to the Bus Station?

10 How long should it take to travel by bus from Piper's Way to New Town?

11 How long should it take to travel by train from Bristol to London (Paddington)?

12 How long should it take to travel by train from Swindon to Reading?

13 How long should it take to travel by train from Bath to Didcot?

14 The bus timetable is for a bus route in Swindon. It takes five minutes to walk from the bus station to the train platform. Use both timetables to work out which bus and train:

   (a) Gareth catches at Piper's Way to be in London (Paddington) at 09:00

   (b) Susan catches if she needs to be in Reading at 08:30 and she travels by bus from Coate

   (c) Mario catches if he travels by bus from Old Town and needs to be in Didcot at 08:40

   (d) Claudette catches at Drove Road to be in London (Paddington) by 10:00

   (e) Bridgette catches if she needs to be in Reading at 09:30 and she travels by bus from Old Town

   (f) Katrina caught if she travelled from Drove Road and arrived in Reading at 08:45.

Mixed exercise 14

1 Put these measurements in order, smallest first.
   (a) 12 cm, 15 mm, 5 m, 6.5 cm, 60 mm
   (b) 2.5 km, 3000 m, 1800 m, 3.6 km

2 Sarah and her boyfriend drove 50 miles to Bristol.
About how many kilometres is 50 miles?

3 Siân bought 5 kg of potatoes.
About how many pounds of potatoes was this?

4 Michelle filled her car's petrol tank with 50 *l* of petrol.
About how many gallons of petrol was this?

5 Dick travelled from Manchester to London.
He set off at 07:25. The journey took 3 hours 40 minutes.
At what time did he arrive in London?

6 Here is part of a railway timetable.

A train leaves Manchester at 10 35.

Manchester	07 53	09 17	10 35	11 17	13 30	14 36	16 26
Stockport	08 01	09 26	10 43	11 25	13 38	14 46	16 39
Macclesfield	08 23	09 38	10 58	11 38	13 52	14 58	17 03
Congleton	08 31	–	–	11 49	–	15 07	17 10
Kidsgrove	08 37	–	–	–	–	–	17 16
Stoke-on-Trent	08 49	10 00	11 23	12 03	14 12	15 19	17 33

(a) At what time should this train arrive in Stoke-on-Trent?

Doris has to go to a meeting in Stoke-on-Trent.
She will catch the train in Stockport.
She needs to arrive in Stoke-on-Trent before 2 pm for her meeting.

(b) Write down the time of the latest train she can catch in Stockport.

(c) Work out how many minutes it should take the 14 36 train from Manchester to get to Stoke-on-Trent.

The 14 36 train from Manchester to Stoke-on-Trent takes less time than the 16 26 train from Manchester to Stoke-on-Trent.

(d) How many minutes less?　　　　　　　　　　　[E]

7

This signpost is on the road from Paris to Dijon.

(a) Work out the distance, in kilometres, from Paris to Dijon along this road.

(b) Work out the approximate distance, in miles, from the signpost to Paris.　　　　　[E]

8 Here is a timetable for Amina's school bus.
Amina catches the bus at Grange Drive.

Bus stop	Time
Bus Station	08 00
Station Road	08 15
Grange Drive	08 20
Holley Ave	08 30
King's Road	08 40
School Road	08 45

(a) At what time should the bus be at Grange Drive?

(b) How long should the bus take to get from Grange Drive to School Road?　　　　　[E]

9 Chippy the carpenter marks a 3 metre length of wood into three pieces.

One piece is 1.40 metres long.
Another piece is 84 centimetres long.
How long is the third piece of wood?

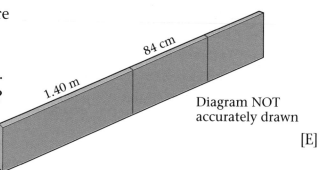

Diagram NOT accurately drawn

[E]

Summary of key points

1

Length	Weight	Capacity
10 mm = 1 cm 100 cm = 1 m 1000 mm = 1 m 1000 m = 1 km	1000 mg = 1 g 1000 g = 1 kg 1000 kg = 1 tonne	100 c*l* = 1 litre 1000 m*l* = 1 litre 1000 *l* = 1 cubic metre

2 When you change from small units to large units you divide.

3 When you change from large units to small units you multiply.

4

Metric	Imperial
8 km	5 miles
1 kg	2.2 pounds
25 g	1 ounce
1 *l*	$1\frac{3}{4}$ pints
4.5 *l*	1 gallon
1 m	39 inches
30 cm	1 foot
2.5 cm	1 inch

These conversions are only approximate.

5
60 seconds = 1 minute   60 minutes = 1 hour
24 hours   = 1 day   365 days   = 1 year
366 days   = 1 leap year   3 months   = 1 quarter
12 months   = 1 year

6 30 days hath September, April, June and November.
All the rest have 31 except for February alone
which has just 28 days clear and 29 in each leap year.

Answers

Chapter 1 Understanding whole numbers

Exercise 1A

1

	Ten thousands	Thousands	Hundreds	Tens	Units
(a)		4	x	x	x
(b)				3	x
(c)	x	x	1	x	x
(d)			x	x	9
(e)		x	x	0	x
(f)	x	x	4	x	x
(g)			7	7	7
(h)		6	x	x	6

2 Five numbers each:
$5x$, $xy4$, $x2yz$
3 (a) 60   (b) 600   (c) 60 000 (d) 6   (e) 6000

Exercise 1B

1 (a) Thirty-six (b) Ninety-five (c) Five hundred and
ninety-eight (d) Two hundred and forty-six
(e) Five thousand six hundred and twenty-three
(f) One thousand two hundred and fifty-one
2 (a) Seven hundred and nine (b) Eight hundred and ninety
(c) Six thousand and fifty-four (d) Nine thousand two
hundred and one (e) Twenty-six thousand and seven
(f) Forty thousand two hundred (g) Thirty-two thousand
(h) Seventy thousand and ninety
(i) Thirteen thousand four hundred and six
3 (a) 63   (b) 708   (c) 7000
(d) 18 600   (e) 75 000   (f) 809 000
(g) 4 000 000 (h) 1 001 000 (i) 9020
(j) 40 600
4 (a) Ten million, three hundred and forty-eight thousand,
two hundred and seventy-six
(b) Four hundred and sixty-two thousand, six hundred and
ninety
(c) Forty million, two hundred and eighty thousand, seven
hundred and eighty
(d) Ten million, five hundred and twenty-four thousand,
one hundred and forty-five
(e) Sixty million, four hundred and twenty-four thousand,
two hundred and thirteen
5 (a) 69   1010   2306
(b) 76 152   70 363   151 400
(c) 294 000   682 000   2 600 000   3 990 000
6 (a) 200   114   104   88   86   79
(b) 330 000   30 300   3033   3003   3000
(c) 6 102 000   6 000 006   990 000   660 000   600 006
7 7   23   56   93   234   469   614
8 Toyota MR2   £3650   Volvo V70   £12 375
Volkswagen Polo £5423 Landrover Discovery £15 560
Vauxhall Nova   £6755   Jaguar XK8   £19 650
Ford Focus   £7670   Mercedes 500SL   £21 200
9 (a) 2005 (b) 2001   (c) 2003   (d) 2005
10 (a) Belgium   Thirty thousand, five hundred and
thirteen km^2
Luxembourg Two thousand, five hundred and seventy-
six km^2
Spain   Five hundred and four thousand, seven
hundred and eighty-two km^2

Portugal   Ninety-two thousand and eighty-two km^2
France   Five hundred and forty-seven thousand
and twenty-six km^2
(b) France   Spain   Portugal   Belgium   Luxembourg

Exercise 1C

1 (a) 7   (b) 9   (c) 19   (d) 13   (e) 15
2 (a) 9   (b) 1   (c) 11   (d) 3   (e) 7
3 (a) 4   (b) 8   (c) 2   (d) 2   (e) 3
4 (a) 3   (b) 7   (c) 9   (d) 15   (e) 11
5 (a) increase of 5
(b) increase of 6
(c) decrease of 5
(d) decrease of 9
(e) decrease of 20

Exercise 1D

1 43   **2** 80   **3** 331   **4** 270   **5** 45
6 96   **7** 84   **8** 216   **9** 401   **10** 416

Exercise 1E

1 305   **2** 3166   **3** 1003   **4** 12
5 (a) 19   (b) 17   (c) 36
6 (a) 88   (b) 59   (c) 133
7 (a) £38 364   (b) £57 272   (c) £14 874

Exercise 1F

1 (a) (i) 50   (ii) 500   (iii) 5000
(b) (i) 430   (ii) 4300   (iii) 43 000
(c) (i) 3570   (ii) 35 700   (iii) 357 000
(d) (i) 850   (ii) 8500   (iii) 85 000
(e) (i) 30 000   (ii) 300 000   (iii) 3 000 000
2 (a) (i) 500   (ii) 50   (iii) 5
(b) (i) 7400   (ii) 740   (iii) 74
(c) (i) 86 500   (ii) 8650   (iii) 865
(d) (i) 400 000   (ii) 40 000   (iii) 4000
3 (a) 700   (b) 5200   (c) 3660   (d) 63 900
(e) 1880   (f) 144 000 (g) 107 500 (h) 2 190 000
4 (a) 30   (b) 40   (c) 300   (d) 30
(e) 2   (f) 200   (g) 200   (h) 500

Exercise 1G

1 (a) 680   (b) 455   (c) 159   (d) 1884
(e) 3661   (f) 884   (g) 730   (h) 264
2 (a) 408   (b) 975   (c) 1749   (d) 5024
(e) 24 581 (f) 14 144 (g) 7738   (h) 3300
3 1080   **4** 4494   **5** 456 m   **6** 2268
7 (a) 1500 m   (b) 2800 m   (c) 18 000 m   56 000 m
8 36   108   216
9 (a) 204 miles (b) 2040 miles (c) 10 608 miles

Exercise 1H

1 (a) 24   (b) 23   (c) 14   (d) 16
(e) 160   (f) 113   (g) 18   (h) 89
(i) 92   (j) 91   (k) 204   (l) 340
2 (a) 16   (b) 44   (c) 16   (d) 41
(e) 21   (f) 34   (g) 40   (h) 300

3 (a) 21   (b) 15   (c) 40   (d) 20   (e) 14
4 £480
5 (a) 10   (b) 30   (c) 36
6 (a) 7   (b) 13   (c) 36
7 (a) 12   (b) 41   (c) 80

Exercise 1I

1 2910   **2** 227   **3** 9792   **4** 6696
5 181   **6** 49572   **7** 135   **8** 27897
9 502   **10** 69865   **11** 736   **12** 431
13 10848   **14** 333   **15** 10656

Exercise 1J

1 33   **2** 368   **3** 2016   **4** 49
5 (a) 3   (b) 2   (c) 8   (d) 12
6 (a) 90   (b) 19
7 (a) 561   (b) 23   (c) 6   (d) 1683
8 (a) 576   (b) 458

Exercise 1K

1 (a) 60   (b) 60   (c) 190   (d) 190
   (e) 990   (f) 2410
2 (a) 300   (b) 700   (c) 2400   (d) 3100
   (e) 8800   (f) 29500
3 (a) 2000   (b) 36000   (c) 29000   (d) 322000
   (e) 717000   (f) 2247000
4 (a) 150   90   90   50   180
   (b) 36100   130000   50300   12600   496000
   (c) 560   580   400   270   620

5

Area	Population
132000	10600000
301000	57400000
34000	16300000
357000	83300000
70000	3900000

6 (a) 100 to nearest hundred
   (b) 300 to nearest hundred
   (c) 6300 to nearest 100 or 6000 to nearest 1000
   (d) 40200 to nearest 100, 40000 to nearest 1000 or 10000
   (e) £45000000 to nearest million or £45400000 to nearest 100000
   (f) 13300 to nearest 100 or 13000 to nearest 1000

Exercise 1L

1 (a) 10   (b) 50   (c) 4   (d) 200
   (e) 5000   (f) 500   (g) 3000   (h) 70
   (i) 6000   (j) 9000   (k) 80000   (l) 80000
2 200   **3** 2000
4 (a) $\dfrac{60 \times 60}{30} = 120$ (b) $\dfrac{200 \times 300}{150} = 400$
   (c) $\dfrac{10 \times 30 \times 100}{300} = 100$ (d) $\dfrac{2000}{10 \times 100} = 2$
   (e) $\dfrac{500}{10 \times 50} = 1$ (f) $\dfrac{100 \times 90}{20 \times 30} = 15$
5 (a) 378.35294 $\dfrac{200 \times 100}{50} = 400$
   (b) 22.155242 $\dfrac{10 \times 1000}{500} = 20$
   (c) 107.91304 $\dfrac{140 \times 50}{70} = 100$

   (d) 9.2592593 $\dfrac{1000}{10 \times 10} = 10$
   (e) 5.6772082 $\dfrac{5200}{130 \times 10} = 4$
   (f) 6.3631902 $\dfrac{900 \times 80}{40 \times 300} = 6$
6 (a) $50 \times 100 = 5000$
   (b) Bigger – numbers both rounded up
7 $1350 \div 50 = 27$
8 $900 \times 400 \div 1000 = 360$ Answer wrong
9 $16 \times 2 \times 195 \approx 30 \times 200 = 6000$
10 $120 \times 40 \times 50 = 240000$

Mixed exercise 1

1 (a) 46   (b) 420
2 9, 37, 56, 59, 75
3 £29
4 (a) 54000   (b) fifty thousand
5 (a) 250000   (b) 7 million or 7000000
6 14
7 656
8 8760
9 (a) 20   (b) 5   (c) 2
10 (a) 80   (b) 640   (c) 20
   (d) 4560   (e) 110   (f) 7000
11 (a) 1459   (b) 9541   (c) $9 + 5 = 14$ (d) 0
12 (a) 232   (b) 5800p   (c) £58   (d) £70

Chapter 2 Number facts

Exercise 2A

1 (a) 5, −10 (b) 0, −13 (c) 13, −15 (d) −2, −21
2 (a) 0, −1 (b) −2, −5 (c) 3, 7
   (d) −7, −12   (e) −15, −24   (f) −1, 2
3 (a) 7   (b) −3   (c) −1   (d) −5   (e) −6
   (f) 3   (g) 0   (h) −7   (i) −5   (j) 0
4 (a) −40   (b) −70   (c) 30   (d) −30   (e) −160
   (f) 270   (g) −30   (h) 0   (i) 120   (j) −400
5 (a) Minsk   (b) Minsk   (c) Tripoli
6 22°C   **7** 6°C

Exercise 2B

1 (a) −12°C, −7°C, −5°C, −1°C, 0°C, 2°C, 4°C, 7°C, 9°C
   (b) −9°C, −8°C, −3°C, −2°C, 0°C, 2°C, 5°C, 8°C, 10°C
   (c) −7°C, −6°C, −4°C, −3°C, −1°C, 3°C, 5°C, 7°C, 8°C
   (d) −8°C, −4°C, −3°C, −2°C, 1°C, 4°C, 6°C, 7°C, 9°C
   (e) −9°C, −7°C, −5°C, −3°C, −1°C, 0°C, 4°C, 5°C, 7°C, 8°C
2 (a) 5°C   (b) 3°C   (c) 6°C   (d) 10°C   (e) 10°C
   (f) 8°C   (g) 5°C   (h) 13°C
3 (a) −2°C   (b) −3°C   (c) −7°C   (d) 3°C   (e) 3°C
   (f) −6°C   (g) −9°C

Exercise 2C

1 (a) 0   (b) −4   (c) −14   (d) −4
2 (a) +1   (b) +17   (c) 2   (d) +10
3 (a) −5   (b) +5   (c) −2   (d) −6
4 (a) −11   (b) +3   (c) +17   (d) −5
5 (a) −14   (b) +3   (c) −5   (d) −9

Answers   A3

Exercise 2D

1–3

First number

−5	−4	−3	−2	−1	0	1	2	3	4	5	×
−25	−20	−15	−10	−5	0	5	10	15	20	25	5
−20	−16	−12	−8	−4	0	4	8	12	16	20	4
−15	−12	−9	−6	−3	0	3	6	9	12	15	3
−10	−8	−6	−4	−2	0	2	4	6	8	10	2
−5	−4	−3	−2	−1	0	1	2	3	4	5	1
0	0	0	0	0	0	0	0	0	0	0	0
5	4	3	2	1	0	−1	−2	−3	−4	−5	−1
10	8	6	4	2	0	−2	−4	−6	−8	−10	−2
15	12	9	6	3	0	−3	−6	−9	−12	−15	−3
20	16	12	8	4	0	−4	−8	−12	−16	−20	−4
25	20	15	10	5	0	−5	−10	−15	−20	−25	−5

Second number

4 (a) +10   (b) −12   (c) −8   (d) +15   (e) +3
  (f) −6   (g) −20   (h) +4

Exercise 2E

1   First number

×	+5	+3	−6	−2
+2	+10	+6	−12	−4
+8	+40	+24	−48	−16
−3	−15	−9	+18	+6
−4	−20	−12	+24	+8

Second number

2   First number

÷	+6	−12	−18	+24
+3	+2	−4	−6	+8
−2	−3	+6	+9	−12
−6	−1	+2	+3	−4
+1	+6	−12	−18	+24

Second number

Exercise 2F

1 (a) −3   (b) −3   (c) +4   (d) +12   (e) −4
  (f) −12
2 (a) −90   (b) +4   (c) +5   (d) −14   (e) −2
  (f) +12
3 (a) −20   (b) +2   (c) −20   (d) +6   (e) +9
  (f) −42
4 (a) +24   (b) −15   (c −4   (d) +27   (e) −40
  (f) +3
5 (a) +10   (b) −56   (c) +36   (d) +21   (e) −3
  (f) −42

Exercise 2G

1 2   18   1110   73 536   500 000
2 537   811   36 225
3 17   19   23   29   31   37   41
4 (a) 450   (b) 71   (c) 71
5 (a) 3   (b) 2, 3, 4, 6, 8 or 12
  (c) 2, 4, 8 or 16   (d) 5 or 11
  (e) 2, 3, 4, 6, 9, 12, 18, 27, 36 or 54
  (f) 5, 25 or 125
6 1, 2, 3, 4, 6, 12
7 (a) 1, 2, 4, 8, 16, 32
  (b) 1, 2, 4, 5, 8, 10, 20, 25, 40, 50, 100, 200
  (c) 1, 2, 1, 5, 10, 17, 20, 34, 68, 85, 170, 340
  (d) 1, 2, 4, 5, 8, 10, 20, 25, 40, 50, 100, 125, 200, 250, 500, 1000

8 (a) 1 and 2   (b) 1 and 3   (c) 1 and 5
  (d) 1 and 2   (e) 1 and 7
9 (a) 1, 2, 5 and 10   (b) 1, 2, 5 and 10   (c) 1, 2 and 4
  (d) 1, 2, 3 and 6   (e) 1, 3 and 9
10 (a) 1, 2, 5 or 10   (b) 1, 2 or 4   (c) 1, 5, 7 or 35
  (d) 1, 2, 3 or 6   (e) 1, 2, 3 or 6
11 9, 18, 27 . . .   **12** 99
13 (a) 54, 60, 66, etc   (b) 1020, 1040, 1060, etc
  (c) 105, 120, 135, etc
14 (a) 16, 24, 32, etc   (b) 150, 300, 450, etc.
  (c) 3, 5, 15, 27, etc
15 10   20   ~~30~~   40   50
  ~~60~~   70   80   ~~90~~   100
  110   ~~120~~   130   140   ~~150~~
  160   170   ~~180~~   190   200
  ~~210~~   220   230   ~~240~~   250
  (f) 180

Exercise 2H

1 (a) 64   (b) 343   (c) 144   (d) 1000
  (e) 1, 4, 9, 16, 25, 36, 49, 64, 81, 100, 121, 144
  (f) 1, 8, 27, 64, 125, 216, 343, 512
2 (a) (i) 1, 9, 49, 64   (ii) 1, 8, 64
  (b) (i) 4, 16   (ii) 27, 125
  (c) (i) 64, 81, 144   (ii) 64, 125
  (d) (i) 81, 100, 169   (ii) 125, 216

Exercise 2I

1 (a) 169   (b) 12.25   (c) 1600   (d) 75.69
  (e) 384.16 (f) 3294.76
2 (a) 216   (b) 13.824   (c) 8000   (d) −2.197
  (e) −2406.104   (f) 47 437.928
3 (a) 11   (b) 15   (c) 130   (d) 1.7
  (e) 0.7   (f) 5.8
4 (a) 15.91   (b) 4.29   (c) 5.43
5 (a) 4.08   (b) 2.98   (c) 9.59

Exercise 2J

1 2.65   **2** 2.47   **3** 2.29   **4** 3.16
5 4.47   **6** 5.66   **7** 3.11   **8** 3.48
9 3.61   **10** 3.68   **11** 5.29   **12** 3.21

Exercise 2K

1 (a) $45 = 3 \times 3 \times 5 = 3^2 \times 5$
  (b) $36 = 2 \times 2 \times 3 \times 3 = 2^2 \times 3^2$
  (c) $29 = 29$
  (d) $100 = 2 \times 2 \times 5 \times 5 = 2^2 \times 5^2$
2 (a) $24 = 2 \times 2 \times 2 \times 3 = 2^3 \times 3$
  (b) $32 = 2 \times 2 \times 2 \times 2 \times 2 = 2^5$
  (c) $18 = 2 \times 3 \times 3 = 2 \times 3^2$
  (d) $13 = 13$

Exercise 2L

1 (a) 4   (b) 3   (c) 6   (d) 6   (e) 7
2 (a) 12   (b) 12   (c) 14   (d) 30
3 (a) 60   (b) 144   (c) 850
4 (a) 6, 36   (b) 60, 360   (c) 12, 168   (d) 13, 910
  (e) 24, 288   (f) 20, 120

Mixed exercise 2

1 $-10, -6, -4, 2, 5$
2 (a) 6, 12   (b) 4, 16   (c) 3, 4, 6, 12   (d) 8, 27
3 (a) Edinburgh and Plymouth
   (b) Belfast and Cardiff, London and Plymouth
4 (a) (i) $7°C$ (ii) $-10°C$
   (b) (i) $6°C$ (ii) $8°C$
   (c) $-7°C$
5 (a) $2^2 \times 3^3$ (b) 12
6 (a) (i) $2 \times 2 \times 3 \times 5$ (ii) $2 \times 2 \times 2 \times 2 \times 2 \times 3$
   (b) 12
   (c) 480
7 (a) 5, 9, 27, 35, 37   (b) 9, 12, 27, 36   (c) 4, 8, 12, 16,
   (d) 5, 37   (e) 4, 9, 16, 36   (f) 8, 27
8 (a) 2   (b) -2 (c) 0
   (d) 1   (e) -5 (f) -2
   (g) -10 (h) 0   (i) -1
   (j) 7   (k) 3   (l) 7
   (m) -9 (n) 2   (o) -13
   (p) -4
9 (a) -8 (b) 6   (c) -30
   (d) 12   (e) -4 (f) 6
   (g) -4 (h) 5   (i) -3
   (j) 3   (k) -8 (l) 7

Chapter 3 Essential algebra

Exercise 3A

1 $a + 3$ **2** $x + 4$ **3** $x + 7$ **4** $b - 2$ **5** $c - 3$
6 $q - p$ **7** $x + y$ **8** $a + 4$ **9** $3b - 6$ **10** $d + 3$
11 $a - 2$ **12** $£x - £5$

Exercise 3B

1 $6a$ **2** $4p$ **3** $5b$ **4** $6q$
5 $2c$ **6** $3n$ **7** $5w$ **8** $5y$
9 $7z$ **10** $7a$ **11** $5b$ **12** $8p$
13 $a + a + a + a$ **14** $p + p$ **15** $p + p + p + p + p$
16 $a + a + a + a + a + a$ **17** $y + y$ **18** $q + q + q + q$
19 $c + c + c$ **20** $d + d + d + d + d$
21 $a + a + a + a + a + a + a + a + a + a$
22 $h + h + h + h + h$ **23** $g + g + g + g + g + g$
24 $z + z + z + z$

Exercise 3C

1 $6a$ **2** $7b$ **3** $7c$ **4** $2d$ **5** $4e$
6 $4f$ **7** $7a$ **8** $8a$ **9** $12c$ **10** $14g$
11 $4g$ **12** $3s$ **13** $14q$ **14** $18p$ **15** $6p$

Exercise 3D

1 $7a + 6b$ **2** $9m + 7n$ **3** $p + 5q$ **4** $6c + 16e$
5 $12p + 2y$ **6** $4a + 13g$ **7** $9k + q$ **8** $d + 10f$
9 $3h + 10$ **10** $2e + 5f$ **11** $4g + 7n$ **12** $4 + 2g$
13 $14a$ **14** $5b$ **15** $4c$ **16** $5d$
17 $7a + b$ **18** $8b + 6c$ **19** $p + 1$ **20** $14y + 4z$
21 $17a$ **22** 0 **23** $7s$ **24** a

Exercise 3E

1 $p \times q$ **2** $r \times s \times t$ **3** $2 \times e \times f$
4 $5 \times a \times b \times c$ **5** $7 \times k \times l \times m$ **6** $9 \times a \times b$
7 $15 \times a \times b \times c$ **8** $3 \times p \times q \times r \times s$ **9** $16 \times s \times t$
10 $6 \times y \times z$ **11** $8 \times d \times e \times f \times g$
12 $20 \times a \times b \times c \times d$ **13** pq **14** efg **15** rst
16 $2ef$ **17** $2cd$ **18** hds **19** $2sf$ **20** $3def$
21 $4pq$ **22** $3hj$ **23** $5kv$ **24** $12rst$

Exercise 3F

1 $8ab$ **2** $15cd$ **3** $12pq$ **4** $20st$ **5** $30fg$
6 $28pq$ **7** $36mn$ **8** $24abc$ **9** $24rst$ **10** $20pq$
11 $12ab$ **12** $40pqr$ **13** $12st$ **14** $28pt$ **15** $45ce$
16 $64gqr$ **17** $48dr$ **18** $60st$ **19** $30ty$ **20** $40rst$

Exercise 3G

1 $4p$ **2** p **3** 5   **4** $4n$ **5** $2e$
6 15   **7** $4b$ **8** $7a$ **9** $6s$ **10** $6y$
11 30   **12** $4ab$ **13** $3c$ **14** $15x$ **15** $6pq$

Exercise 3H

1 (a) 9   (b) 8   (c) 1   (d) 625
   (e) 32   (f) 64   (g) 16   (h) 128
   (i) 216   (j) 125   (k) 25   (l) 100 000
2 (a) 729   (b) 3125   (c) 0   (d) 6561
3 (a) 16   (b) 1000   (c) 59 049   (d) 73
4 (a) 1728   (b) 81   (c) 196   (d) 512
5 (a) 3   (b) 3   (c) 5
6 (a) 4   (b) 3   (c) 4
7 (a) 2   (b) 6   (c) 3
8 (a) 10   (b) 3   (c) 2

Exercise 3I

1 (a) 6^{11} (b) 8^8 (c) 2^6
2 (a) 4   (b) 6^3 (c) 7^4
3 (a) 4^5 (b) 5^2 (c) 3
4 (a) 5^{13} (b) 2^{11}
5 (a) 10^5 (b) 9^0
6 (a) 6^{11} (b) 5^6
7 (a) 3^8 (b) 4^6
8 (a) 6^3 (b) 5^5 (c) 4^2
9 (a) 5^6 (b) 7^8

Exercise 3J

1 (a) b^3 (b) p^2 (c) r^7 (d) s^5 (e) q^4 (f) c^5
2 (a) a^4 (b) s^3 (c) t^6 (d) v^3 (e) f^5 (f) y^5
3 (a) $a \times a \times a$ (b) $a \times a \times a \times a$ (c) $d \times d$
   (d) $e \times e \times e \times e \times e$ (e) $f \times f \times f \times f$
   (f) $p \times p \times p \times p \times p$ (g) $a \times a \times a \times a \times a \times a \times a$
   (h) $s \times s$ (i) $k \times k \times k \times k \times k \times k$ (j) $n \times n \times n$
   (k) $n \times n \times n \times n \times n \times n \times n$
   (l) $a \times a \times a \times a \times a \times a \times a \times a \times a \times a \times a \times a$
4 (a) a^5 (b) b^6 (c) c^2 (d) d^3 (e) e^7

Exercise 3K

1 (a) x^{10} (b) y^{11} (c) w^{14}
2 (a) a^8 (b) b^6 (c) d^{11}
3 (a) p^3 (b) q^{10} (c) t^4
4 (a) j^6 (b) k (c) n^2
5 (a) x^9 (b) y^9 (c) z^{10}
6 (a) $6x^5$ (b) $15y^{29}$ (c) $24z^{10}$
7 (a) $3p^5$ (b) $5q^2$ (c) $2r^3$

Exercise 3L

1 (a) d^{12} (b) e^{10} (c) f^9 (d) g^{63}
2 (a) g^{24} (b) h^4 (c) 1   (d) 1
3 (a) $2187d^{14}$ (b) $64e^3$ (c) 1
4 (a) 1   (b) b^4 (c) 1
5 (a) $8d^{10}$ (b) $2e^4$ (c) $16f^4$

Exercise 3M

1 (a) 9   (b) 1   (c) 25   (d) 13   (e) 21
  (f) 15   (g) 6   (h) 4   (i) 8   (j) 5
  (k) 6   (l) 2   (m) 1   (n) 5   (o) 4
2 (a) $4 + 5 = 9$ (b) $4 \times 5 = 20$
  (c) $(2 + 3) \times 4 = 20$ (d) $(3 - 2) \times 5 = 5$
  (e) $(5 - 2) \times 3 = 9$ (f) $4 - 2 + 8 = 10$
  (g) $5 \times 4 + 5 + 2 = 27$ (h) $5 \times 4 + 5 - 2 = 23$
3 (a) 49   (b) 25   (c) 243   (d) 123   (e) 72
  (f) 17   (g) 22   (h) 7   (i) 7   (j) 0
  (k) 7   (l) 0

Exercise 3N

1 $2p + 2q$ 2 $3c + 3d$ 3 $5y - 5n$
4 $3t + 3u$ 5 $14p + 7q$ 6 $6a - 4b$
7 $8a + 4b$ 8 $3a - 6b$ 9 $12r - 15s$
10 $10a - 70b$ 11 $24s + 16t$ 12 $30p + 20q - 10r$
13 $36a + 48b$ 14 $28s - 35t$ 15 $15a - 12b + 6c$

Exercise 3O

1 $5a + 5b$ 2 $11a + 6b$ 3 $18a - b$
4 $7p + 7q$ 5 $26a + 2c$ 6 $18p$
7 $s + 44t$ 8 $2d + 33e$ 9 $9b + 7z$
10 $8a + 11b + c$ 11 $17a - b$ 12 $12p + 4q$
13 $22a$ 14 $5g + 24h$ 15 $21a + 5b + 10c$

Exercise 3P

1 (a) 5   (b) 17   (c) 10   (d) 3
  (e) 4   (f) 4   (g) 0   (h) 14
2 (a) $-p - q$ (b) $-p + q$
  (c) $-a - b - c$ (d) $-a - b + c$
  (e) $-r - s$ (f) $-r + s$
  (g) $-p - q + r$ (h) $-p + q - r$

Exercise 3Q

1 $3a + 2b$ 2 $4p + q$ 3 $3a + 7$ 4 $y - 4z$
5 $7r + 10s$ 6 7   7 $6s + 7t$ 8 $6a - 11b$
9 $5n$ 10 $12h - 23k$ 11 c 12 $a - 5b$

Exercise 3R

1 $3a + 4b$ 2 $4p + 3q$ 3 $3a + 17$ 4 $y - 2z$
5 $7r + 14s$ 6 23   7 $6s + 23t$ 8 $6a + 19b$
9 $7n$ 10 $12h - 7k$ 11 $c + 12d$ 12 $a + 5b$

Exercise 3S

1 (a) $ax + 2x$ (b) $3y - xy$ (c) $abx + 2acx$
  (d) $2a^3 + a$ (e) $a^2b + ab^2$ (f) $a^2x + a^2y$
  (g) $6p^2 - 8pq$ (h) $6a^2 + 9ab$
  (i) $3abc - a^2bc - ab^2c^2$ (j) $pq + pqr$
2 (a) $ab + 2ac + bc$ (b) $b + b^2$ (c) $x - 3x^2$
  (d) $5r^2s - r^3 - 2rs^2$ (e) $2p + 6q - pq$ (f) $px - xy$

Exercise 3T

1 (a) $x(x + 3)$ (b) $a(a - b)$ (c) $p(p + q)$
  (d) $3(a + 4b)$ (e) $5(a + 2)$ (f) $2(b - 2c)$
  (g) $4(1 + 2a)$ (h) $2(a - 1)$ (i) $3(a + 3)$
  (j) $5(p + 5)$ (k) $4(a + 4)$ (l) $4(p - 2)$
  (m) $7(x - 2)$ (n) $7(y + 1)$ (o) $y(7y + 1)$
  (p) $5(q - 3)$ (q) $x(x + 2)$ (r) $y(y + 3)$
  (s) $3(a - 1)$ (t) $a(2a^3 + 3)$ (u) $x(3y - 4z)$
  (v) $a(4a - 5)$ (w) $a(5a^4 - 4)$ (x) $x(5x + 4)$

2 (a) $2(x + 3)$ (b) $2(3y + 1)$ (c) $5(3b - 1)$
  (d) $2(2r - 1)$ (e) $x(3 + 5y)$ (f) $4(3x + 2y)$
  (g) $4(3x - 4)$ (h) $3(3 - x)$ (i) $3(3 + 5g)$
3 (a) $x(3x + 4)$ (b) $y(5y - 3)$ (c) $a(2a + 1)$
  (d) $b(5b - 2)$ (e) $c(7 - 3c)$ (f) $d(d + 3)$
  (g) $m(6m - 1)$ (h) $x(4y + 3)$ (i) $n^2(n - 8)$
4 (a) $4x(2x + 1)$ (b) $3p(2p + 1)$ (c) $3x(2x - 1)$
  (d) $3b(b - 3)$ (e) $3a(4 + a)$ (f) $5c(3 - 2c)$
  (g) $7x^3(3x + 2)$ (h) $4y^2(4y - 3)$ (i) $2d^2(3d^2 - 2)$
5 (a) $ax(x + 1)$ (b) $pr(r - 1)$ (c) $ab(b - 1)$
  (d) $q(r^2 - q)$ (e) $ax(a + x)$ (f) $by(b - y)$
  (g) $3a^2(2a - 3)$ (h) $4x^3(2 - x)$ (i) $6x^3(3 + 2x^2)$
6 (a) $6ab(2a + 3b)$ (b) $2xy(2x - y)$ (c) $4ab(a + 2b + 3)$
  (d) $2xy(2x + 3y - 1)$ (e) $3ax(4x + 2a - 1)$ (f) $abc(a + b + c)$
7 (a) $5(x + 4)$ (b) $2(6y - 5)$ (c) $x(3x + 5)$
  (d) $y(4 - 3y)$ (e) $2a(4 + 3a)$ (f) $4b(3b - 2)$
  (g) $cy(y + 1)$ (h) $3dx(x - 2)$ (i) $3cd(3c + 5d)$

Mixed exercise 3

1 (a) (i) $4c$ (ii) p^4 (iii) $8g$ (iv) $10pr$
  (b) $10y - 15$ (c) $5(3a + 2)$
2 (a) $2n$ (b) $2n + 15$ (c) $20q$
3 (a) $6x$ (b) $x - 4$ (c) $12(x - 4)$ (d) $18x - 48$
4 (a) $2y$ (b) $3p^2$ (c) $x(x - 3)$ (d) $10q + 35$
5 (a) $5(x + 2)$ (b) $3(y - 3)$ (c) $a(4 + 9b)$
  (d) $y(10x - 11)$ (e) $2x(y + 2)$ (f) $3a(2 - 3b)$
  (g) $4x(x - 2)$ (h) $2xy(6y + 2x - 1)$
6 (a) x^8 (b) $20y^8$ (c) $4p^3$
7 (a) $5^2 = 25$ (b) 4   (c) 81
8 6

Chapter 4 Patterns and sequences

Exercise 4A

1 12, 15; $+3$ 2 25, 30; $+5$ 3 5, 6; $+1$ 4 35, 42; $+7$
5 18, 24; $+6$ 6 40, 50; $+10$ 7 13, 15; $+2$ 8 16, 19; $+3$
9 23, 28; $+5$ 10 17, 21; $+4$

Exercise 4B

1 9, 6; -3 2 12, 8; -4 3 15, 10; -5 4 21, 14; -7
5 13, 10; -3 6 17, 12; -5 7 13, 11; -2 8 13, 9; -4
9 18, 13; -5 10 17, 10; -7

Exercise 4C

1 27, 81; $\times 3$ 2 64; $\times 4$ 3 5, 625; $\times 5$
4 1000, 10000; $\times 10$ 5 24, 48; $\times 2$ 6 54, 162; $\times 3$
7 128, 512; $\times 4$ 8 2000, 20000; $\times 10$ 9 250; $\times 5$
10 375; $\times 5$

Exercise 4D

1 16, 2; $\div 2$ 2 16; $\div 4$ 3 1000, 100; $\div 10$
4 25; $\div 5$ 5 12, 6; $\div 2$ 6 18, 6; $\div 3$
7 32, 8; $\div 4$ 8 200, 20; $\div 10$ 9 10; $\div 5$
10 15; $\div 5$

Exercise 4E

1 add 2, 11   2 add 4, 21   3 cube numbers, 216
4 add 2, 12   5 add 3, 17   6 add 4, 23
7 add two previous numbers, 26
8 add two previous numbers, 39   9 add 2, 15
10 add 3, 19   11 add 5, 27   12 add 5, 28

Exercise 4F

1 (a)

13 matches   16 matches

(b)

Term number	1	2	3	4	5
Matches used	4	7	10	13	16

(c) (term number) $\times 3 + 1 = (6 \times 3) + 1$ (d) $3n + 1$

2 (i) (a)
XXXXX   XXXXXX
XXXXX   XXXXXX

(b) add 2 crosses
(c) $2n$
(d) 20 crosses

(ii) (a)
XXXXXX   XXXXXXX
XXXXXX   XXXXXXX

(b) add 3 crosses
(c) $3n$
(d) 30 crosses

(iii) (a)

(b) add another set of 6 matches
(c) $6n$ (d) 60 matches

(iv) (a)

(b) add 2 matches
(c) $2n + 1$ (d) 21 matches

(v) (a)
XXXXX   XXXXX
XXXXX   XXXXX

(b) add 2 crosses
(c) $2n - 1$ (d) 19 crosses

(vi) (a)
XXXXX   XXXXX
XXXXX   XXXXXX

(b) add 2 crosses
(c) $2n + 1$ (d) 21 crosses

3 $5n + 1$

4 (a) $3n$, 60   (b) $5n$, 100   (c) n, 20
(d) $7n$, 140   (e) $6(n - 1)$, 114   (f) $10n$, 200
(g) $2n + 3$, 43   (h) $3n + 1$, 61   (i) $5n - 2$, 98
(j) $4n - 3$, 77   (k) $2n - 1$, 39   (l) $2n + 1$, 41
(m) $3n - 1$, 59   (n) $3n + 2$, 62   (o) $4n - 3$, 77
(p) $4n - 2$, 78   (q) $5n - 3$, 97   (r) $5n - 1$, 99
(s) $45 - 5n$, −55   (t) $40 - 2n$, 0

Exercise 4G

For example:
1 All odd numbers from 1, so 21 is in but not 34.
2 All odd numbers from 3, so 63 is in but not 62.
3 General term is $3n - 1$, so 50 is the 17th term but 60 is not in the pattern.
4 General term is $3n + 2$, so 101 is the 33rd term and 98 is the 32nd term.
5 General term is $4n - 3$, so 101 is the 26th term but 150 is not in the pattern.
6 General term is $4n - 2$, so 101 is not the pattern but 98 is the 25th term.
7 General term is $5n - 3$, so 97 is the 20th term but 120 is not in the pattern.
8 The pattern contains all whole numbers ending in 4 and 9, so 168 is not in the pattern, but 169 is.
9 The pattern contains all mutliples of 5 that are 40 or less, so 85 and 4 are not in the pattern.
10 The pattern contains all even numbers less than 40 so 71 and 82 are not in the pattern.

Exercise 4H

1 1 EXE Ans + 2 EXE EXE EXE …
2 5 EXE Ans + 5 EXE EXE EXE …
3 2 EXE Ans × 2 EXE EXE EXE …
4 3 EXE Ans × 3 EXE EXE EXE …
5 1 0 EXE Ans − 1 EXE EXE EXE …
6 1 6 EXE Ans ÷ 2 EXE EXE EXE …
7 2 0 0 EXE Ans ÷ 1 0 EXE EXE EXE …
8 (−) 5 EXE Ans − 2 EXE EXE EXE …

Exercise 4I

5 They are consecutive multiples of 4.
6 They are consecutive square numbers starting with 4.

Mixed exercise 4

1 (a) row 4, $\dfrac{4 \times 5}{2}$; row 8, $1 + 2 + 3 + 4 + 5 + 6 + 7 + 8$, $\dfrac{8 \times 9}{2}$
(b) $\dfrac{100 \times 101}{2} = 5050$

2 (a) 28, 33   (b) add 5
(c) 387 is not in the sequence because all members of the sequence end in 3 or 8

3 (a) pattern has 7 dots in vertical and 6 dots in horizontal
(b) 22, 26   (c) 46

4 (a)
XXXXX
XXXXX
XXXXX

(b) $5 \to 17$, $6 \to 20$ (c) 8
(d) 32   (e) $C = 3n + 2$

Chapter 5 Decimals

Exercise 5A

1

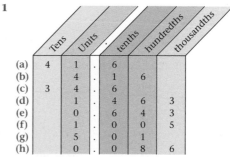

	Tens	Units	.	tenths	hundredths	thousandths
(a)	4	1	.	6		
(b)		4	.	1	6	
(c)	3	4	.	6		
(d)		1	.	4	6	3
(e)		0	.	6	4	3
(f)		1	.	0	0	5
(g)		5	.	0	1	
(h)		0	.	0	8	6

2 (a) Unit   (b) Tenth   (c) Tenth
(d) Hundredth   (e) Ten   (f) Thousandth
(g) Hundredth   (h) Ten thousandth   (i) Hundredth
(j) Tenth   (k) Thousandth   (l) Hundredth

Exercise 5B

1 (a) 0.9, 0.76, 0.71, 0.68, 0.62
(b) 3.75, 3.4, 3.12, 2.13, 2.09
(c) 0.42, 0.407, 0.3, 0.09, 0.065
(d) 6.52, 6.08, 3.7, 3.58, 3.0
(e) 0.13, 0.105, 0.06, 0.024, 0.009
(f) 2.2, 2.09, 1.3, 1.16, 1.08

2 (a) 4.09, 4.85, 5.16, 5.23, 5.9
  (b) 0.021, 0.09, 0.34, 0.37, 0.4
  (c) 5, 5.009, 5.01, 7.07, 7.23
  (d) 0.07, 0.23, 1.001, 1.08, 1.14
3 £1.09, £1.13, £1.18, £1.20, £1.29, £1.31
4 Latif, Sheila, Ira, Jean, Naomi, Rachel.
5 52.037, 53.027, 53.072, 53.207, 53.702, 57.320
6 0.0014 g, 0.0015 g, 0.002 g, 0.014 g, 0.02 g, 1.5 g

Exercise 5C

1	(a) 8	(b) 13	(c) 14	(d) 6
	(e) 11	(f) 20	(g) 1	(h) 20
	(i) 1	(j) 100	(k) 20	(l) 2
2	(a) 3.6	(b) 5.3	(c) 0.1	(d) 9.3
	(e) 10.7	(f) 8.0	(g) 2.1	(h) 0.5
	(i) 2.5	(j) 125.7	(k) 0.1	(l) 9.9
3	(a) 14 mm	(b) 80 m	(c) 1 kg	(d) £204
	(e) 4 lb	(f) 2 tonnes	(g) 11 g	(h) 8 min

Exercise 5D

1 (a) (i) 4.226 (ii) 4.23 (b) (i) 9.787 (ii) 9.79
  (c) (i) 0.416 (ii) 0.42 (d) (i) 0.058 (ii) 0.06
2 (a) (i) 10.517 (ii) 10.52 (b) (i) 7.503 (ii) 7.50
  (c) (i) 21.730 (ii) 21.73 (d) (i) 9.089 (ii) 9.09
3 (a) (i) 15.598 (ii) 15.60 (b) (i) 0.408 (ii) 0.41
  (c) (i) 7.247 (ii) 7.25 (d) (i) 6.051 (ii) 6.05
4 (a) (i) 29.158 (ii) 29.16 (b) (i) 0.055 (ii) 0.05
  (c) (i) 13.379 (ii) 13.38 (b) (i) 5.998 (ii) 6.00
5 (a) 5.617 (b) 0.0 (c) 0.9240 (d) 0.86 (e) 9.7

Exercise 5E

1 (a) (i) 0.06 (ii) 0.0618 (b) (i) 0.2 (ii) 0.165
  (c) (i) 100 (ii) 96.3 (d) (i) 40 (ii) 41.5
2 (a) (i) 700 (ii) 735 (b) (i) 0.08 (ii) 0.0795
  (c) (i) 6 (ii) 5.69 (d) (i) 600 (ii) 586
3 (a) (i) 0.01 (ii) 0.0145 (b) (i) 2000 (ii) 2220
  (c) (i) 80 (ii) 76.2 (d) (i) 0.4 (ii) 0.380
4 (a) (i) 8 (ii) 8.38 (b) (i) 40 (ii) 36.0
  (c) (i) 200 (ii) 187 (d) (i) 0.07 (ii) 0.0666
5 (a) (i) 90 (ii) 94.7 (b) (i) 900 (ii) 851
  (c) (i) 6 (ii) 6.25 (d) (i) 0.06 (ii) 0.0626
6 (a) 0.098 (b) 54.88 (c) 8 (d) 3100
  (e) 6000 (f) 53.0

Exercise 5F

1 6.1	2 3.25	3 68.9	4 126.02
5 1.0	6 18.725	7 19.8	8 11.001
9 1.914	10 118.17	11 31.97	12 28.71
13 19.122	14 18.326	15 11.064	16 31.006
17 15.0976	18 178.585		

Exercise 5G

1	(a) 6.20	(b) 4.14	(c) 14.10	(d) 97.30
	(e) 0.11	(f) 0.35	(g) 6.19	(h) 11.14
	(i) 0.90	(j) 4.07	(k) 14.03	(l) 13.25
2	(a) 1.225	(b) 11.649	(c) 2.254	(d) 168.58

Exercise 5H

1	(a) £13.50	(b) £5.48	(c) £5.20	(d) £1.20
2	(a) 30.4	(b) 3.04	(c) 0.304	
	(d) 11.25	(e) 1.125	(f) 0.1125	
	(g) 1.125	(h) 0.011 25	(i) 0.001 125	
3	(a) 172.2 kg	(b) 0.0945 s	(c) 0.0144 m	
	(d) 0.04 miles	(e) 0.9 l	(f) 0.0012 hours	
4	(a) 64.2	(b) 642	(c) 6.42	
	(d) 562.3	(e) 56.23	(f) 0.5623	

Figures have moved one column left.

5 (a) 4.5 (b) 45.0 (c) 450
  (d) 2.03 (e) 20.3 (f) 203
Figures have moved two columns left.
6 (a) £116.25 (b) £167.40 (c) £255.75
7 (a) £117.75 (b) £196.25 (c) £337.55
8 (a) 68.25 l (b) 113.75 l (c) 295.75 l

Exercise 5I

1 (a) 16.12 (b) 0.633 (c) 14.84
  (d) 34.221 (e) 5.027 (f) 0.046
2 (a) 3.45 (b) 0.345 (c) 0.0345
  (d) 7.8 (e) 0.78 (f) 0.078
  (g) 6.5 (h) 0.65 (i) 0.065
Figures have moved right by number of noughts in the division.
3 (a) 2.5 (b) 1.2 (c) 0.875
  (d) 0.24 (e) 0.52 (f) 0.155
  (g) 1.2 (h) 0.1625
4 £15.40 5 15 jugs

Exercise 5J

1 3.1	2 3.6	3 1.7	4 1.5	5 4.3
6 2.7	7 10.7	8 1.01	9 2.5	
10 (a) 0.6	(b) 0.75	(c) 0.25	(d) 0.2	
(e) 0.2	(f) 0.2	(g) 3.125	(h) 0.4	

11 £420.83
12 25 cm or 0.25 m
13 5

Mixed exercise 5

1 (a) 346 000 (b) 3480 (c) 3.58 (d) 0.004 50
2 (a) 3.48 (b) 0.06 (c) 23.88 (d) 456.75
3 (a) 42.16 (b) 59.95 (c) 4.32 (d) 4.83
  (e) 1.45 (f) 19.44 (g) 3.648 (h) 14.375
  (i) 2.5 (j) 0.36 (k) 61.5 (l) 0.25
4 9.253, 3.510, 0.727, 0.660, 0.606
5 (a) 110 miles (b) £21 (c) £13
6 £1.60, £2.05

Chapter 6 Angles and turning

Exercise 6A

1 (a), (b), (c) and (f)
2 (a) South (b) North (c) West
  (d) West $\frac{1}{2}$ turn clockwise = $\frac{1}{2}$ turn anticlockwise
3 (a) North-West (b) North-East (c) South-East
4 (a) $\frac{1}{4}$ turn (b) $\frac{1}{2}$ turn (c) $\frac{1}{4}$ turn

Exercise 6B

1 a is acute
2 b is a right angle
3 c is obtuse
4 d is a right angle, e is acute
5 f is obtuse, g is acute, h is obtuse, i is acute
6 j is obtuse, k is acute
7 l is reflex, m is a right angle, n is reflex
8 o is reflex
9 40° 10 135°
11 50° 12 135°
13 75° 14 90°
15 270°, 270° 16 220°

Exercise 6C

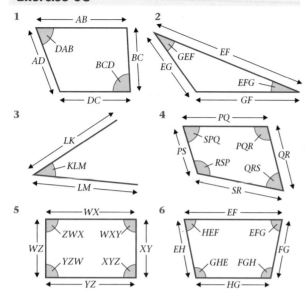

Exercise 6D

1 angle $ABC = 50°$
2 angle $EFG = 135°$
3 angle $ABC = 61°$, angle $ABD = 119°$
4 angle $EFG = 119°$, angle $GFH = 61°$
5 angle $SPQ = 142°$, angle $PQR = 65°$, angle $QRS = 98°$, angle $RSP = 55°$
6 angle $ZXY = 62°$, angle $XYZ = 80°$, angle $YZX = 38°$
7 angle $ABC = 50°$, angle $BCA = 83°$, angle $CAB = 47°$
8 angle $RST = 124°$, angle $STU = 59°$, angle $TUR = 121°$, angle $URS = 56°$
9 angle $RPQ = 105°$, angle $PQR = 45°$, angle $QRP = 30°$
10 angle $ZXY = 47°$, angle $XYZ = 53°$, angle $YZX = 80°$

Exercise 6F

1 $a = 85°$ 2 $b = 102°$ 3 $c = 46°$
4 $d = 99°$ 5 $e = 60°$ 6 $f = 45°$

Exercise 6G

1 $a = 90°$, angles at a point add up to 360°
2 $b = 120°$, vertically opposite angles are equal, $c = 60°$, angles on a straight line add up to 180°, $d = 60°$, vertically opposite angles are equal
3 $e = 38°$, angles at a point add up to 360°
4 $f = 261°$, angles at a point add up to 360°
5 $g = 33°$, vertically opposite angles are equal, $h = 147°$, angles on a straight line add up to 180°, $i = 147°$, vertically opposite angles are equal
6 $j = 132°$, vertically opposite angles are equal, $k = 48°$, angles on a straight line add up to 180°, $l = 48°$, vertically opposite angles are equal
7 $m = 135°$, angles at a point add up to 360°
8 $n = 60°$, angles on a straight line add up to 180°, $p = 60°$, angles on a straight line add up to 180°, $q = 120°$, angles on a straight line add up to 180°
9 $r = 36°$, angles at a point add up to 360°, $3r = 108°$

Exercise 6H

1 $a = 30°$, angles of a triangle add up to 180°
2 $b = 70°$, angles of a quadrilateral add up to 360°
3 $c = 97°$, angles of a triangle add up to 180°
4 $e = 25°$, angles of a triangle add up to 180°

5 $f = 74°$, angles of a quadrilateral add up to 360°
6 $g = 66°$, angles of a quadrilateral add up to 360°
7 $h = 40°$, angles of a triangle add up to 180°
8 $i = 85°$, angles of a quadrilateral add up to 360°
9 $j = 60°$, angles of a triangle add up to 180°

Exercise 6I

1 45°, angles on a straight line add up to 180°
2 134°, angles at a point add up to 360°
3 $a = 128°$, angles on a straight line add up to 180°, $b = 55°$, angles of a triangle add up to 180°
4 57°, vertically opposite angles are equal
5 44°, angles of a quadrilateral add up to 360°
6 (a) 25°, base angle of isosceles triangle   (b) 130°
7 32°   **8** 84°
9 (a) 68°   (b) 112°   (c) 136°
10 (a) $a = 62°$, $b = 56°$, angles of a triangle add up to 180°, $c = 124°$, angles on a straight line add up to 180°, $d = 56°$, vertically opposite angles are equal, $e = 124°$
   (b) $a = 56°$, angles on a straight line add up to 180° $b = 87°$, angles of a quadrilateral add up to 360° $c = 93°$, angles on a straight line add up to 180°
   (c) $a = 42°$, base angle of isosceles triangle $b = 96°$, angles of a triangle add up to 180° $c = 138°$, angles on a straight line add up to 180° $d = 62°$, $e = 62°$, angles of a triangle add up to 180°, base angle of isosceles triangle
   (d) $p = 132°$, angles on a straight line add up to 180°, $q = 66°$, $r = 66°$, angles of a triangle add up to 180°, base angle of isosceles triangle, $s = 114°$, angles on a straight line add up to 180°, $t = 66°$, vertically opposite angles are equal, $u = 114°$, vertically opposite angles are equal
   (e) $x = 47°$, angles on a straight line add up to 180°, $y = 123°$, angles of a quadrilateral add up to 360°
   (f) $a = 13°$, angles of a triangle add up to 180° $b = 54°$, angles on a straight line add up to 180° $c = 54°$, base angle of isosceles triangle $d = 72°$, angles of a triangle add up to 180°

Exercise 6J

1 A/B C/E D/F G/H I/J K/L
3 b and e
4 c and e
5 (a) $a = 50°$, alternate angles
   (b) $b = 35°$, corresponding angles
   (c) $c = 110°$, alternate angles
   (d) $d = 140°$, corresponding angles
   (e) $e = 115°$, angles on a straight line; $f = 115°$, alternate angles; $g = 65°$, angles on a straight line
   (f) $h = 55°$, angles on a straight line; $i = 55°$, alternate angles; $j = 55°$, corresponding angles (or opposite angles)
6 (a) $x = 123°$, corresponding angles, $y = 57°$, angles on a straight line
   (b) $p = 39°$, angles on a straight line, $q = 141°$, corresponding angles
   (c) $a = 36°$, alternate angles $b = 144°$, angles on a straight line
   (d) $p = 137°$, alternate angles $m = 43°$, angles on a straight line
   (e) $x = 51°$, angles of a triangle, $y = 76°$, corresponding angles
   (f) $a = 62°$, corresponding angles, $b = 62°$, vertically opposite angles, $c = 33°$, angles of a triangle
   (g) $a = 74°$, alternate angles, $b = 106°$, angles on a straight line, $c = 74°$, base angle of isosceles triangle, $d = 106°$, angles on a straight line, $e = 32°$, angles of a triangle, $f = 74°$, angles on a straight line
   (h) $p = 48°$, angles on a straight line, $q = 132°$, vertically opposite angles, $r = 48°$, vertically opposite angles, $s = 48°$, alternate angles
7 (a) 64°   (b) 52°
8 (a) (i) 109°   (ii) Angles on a straight line add up to 180°
   (b) (i) 24°   (ii) Alternate angles

Exercise 6K

1 (a) $x = 180° − (90° + 45°) = 45°$, angles of a triangle
   (b) $2x + 90° = 180°$, angles of isosceles triangle, $x = 45°$
2 (a) Vertically opposite angle is 30°, $y = 30°$, corresponding angle
   (b) $y = 180° − 2 × 75° = 30°$, angles of isosceles triangle
3 (a) Angle $ABC = p$, corresponding angles
      Two angles are equal so ABC is isosceles
   (b) Angles ABC and $ACB = x$, corresponding angles
      Two angles are equal so ABC is isosceles

Exercise 6L

1 (a) 72°   (b) 60°   (c) 45°
2 (a) 108°   (b) 120°   (c) 135°
3 (a) 6   (b) 8   (c) 9
4 (a) 6   (b) 8   (c) 5
5 (a) 101°   (b) 79°
6 125°   7 144°

Exercise 6M

1 (a) 044°   (b) 134°   (c) 305°
   (d) 063°   (e) 110°   (f) 320°
   (g) 145°   (h) 230°   (i) 080°
2 (a) 070°   (b) 117°   (c) 233°
4 (a) 050°   (b) 230°   (c) 090°   (d) 270°

Mixed exercise 6

1 (c) (i) acute   (ii) reflex
2 (a) 54°
   (b) (i) 72°
      (ii) angle $Q = 54°$, isosceles triangle, $y = 180° − 2 × 54°$
         angles of a triangle
3 (a) 60°
   (b) 3 angles in a triangle = 60° means equilateral triangle
4 (a) 130°
   (b) angle $SQR = 50°$ (isosceles triangle) $x = 180° − 50°$ since 180° in straight line
5 64°, alternate angles
6 (a) pentagon   (b) 72°
7 (a) (i) acute   (ii) obtuse   (iii) reflex
   (b) 120° + 230° = 350°, but angles around a point add up to 360°
8 (a) 297°   (b) 081°   (c) 207°

Chapter 7 2-D shapes

Exercise 7A

1 (c) 2, 2   (d) 90°   (e) 4
   (f) 90°, equal   (g) equal, 90°   (h) sides, equal
   (i) opposite, equal, opposite
   (j) sides, equal, opposite   (k) parallel
2 (a) trapezium   (b) parallelogram (c) trapezium
   (d) kite   (e) square   (f) trapezium
3 (b) L   (c) B, S, Q, T   (d) rectangle
   (e) E, M   (f) F, K   (g) P
   (h) isosceles   (i) L   (j) C, G, H, U, R
4 (a) Square   (b) kite   (c) parallelogram
   (d) right-angled triangle   (e) trapezium
   (f) rhombus   (g) hexagon
   (h) isosceles triangle   (i) octagon
5 (a) equilateral triangle   (b) pentagon
   (c) regular octagon   (d) isosceles triangle
   (e) decagon

6 (a) square   (b) trapezium   (c) kite
7 (a) rectangle, square
   (b) parallelogram, rhombus, rectangle, square
   (c) rhombus, square
   (d) parallelogram, rectangle, kite
8 (a) rectangle, square
   (b) parallelogram, rhombus, rectangle, square
   (c) rhombus, square, kite
   (d) rhombus, square
   (e) trapezium, parallelogram, rhombus, rectangle, square
9 (a) 133°   (b) (i) 47°   (ii) 47°
10 (a) 32°   (b) 64°
11 (a) 15 cm²   (b) 30 cm²

Exercise 7C

1 A and D   2 A and C, B and D   3 B and D
4 A and D, B and C   5 B and C   6 A and B
8 B and H, O and M, L and E, G and J

Exercise 7E

2 (b) 103°   3 (b) 1.6 cm
5 (a) not possible   (b) 2 possible triangles
   (c) 1 triangle

Exercise 7F

1 11 km
2 (a) 1.4 km   (b) 17.4 cm
5 (a) (i) 12 500 cm   (ii) 125 m
   (b) (i) 6.3 cm   (ii) 157.5 m
6 (a) 2.7 km   (b) 258°
7 (b) (i) 2.33 km   (ii) 080°
8 20 km, 344°
9 108 yards, 017°
10 096°, 125 km

Exercise 7H

1 Circle, centre P, radius 5 cm
2 A pair of parallel lines, 5 cm either side of AB, joined by semicircles with centres at A and B
3 The perpendicular bisector of PQ
4 Two perpendicular lines that bisect the angles between AB and CD
5 4 straight lines 4 cm long and 5 cm outside the sides of the square, joined by 4 quarter circles, radius 5 cm, centres the vertices of the square
6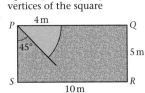
7 (b) The perpendicular bisector of AB
8 (b) The perpendicular bisector of DE
   (c) Circle, centre D, radius 4 cm

Mixed exercise 7

1 (a) rectangle   (b) regular hexagon   (c) rhombus
2 A, C, E, F
4 (b) 63°
6 (a) 89 km   (b) 157°
9 (a) 60°   (b) 120°

Chapter 8 Fractions

Exercise 8A

1 $\frac{1}{2}, \frac{1}{2}, \frac{1}{4}, \frac{3}{4}, \frac{2}{5}, \frac{3}{5}, \frac{3}{10}, \frac{7}{10}, \frac{5}{8}, \frac{3}{8}, \frac{4}{9}, \frac{5}{9}$
2 (a) Rectangle with 1 cell shaded
   (b) rectangle with 3 cells shaded
   (c) rectangle with 8 cells shaded
   (d) rectangle all shaded
3 (a) Circle with 1 sector shaded
   (b) circle with 3 sectors shaded
   (c) circle with 3 sectors shaded
4

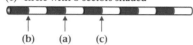

      (b)   (a)   (c)

Exercise 8B

1 (a) $\frac{15}{28}$ (b) $\frac{13}{28}$
2 (a) 75   (b) $\frac{28}{75}$ (c) $\frac{47}{75}$
3 (a) $\frac{37}{51}$ (b) $\frac{10}{51}$ (c) $\frac{4}{51}$
4 (a) $\frac{298}{317}$ (b) $\frac{19}{317}$
5 (a) 16   (b) $\frac{7}{16}$ (c) $\frac{3}{16}$ (d) $\frac{5}{16}$ (e) $\frac{1}{16}$
6 (a) 17   (b) $\frac{5}{17}$ (c) $\frac{6}{17}$ (d) $\frac{4}{17}$ (e) $\frac{2}{17}$
7 (a) $\frac{6}{11}$ (b) $\frac{4}{11}$ (c) $\frac{1}{11}$

Exercise 8C

1 (a) $2\frac{1}{2}$ (b) $1\frac{3}{4}$ (c) $1\frac{2}{7}$ (d) $1\frac{3}{8}$
   (e) $1\frac{1}{8}$ (f) $3\frac{1}{5}$ (g) $2\frac{3}{10}$ (h) $4\frac{4}{5}$
   (i) $2\frac{2}{7}$ (j) $2\frac{2}{5}$ (k) $6\frac{2}{3}$ (l) $1\frac{7}{9}$
   (m) $9\frac{3}{4}$ (n) $5\frac{2}{5}$ (o) $2\frac{8}{9}$ (p) $1\frac{7}{10}$
2 (a) $\frac{3}{2}$ (b) $\frac{11}{3}$ (c) $\frac{11}{4}$ (d) $\frac{5}{3}$
   (e) $\frac{13}{4}$ (f) $\frac{22}{5}$ (g) $\frac{37}{10}$ (h) $\frac{26}{5}$
   (i) $\frac{31}{4}$ (j) $\frac{9}{4}$ (k) $\frac{19}{10}$ (l) $\frac{28}{3}$
   (m) $\frac{17}{6}$ (n) $\frac{43}{8}$ (o) $\frac{29}{8}$ (p) $\frac{109}{100}$

Exercise 8D

1 (a) 35   (b) £26   (c) 24 kg   (d) 64   (e) £21
   (f) 45p   (g) £1.70   (h) 63p   (i) £2.80
2 (a) 9   (b) 30   (c) 28 litres
   (d) 21 pints
3 (a) 27 lb   (b) £2.22   (c) 660 km
   (d) 280 people
4 (a) 34   (b) 51
5 46
6 62
7 375 kg
8 140 ham, 224 salad, 70 tuna, 126 cheese
9 (a) 350   (b) 2450   (c) 700
10 (a) 320   (b) 120   (c) 40
11 140 days
12 21

Exercise 8E

1 (a) $\frac{2}{3}$ (b) $\frac{3}{5}$ (c) $\frac{4}{7}$ (d) $\frac{3}{4}$ (e) $\frac{2}{3}$
2 (a) $\frac{3}{4}$ (b) $\frac{5}{6}$ (c) $\frac{5}{6}$ (d) $\frac{5}{7}$ (e) $\frac{5}{9}$
3 (a) $\frac{5}{8}$ (b) $\frac{3}{4}$ (c) $\frac{7}{9}$ (d) $\frac{2}{5}$ (e) $\frac{2}{3}$
4 (a) $\frac{2}{3}$ (b) $\frac{1}{2}$ (c) $\frac{1}{2}$ (d) $\frac{1}{3}$ (e) $\frac{2}{5}$
   (f) $\frac{2}{3}$ (g) $\frac{2}{3}$ (h) $\frac{3}{4}$ (i) $\frac{7}{11}$ (j) $\frac{6}{7}$
   (k) $\frac{3}{4}$ (l) $\frac{5}{6}$

5 $\frac{2}{4}, \frac{1}{2}, \frac{2}{8}, \frac{1}{4}, \frac{4}{10}, \frac{2}{5}, \frac{3}{12}, \frac{1}{4}, \frac{3}{9}, \frac{1}{3}, \frac{6}{16}, \frac{3}{8}$
6 (a) $\frac{2}{7}$ (b) $\frac{5}{7}$
7 (a) $\frac{2}{7}$ (b) $\frac{1}{2}$ (c) $\frac{3}{14}$
8 (a) $\frac{13}{28}$ (b) $\frac{5}{28}$ (c) $\frac{3}{28}$ (d) $\frac{1}{4}$

Exercise 8F

1 (a) $\frac{3}{4}, \frac{6}{8}$ (b) $\frac{1}{3}, \frac{2}{6}$ (c) $\frac{3}{12}, \frac{1}{4}$ (d) $\frac{3}{8}, \frac{6}{16}$ (e) $\frac{4}{12}, \frac{1}{3}$
   (f) $\frac{8}{12}, \frac{2}{3}, \frac{4}{6}$ (g) $\frac{6}{12}, \frac{1}{2}, \frac{3}{6}$ (h) $\frac{9}{12}, \frac{3}{4}$ (i) $\frac{8}{12}, \frac{2}{3}, \frac{4}{6}$ (j) $\frac{6}{18}, \frac{1}{3}$
2 (a) $\frac{3}{4} = \frac{6}{8} = \frac{9}{12} = \frac{12}{16} = \frac{15}{20} = \frac{18}{24}$
   (b) $\frac{2}{7} = \frac{4}{14} = \frac{6}{21} = \frac{8}{28} = \frac{10}{35} = \frac{12}{42}$
   (c) $\frac{4}{5} = \frac{8}{10} = \frac{12}{15} = \frac{16}{20} = \frac{20}{25} = \frac{24}{30}$
   (d) $\frac{1}{3} = \frac{3}{9} = \frac{6}{18} = \frac{9}{27} = \frac{12}{36} = \frac{15}{45}$
3 (a) $\frac{1}{6} = \frac{3}{18}$ (b) $\frac{3}{7} = \frac{6}{14}$ (c) $\frac{3}{8} = \frac{18}{48}$ (d) $\frac{4}{7} = \frac{12}{21}$
   (e) $\frac{5}{6} = \frac{30}{36}$ (f) $\frac{2}{3} = \frac{6}{9}$ (g) $\frac{4}{9} = \frac{24}{54}$ (h) $\frac{5}{7} = \frac{40}{56}$
   (i) $\frac{9}{10} = \frac{90}{100}$ (j) $\frac{7}{12} = \frac{84}{144}$ (k) $\frac{7}{8} = \frac{49}{56}$ (l) $\frac{2}{9} = \frac{18}{81}$
4 (a) $\frac{3}{6}, \frac{2}{6}$
   (b) (i) $\frac{12}{30}, \frac{15}{30}$ (ii) $\frac{7}{70}, \frac{10}{70}$ (iii) $\frac{3}{12}, \frac{10}{12}$ (iv) $\frac{5}{10}, \frac{6}{10}$
        (v) $\frac{16}{24}, \frac{3}{24}$ (vi) $\frac{15}{20}, \frac{12}{20}$

Exercise 8G

1 (a) 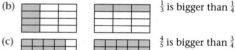 $\frac{3}{4}$ is bigger than $\frac{1}{2}$
   (b) $\frac{1}{3}$ is bigger than $\frac{1}{4}$
   (c) $\frac{4}{5}$ is bigger than $\frac{3}{4}$
   (d) $\frac{5}{6}$ is bigger than $\frac{4}{5}$

2 (a) $\frac{2}{5} = \frac{8}{20}, \frac{1}{4} = \frac{5}{20}, \frac{1}{4}$ is smaller
   (b) $\frac{3}{4} = \frac{15}{20}, \frac{4}{5} = \frac{16}{20}, \frac{3}{4}$ is smaller
   (c) $\frac{2}{3} = \frac{8}{12}, \frac{3}{4} = \frac{9}{12}, \frac{2}{3}$ is smaller
   (d) $\frac{3}{5} = \frac{6}{10}, \frac{3}{5}$ is smaller than $\frac{7}{10}$
3 (a) $\frac{3}{6}$ (b) $\frac{1}{7}$ (c) $\frac{5}{6}$ (d) $\frac{3}{5}$
   (e) $\frac{2}{3}$ (f) $\frac{3}{4}$
4 (a) $\frac{1}{2}, \frac{2}{3}, \frac{3}{4}$ (b) $\frac{7}{15}, \frac{4}{5}, \frac{5}{6}$ (c) $\frac{1}{2}, \frac{3}{4}, \frac{4}{5}$ (d) $\frac{5}{14}, \frac{3}{7}, \frac{1}{2}, \frac{4}{7}$
5 $\frac{7}{8}, \frac{3}{4}, \frac{1}{2}, \frac{2}{5}, \frac{1}{10}$

Exercise 8H

1 (a) $\frac{7}{8}$ (b) $\frac{7}{9}$ (c) $\frac{1}{2}$ (d) $\frac{8}{9}$ (e) $\frac{3}{4}$
   (f) $\frac{5}{8}$ (g) $1\frac{3}{8}$ (h) $\frac{5}{6}$ (i) $1\frac{1}{6}$ (j) $\frac{7}{10}$
   (k) $1\frac{1}{3}$ (l) $1\frac{1}{10}$ (m) $\frac{1}{2}$ (n) $\frac{6}{7}$ (o) $1\frac{1}{5}$
   (p) $1\frac{3}{5}$ (q) $3\frac{2}{9}$ (r) $2\frac{2}{3}$ (s) $1\frac{3}{4}$ (t) $1\frac{7}{8}$
2 (a) $1\frac{3}{8}$ (b) $\frac{17}{20}$ (c) $\frac{31}{36}$ (d) $1\frac{31}{40}$
   (e) $\frac{17}{30}$ (f) $1\frac{1}{12}$ (g) $\frac{23}{24}$ (h) $1\frac{1}{18}$
   (i) $\frac{7}{8}$ (j) $3\frac{5}{8}$ (k) $\frac{19}{24}$ (l) $6\frac{5}{8}$
   (m) $4\frac{1}{16}$ (n) $4\frac{3}{8}$ (o) $1\frac{1}{16}$ (p) $4\frac{3}{16}$
3 (a) $\frac{5}{6}$ (b) $\frac{17}{30}$ (c) $\frac{33}{40}$ (d) $\frac{31}{36}$
   (e) $1\frac{11}{42}$ (f) $1\frac{13}{70}$ (g) $1\frac{11}{30}$ (h) $1\frac{7}{20}$
   (i) $\frac{23}{40}$ (j) $\frac{11}{30}$ (k) $2\frac{29}{30}$ (l) $\frac{20}{21}$
   (m) $3\frac{19}{42}$ (n) $3\frac{41}{42}$ (o) $5\frac{13}{15}$ (p) $2\frac{8}{9}$
4 $7\frac{1}{12}$ miles
5 (a) $5\frac{3}{4}$ (b) $3\frac{1}{6}$ (c) $4\frac{1}{8}$ (d) $9\frac{1}{12}$ (e) $5\frac{3}{16}$
   (f) $3\frac{2}{3}$ (g) $7\frac{1}{6}$ (h) $7\frac{4}{15}$
6 $\frac{1}{2}$ 7 $\frac{49}{80}$ 8 $17\frac{1}{2}$ in   9 $3\frac{11}{16}$ in
10 $\frac{17}{30}$ 11 $1\frac{22}{35}$ lb

Exercise 8I

1 (a) $\frac{2}{11}$ (b) $\frac{2}{9}$ (c) $\frac{6}{8}=\frac{3}{4}$ (d) $\frac{2}{12}=\frac{1}{6}$
(e) $\frac{1}{2}$ (f) $\frac{1}{4}$ (g) $\frac{1}{2}$ (h) $\frac{3}{7}$
2 (a) $\frac{1}{4}$ (b) $\frac{1}{8}$ (c) $\frac{1}{8}$ (d) $\frac{5}{8}$
(e) $\frac{1}{2}$ (f) $\frac{1}{4}$ (g) $\frac{1}{2}$ (h) $\frac{1}{5}$
(i) $\frac{1}{8}$ (j) $\frac{3}{8}$ (k) $\frac{1}{6}$ (l) $2\frac{3}{8}$
3 (a) $\frac{1}{6}$ (b) $\frac{7}{24}$ (c) $\frac{1}{30}$ (d) $\frac{13}{30}$
(e) $\frac{2}{15}$ (f) $\frac{3}{20}$ (g) $\frac{11}{30}$ (h) $\frac{3}{20}$
4 (a) $5\frac{3}{20}$ (b) $7\frac{1}{6}$ (c) $1\frac{1}{4}$ (d) $2\frac{1}{5}$
(e) $2\frac{7}{10}$ (f) $\frac{9}{10}$ (g) $\frac{3}{4}$ (h) $2\frac{4}{5}$
(i) $3\frac{5}{24}$ (j) $2\frac{4}{9}$ (k) $3\frac{17}{40}$ (l) $3\frac{6}{35}$
5 $\frac{9}{16}$ 6 $\frac{3}{5}$ 7 $\frac{1}{12}$ acre   8 $4\frac{5}{8}$ kg
9 $3\frac{1}{8}$ million   10 $2\frac{1}{8}$ ft   11 $\frac{1}{12}$

Exercise 8J

1 (a) $\frac{3}{8}$ (b) $\frac{3}{32}$ (c) $\frac{8}{25}$ (d) $\frac{9}{32}$
(e) $\frac{5}{36}$ (f) $\frac{21}{40}$ (g) $\frac{9}{50}$ (h) $\frac{4}{9}$
(i) $\frac{3}{16}$ (j) $\frac{8}{15}$ (k) $\frac{4}{21}$ (l) $\frac{4}{15}$
(m) $\frac{2}{35}$ (n) $\frac{10}{21}$ (o) $\frac{3}{8}$ (p) $\frac{1}{5}$
2 (a) $\frac{2}{5}$ (b) $\frac{3}{5}$ (c) $\frac{1}{2}$ (d) $\frac{6}{25}$
(e) $\frac{5}{8}$ (f) $\frac{1}{8}$ (g) $\frac{4}{15}$ (h) $\frac{4}{7}$
(i) $\frac{2}{7}$ (j) $\frac{5}{14}$ (k) $\frac{2}{5}$ (l) $\frac{1}{6}$
(m) $\frac{1}{7}$ (n) $\frac{2}{5}$ (o) $3\frac{1}{2}$ (p) $\frac{13}{20}$
3 (a) $3\frac{1}{2}$ (b) $3\frac{1}{3}$ (c) $4\frac{4}{5}$ (d) 6 (e) 14 (f) 6
(g) 4 (h) 10 (i) $\frac{8}{9}$ (j) $\frac{14}{15}$ (k) $\frac{3}{8}$ (l) $3\frac{3}{4}$
4 (a) $1\frac{5}{8}$ (b) 3 (c) $1\frac{1}{9}$ (d) $1\frac{1}{4}$ (e) $5\frac{1}{4}$ (f) $5\frac{13}{24}$
(g) $4\frac{1}{5}$ (h) $5\frac{1}{4}$ (i) $\frac{5}{8}$ (j) $1\frac{13}{15}$ (k) 16 (l) 3
5 Jamie $11\frac{1}{4}$ hours, Claire $8\frac{3}{4}$ hours   6 $82\frac{1}{2}$ mins
7 $7\frac{5}{16}$ cm²   8 $20\frac{5}{8}$ lb   9 $14\frac{5}{8}$ min
10 20 min   11 $9\frac{4}{5}$ h   12 $24\frac{1}{6}$ m²

Exercise 8K

1 (a) $1\frac{1}{3}$ (b) $\frac{3}{4}$ (c) $1\frac{1}{2}$ (d) $\frac{5}{7}$
(e) $3\frac{1}{3}$ (f) $1\frac{7}{8}$ (g) $1\frac{1}{9}$ (h) $\frac{7}{8}$
(i) $\frac{4}{9}$ (j) $\frac{8}{15}$ (k) $\frac{9}{16}$ (l) 2
2 (a) 5 (b) $1\frac{3}{10}$ (c) $1\frac{2}{3}$ (d) $\frac{39}{76}$
(e) $\frac{1}{2}$ (f) 2 (g) $\frac{17}{27}$ (h) $\frac{21}{40}$
3 (a) $\frac{3}{32}$ (b) $\frac{5}{12}$ (c) $\frac{1}{10}$ (d) $\frac{4}{25}$
(e) $\frac{1}{3}$ (f) $\frac{13}{24}$ (g) $\frac{17}{60}$ (h) $\frac{1}{2}$
(i) $\frac{2}{9}$ (j) $\frac{1}{9}$ (k) $1\frac{1}{6}$ (l) $1\frac{3}{4}$
4 (a) 16 (b) 16 (c) 10 (d) $9\frac{1}{7}$
(e) 5 (f) $1\frac{5}{7}$ (g) 15 (h) 24
5 (a) $\frac{8}{9}$ (b) $7\frac{1}{2}$ (c) $6\frac{9}{10}$ (d) $1\frac{13}{20}$
(e) $\frac{3}{5}$ (f) $1\frac{1}{9}$ (g) $\frac{4}{9}$ (h) $\frac{9}{10}$
6 16   7 36   8 $11\frac{2}{11}$ days

Exercise 8L

1 4.95 t   2 289 cars   3 $\frac{2}{9}$ 4 $\frac{17}{45}$
5 $1\frac{3}{5}$ miles   6 605   7 $\frac{9}{16}$ 8 $\frac{27}{55}$

Exercise 8M

1 (a) 0.6 (b) 0.5 (c) 0.7 (d) 0.35
(e) 0.16 (f) 0.06 (g) 0.875 (h) 0.45
(i) 0.76 (j) 0.3125 (k) 0.125 (l) 0.54
(m) 0.09 (n) 0.065 (o) 0.6666 … (p) 0.95
2 (a) $\frac{3}{10}$ (b) $\frac{37}{100}$ (c) $\frac{93}{100}$ (d) $\frac{137}{1000}$
(e) $\frac{293}{1000}$ (f) $\frac{7}{100}$ (g) $\frac{59}{100}$ (h) $\frac{3}{1000}$
(i) $\frac{3}{100\,000}$ (j) $\frac{13}{10\,000}$ (k) $\frac{77}{100}$ (l) $\frac{77}{1000}$
(m) $\frac{39}{100}$ (n) $\frac{41}{10\,000}$ (o) $\frac{19}{1000}$ (p) $\frac{31}{1000}$
3 (a) 0.8 (b) 0.75 (c) 1.125 (d) 0.19
(e) 3.6 (f) 0.52 (g) 0.625 (h) 3.425
(i) 0.14 (j) 4.1875 (k) 3.15 (l) 4.3125
(m) 0.007 (n) 1.28 (o) 15.9375 (p) 2.35
4 (a) $\frac{12}{25}$ (b) $\frac{1}{4}$ (c) $1\frac{7}{10}$ (d) $3\frac{203}{500}$
(e) $4\frac{3}{1000}$ (f) $2\frac{1}{40}$ (g) $\frac{49}{1000}$ (h) $4\frac{7}{8}$
(i) $3\frac{3}{4}$ (j) $10\frac{101}{1000}$ (k) $\frac{5}{8}$ (l) $2\frac{64}{125}$
(m) $\frac{13}{16}$ (n) $14\frac{7}{50}$ (o) $9\frac{3}{16}$ (p) $60\frac{13}{200}$

Exercise 8N

1 (i) 0.833 333 (ii) $0.8\dot{3}$ 2 (i) 1.222 222 (ii) $1.\dot{2}$
3 (i) 3.166 666 (ii) $3.1\dot{6}$ 4 (i) 0.916 666 (ii) $0.91\dot{6}$
5 (i) 5.555 555 (ii) $5.\dot{5}$ 6 (i) 4.818 181 (ii) $4.\dot{8}\dot{1}$
7 (i) 0.068 181 (ii) $0.06\dot{8}\dot{1}$ 8 (i) 2.636 363 (ii) $2.\dot{6}\dot{3}$
9 (i) 9.954 545 (ii) $9.9\dot{5}\dot{4}$ 10 (i) 0.833 33 (ii) $0.\dot{8}\dot{3}$

11 $\frac{1}{7}=0.\dot{1}4285\dot{7}$ $\frac{2}{7}=0.\dot{2}8571\dot{4}$
$\frac{3}{7}=0.\dot{4}2857\dot{1}$ $\frac{4}{7}=0.\dot{5}7142\dot{8}$
$\frac{5}{7}=0.\dot{7}1428\dot{5}$ $\frac{6}{7}=0.\dot{8}5714\dot{2}$
The recurring decimal fractions each consist of the same six digits in the same order, starting with a different digit. The smaller the fractions, the smaller the starting number.
12 $\frac{1}{9}=0.\dot{1}$ $\frac{2}{9}=0.\dot{2}$ $\frac{3}{9}=0.\dot{3}$ $\frac{4}{9}=0.\dot{4}$
$\frac{5}{9}=0.\dot{5}$ $\frac{6}{9}=0.\dot{6}$ $\frac{7}{9}=0.\dot{7}$ $\frac{8}{9}=0.\dot{8}$
The single digit of the recurring decimal is the same as the numerator of the fraction.

Exercise 8O

1 (a) $\frac{1}{5}$ or 0.2 (b) $\frac{1}{4}$ or 0.25 (c) $\frac{1}{6}$ or $0.1\dot{6}$ (d) $\frac{1}{8}$ or 0.125
(e) $\frac{1}{10}$ or 0.1 (f) 4 (g) 8 (h) $\frac{5}{3}, 1\frac{2}{3}$ or $1.\dot{6}$
(i) $\frac{6}{5}, 1\frac{1}{5}$ or 1.2 (j) $\frac{3}{5}$ or 0.6
2 (a) 0.04 (b) 0.02 (c) 0.3 (d) $0.\dot{1}4285\dot{7}$
(e) $0.\dot{1}$ (f) $0.01\dot{3}$ (g) 0.01 (h) 40
(i) 8 (j) 20 (k) 1000 (l) $333.\dot{3}$
(m) 5000 (n) 3.5 (o) $0.\dot{7}1428\dot{5}$

Mixed exercise 8

1 (a) $\frac{3}{4}$ (b) 16 squares shaded
2 $\frac{3}{5}$ shade 9 rectangles, $\frac{2}{3}$ shade 10 rectangles, $\frac{2}{3}>\frac{3}{5}$
3 $\frac{2}{5}, \frac{1}{2}, \frac{2}{3}, \frac{3}{4}$
4 any fraction in range e.g. $\frac{7}{12}$
5 $\frac{7}{20}$
6 (a) $1\frac{1}{15}$ (b) $3\frac{1}{12}$ (c) $3\frac{11}{12}$ (d) $\frac{1}{14}$ (e) $5\frac{1}{6}$ (f) $5\frac{17}{20}$
7 9
8 (a) $5\frac{1}{3}$ (b) $8\frac{3}{4}$ (c) $5\frac{1}{2}$ (d) $6\frac{1}{3}$ (e) $4\frac{3}{13}$
9 (a) $\frac{20}{11}$ (b) $\frac{19}{3}$ (c) $\frac{116}{25}$ (d) $\frac{15}{4}$ (e) $\frac{101}{10}$
10 (a) $\frac{4}{15}$ (b) $2\frac{1}{4}$ (c) $9\frac{1}{3}$ (d) $1\frac{1}{10}$ (e) $4\frac{1}{2}$ (f) 4
11 (a) £45 (b) 45 km (c) 32 kg
12 $7\frac{3}{4}$ miles
13 (a) $\frac{1}{5}$ (b) 0.8 (c) 80%
14 (a) 0.5 (b) 0.25 (c) 0.75 (d) 0.333…
(e) 0.6 (f) $0.\dot{4}2857\dot{1}$ (g) 0.222…
15 (a) $\frac{1}{5}$ (b) $\frac{7}{20}$ (c) $\frac{3}{40}$ (d) $\frac{1}{8}$
16 (a) 2 (b) 1.333… (c) 0.2 (d) 8
(e) 0.002 (f) 20 (g) 5 (h) 0.04
17 (a) $\frac{2}{3}, \frac{4}{6},$ … (b) $\frac{26}{50}, \frac{52}{100},$ … (c) $\frac{2}{6}, \frac{3}{9},$ … (d) $\frac{10}{34}, \frac{20}{68},$ …
18 (a) $\frac{3}{4}$ (b) $\frac{3}{5}$ (c) $\frac{49}{50}$ (d) $\frac{5}{7}$
19 (a) (i) 0.444… (ii) $0.\dot{4}$
(b) (i) 0.428 571 42 (ii) $0.\dot{4}28571\dot{}$
(c) (i) 2.142 857 14 (ii) $2.\dot{1}42857\dot{}$
(d) (i) 5.545 454… (ii) $5.\dot{5}\dot{4}$
(e) (i) 4.615 384 61 (ii) $4.\dot{6}15384\dot{}$

Chapter 9 Estimating and using measures

Exercise 9A

1 (a) 1.8 m   (b) 1.4 m   (c) 2.5 m   (d) 1.5 m
2 (a) 4 m   (b) 10 m
3 (a) 7 m   (b) 7 m
4 (a) 3 m   (b) 2.5 m   (c) 9 m

Exercise 9B

Question	Metric	Imperial
1	570 m*l*	1 pint
2	300 m*l*	$\frac{1}{2}$ pint
3	1 *l*	2 pints
4	150 m*l*	$\frac{1}{4}$ pint
5	570 m*l*	1 pint
6	9 *l*	2 gallons
7	90 *l*	20 gallons

Exercise 9C

Question	Metric	Imperial
1	5 kg	11 pounds
2	250 g	$\frac{1}{2}$ pound
3	2 kg	4 pounds
4	250 g	$\frac{1}{2}$ pound
5	1 kg	2 pounds
6	500 g	1 pound
7	1 kg	2 pounds
8	125 g	$\frac{1}{4}$ pound
9	30 g	1 ounce
10	2 kg	4 pounds

Exercise 9D

Question	Metric	Imperial
1	metres	feet
2	centimetres	inches
3	kilometres	miles
4	metres	feet
5	kilograms	pounds
6	grams	ounces
7	tonnes	tons
8	litres	gallons
9	millilitres	fluid ounces
10	millilitres	fluid ounces/teaspoon
11	millilitres	fluid ounces
12	litres	gallons
13	minutes	minutes
14	seconds	seconds
15	hours	hours
16	days	days
17	centimetres	inches
18	millimetres	inches
19	kilograms	pounds
20	years	years

Exercise 9E

1 (a) Not sensible, 1.8 m
   (b) Not sensible, 1.8 m
   (c) Not sensible, 7 m by 6 m
   (d) Not sensible, 200 g or more
   (e) Not sensible, 300 m*l*
   (f) Could be sensible
2 (a) Sensible
   (b) Sensible
   (c) Sensible
   (d) Not sensible, 300 m*l*
   (e) Not sensible, 300 km
   (f) Not sensible, 10 g
3 (a) Sensible
   (b) Not sensible, 570 m*l*
   (c) Not sensible, 50 *l*
4 (a) Sensible
   (b) Not sensible, 50 *l*
   (c) Not sensible, 125 g
   (d) Sensible

Exercise 9F

1 (a) 9 o'clock   (b) Quarter past 8   (c) Half past 3
   (d) Quarter to 6   (e) Ten past 3   (f) Twenty to 3
   (g) Five to 2   (h) Twenty-five to 9
   (i) Twenty-five past 8   (j) Ten to 3
2 (a)   (b)   (c)
   (d)   (e)   (f)

Exercise 9G

1 (a) Half past eight, eight thirty
   (b) Ten past ten, ten ten
   (c) Five past eleven, eleven oh five
   (d) Quarter to five, four forty-five
   (e) Five to four, three fifty-five
2 (a) 9:15   (b) 3:30   (c) 4:40   (d) 6:45   (e) 5:00

Exercise 9H

1 (a) 10:00   (b) 22:00   (c) 09:30   (d) 21:30
   (e) 20:20   (f) 08:20   (g) 07:00   (h) 20:00
   (i) 15:30   (j) 04:40   (k) 01:08   (l) 13:08
   (m) 17:50   (n) 05:50   (o) 23:00   (p) 08:00
   (q) 08:15   (r) 20:45   (s) 14:55   (t) 06:40
2 (a) 8 am   (b) 9:20 am   (c) 9:30 pm   (d) 1:10 pm
   (e) 12:10 pm   (f) 12:20 am   (g) 1:40 am   (h) 8 am
   (i) 3:45 pm   (j) 6 pm   (k) 4:30 pm   (l) 9:10 pm
   (m) 11:55 pm   (n) 2.02 pm   (o) 6:25 am   (p) midnight
   (q) midnight   (r) noon   (s) 10:55 am   (t) 8:55 pm

Exercise 9I

1 (a) 6 cm   (b) 40 mph   (c) 40 m*l*   (d) 60 m*l*
   (e) 100 mph   (f) 80 mm

Exercise 9J

| 1 7.7 cm | 2 188 cm | 3 46 mph |
| 4 26 m*l* | 5 18 mph | 6 8.6 cm |

Exercise 9K

| 1 7.8 units | 2 5.5 cm | 3 37 mph |
| 4 82 mph | 5 6.7 units | 6 4.4 units |

Exercise 9L

| 1 (a) 2 cm | (b) 3.5 cm | (c) 5.5 cm | (d) 10 cm |
| (e) 7.4 cm | (f) 0.8 cm | (g) 1.8 cm | (h) 6.8 cm |

Exercise 9M

Points marked at these distances from the ends of the lines.

1 (a) 4 cm	(b) 3 cm	(c) 5 cm	(d) 2 cm
2 (a) 2 cm	(b) 2.5 cm	(c) 1 cm
3 (a) 2 cm	(b) 4 cm
4 (a) 3 cm	(b) 9 cm
5 (a) 1 cm	(b) 3 cm	(c) 7 cm	(d) 9 cm

Mixed exercise 9

1 Turkey   kilograms
Swimming pool   litres
Page width   inches
2 (a) 18*l*   (b) 13.5*l*   (c) 6 gallons   (d) 4.4 gallons
4 (a) metres   (b) 10–15 metres
5 (a) 15–20 seconds
6

7 (a) about 20 feet   (b) about 6 m

Chapter 10 Collecting and recording data

Exercise 10A

| 1 (a) X | (b) Y | (c) Y | (d) X |
| (e) Y | (f) X | (g) X | (h) X |

Exercise 10B

1 (a) e.g. It suggests Yes is the right answer.
(b) e.g. Terrible for one person may be Quite good for another.
(c) e.g. It suggests Yes is the right answer.
(d) e.g. Some people have never played football.
(e) e.g. There is no way of answering 'none' or more than 3 hours.
(f) e.g. No tick boxes supplied.
2 (a) e.g. £0–£5, £5.01–£10, £10.01–£15, over £15

Exercise 10C

| 1 C | 2 A | 3 C | 4 B | 5 B |

Exercise 10F

1 (a) 2.7% (b) (i) 1999 (ii) 2005 (c) 2000 and 2001
2 (a) (i) Redbridge (ii) Lambeth (b) Richmond
(c) (i) Redbridge (ii) Camden (d) £54

Exercise 10G

1 (a) Volkswagen   (b) Porsche
(c) Porsche   (d) 4
(e) Suzuki, Proton, Daewoo, Vauxhall
(f) Suzuki
(g) Porsche, Citroen, BMW, Nissan, Seat, Volkswagen, Suzuki, Proton, Daewoo, Vauxhall
2 (a) (i) Chad (ii) Algeria (iii) Algeria (iv) 20 800 000
(b) The other countries have a far greater percentage of urban population (2.5–5.9 times that of Burundi).

Exercise 10H

1 (a) 204 miles	(b) 91 miles	(c) 24 miles
(d) 201 miles	(e) 44 miles	(f) 211 miles
2 (a) 120 miles	(b) 98 miles	(c) 73 miles
(d) 56 miles	(e) 153 miles	(f) 52 miles
3 (a) 410 miles	(b) 47 miles	(c) 132 miles
(d) 413 miles	(e) 176 miles	(f) 574 miles

4

Birmingham			
78	Manchester		
155	191	Norwich	
128	67	178	York

| 5 (a) 3 h 52 min | (b) 2 h 09 min | (c) 40 min |
| (d) 3 h 38 min | (e) 54 min | (f) 3 h 52 min |

Mixed exercise 10

1 Response boxes needed
5 How many hours of television do you watch a day?
Less than 1 ☐   1 to 3 ☐   More than 3 ☐
6 Overlapping groups: 0–1 overlaps 1–2, and Over 5 overlaps Over 10
No time period, eg Age in years
7 Number students and use random numbers
8 (a) e.g. What type(s) of restaurant do you like?
Café ☐   Bistro ☐   Tapas bar ☐   Burger house ☐
(b) e.g. Leading question. Response boxes needed.
9 (a) (i) Biased – students have already shown their preference.
(ii) Not representative – target sample at cinema.
(iii) Self selecting sample – few people at mall without a car.
(iv) Biased – trains may be unusually late due to the snow.
(b) Sending questionnaires to different London offices
10 (a) 78 (b) 201 (c) 108 (d) 210 (e) 393 (f) 292

Chapter 11 Linear equations

Exercise 11A

1 $a = 3$	2 $b = 3$	3 $c = 7$	4 $w = 2$
5 $m = 1$	6 $y = 0$	7 $x = 5$	8 $k = 5$
9 $n = 6$	10 $h = 8$	11 $g = 4$	12 $f = 9$
13 $d = 5$	14 $e = 3$	15 $y = 3$	16 $x = 4$
17 $m = 4$	18 $d = 3$	19 $k = 9$	20 $y = 10$
21 $t = 10$	22 $z = 4$	23 $z = 0$	24 $n = 5$

Exercise 11B

1 $a = 1$	2 $y = 2$	3 $h = 7$	4 $p = 9$
5 $q = 10$	6 $d = 8$	7 $x = 0$	8 $t = 4$
9 $r = 3$	10 $k = 1$	11 $n = 1$	12 $x = 5$
13 $m = 5$	14 $y = 16$	15 $w = 0$	16 $q = 12$
17 $p = 2$	18 $t = 0$	19 $a = 12$	20 $x = 0$
21 $p = 38$	22 $a = 4$	23 $b = 1$	24 $y = 0$

Exercise 11C

1 $a = 5$	**2** $p = 11$	**3** $q = 8$	**4** $x = 8$
5 $y = 13$	**6** $s = 3$	**7** $x = 22$	**8** $y = 21$
9 $s = 27$	**10** $a = 1$	**11** $p = 11$	**12** $c = 4$
13 $a = 1$	**14** $p = 5$	**15** $q = 0$	**16** $a = 2$
17 $b = 2$	**18** $c = 15$	**19** $p = 5$	**20** $y = 21$
21 $t = 5$	**22** $p = 0$	**23** $p = 24$	**24** $p = 0$

Exercise 11D

1 $a = 2$	**2** $p = 2$	**3** $p = 3$	**4** $s = 3$
5 $k = 5$	**6** $u = 4$	**7** $g = 7$	**8** $k = 7$
9 $j = 2$	**10** $f = 4$	**11** $r = 9$	**12** $v = 9$
13 $t = 21$	**14** $d = 12$	**15** $t = 9$	

Exercise 11E

1 $a = 10$	**2** $b = 20$	**3** $s = 12$	**4** $c = 30$
5 $t = 24$	**6** $s = 72$	**7** $h = 72$	**8** $f = 28$
9 $d = 45$	**10** $a = 45$	**11** $b = 40$	**12** $r = 52$
13 $a = 60$	**14** $b = 32$	**15** $k = 48$	

Exercise 11F

1 $a = 1$	**2** $b = 3$	**3** $c = 5$	**4** $p = 9$
5 $q = 4$	**6** $d = 8$	**7** $p = 3$	**8** $r = 2$
9 $t = 4$	**10** $a = 12$	**11** $b = 60$	**12** $s = 20$
13 $r = 3$	**14** $e = 1$	**15** $p = 0$	

Exercise 11G

1 $a = 2$	**2** $a = 3$	**3** $a = 2$	**4** $a = 3$
5 $p = 0$	**6** $p = 2$	**7** $q = 3$	**8** $r = 2$
9 $t = 5$	**10** $f = 3$	**11** $r = 13$	**12** $a = 1$
13 $a = 0$	**14** $d = 3$	**15** $c = 4$	**16** $a = 3$
17 $z = 5$	**18** $r = 18$	**19** $s = 12$	**20** $b = 18$
21 $c = 24$	**22** $f = 27$	**23** $h = 4$	**24** $x = 15$

Exercise 11H

1 $a = 1\frac{1}{2}$	**2** $a = 3\frac{1}{2}$	**3** $a = 2\frac{2}{3}$	**4** $a = 4\frac{1}{3}$
5 $p = 1\frac{3}{5}$	**6** $p = 4\frac{2}{5}$	**7** $e = 0$	**8** $t = 1\frac{1}{2}$
9 $j = 1\frac{1}{2}$	**10** $c = 1\frac{4}{7}$	**11** $k = \frac{1}{4}$	**12** $d = 3\frac{1}{3}$
13 $u = \frac{2}{9}$	**14** $q = 2\frac{1}{4}$	**15** $y = 1\frac{2}{7}$	

Exercise 11I

1 $a = -1$	**2** $a = -2$	**3** $a = -4$	**4** $a = -1$
5 $a = -2$	**6** $p = -2$	**7** $s = -5$	**8** $p = -2$
9 $k = -1$	**10** $h = -1$	**11** $y = -5$	**12** $e = -9$
13 $t = 0$	**14** $w = -1$	**15** $c = -2$	**16** $a = 0$

Exercise 11J

1 $s = 3$	**2** $d = 3$	**3** $m = 5$	**4** $h = 4$
5 $k = 9$	**6** $y = 2$	**7** $p = 1\frac{2}{5}$	**8** $f = 3\frac{1}{4}$
9 $s = 3\frac{2}{3}$	**10** $g = -2\frac{2}{7}$	**11** $f = 4\frac{1}{4}$	**12** $k = 3\frac{3}{5}$
13 $s = -5\frac{2}{3}$	**14** $j = 3\frac{2}{3}$	**15** $b = -\frac{5}{9}$	**16** $r = 3\frac{1}{2}$
17 $t = -5\frac{2}{5}$	**18** $y = -\frac{6}{7}$	**19** $e = -\frac{1}{3}$	**20** $f = -1\frac{1}{4}$
21 $g = -\frac{2}{5}$	**22** $h = -1$	**23** $c = -1\frac{2}{3}$	**24** $s = -\frac{5}{8}$
25 $z = 4$	**26** $x = 25$	**27** $p = 4$	**28** $c = -18$
29 $a = 48$	**30** $e = -24$		

Exercise 11K

1 $p = 1$	**2** $d = 5$	**3** $c = 3$	**4** $b = 2\frac{1}{3}$
5 $g = 3$	**6** $g = 5$	**7** $v = -2$	**8** $s = 1$
9 $d = -\frac{1}{3}$	**10** $t = 5\frac{2}{3}$	**11** $h = 3$	**12** $h = 4$
13 $s = 3$	**14** $y = 3\frac{1}{2}$	**15** $r = 5$	

Exercise 11L

1 $a = 1$	**2** $h = 8$	**3** $g = -3$	**4** $f = 6$
5 $q = 0$	**6** $k = 4$	**7** $g = 1$	**8** $h = -2$
9 $d = -1$	**10** $v = -5\frac{1}{2}$	**11** $s = -5\frac{2}{3}$	**12** $n = 3\frac{1}{2}$
13 $f = -\frac{7}{8}$	**14** $d = 2\frac{3}{7}$	**15** $m = -2\frac{1}{5}$	

Exercise 11M

1 $k = 5$	**2** $s = 3\frac{1}{2}$	**3** $p = 4$	**4** $g = -1$
5 $t = 3\frac{2}{3}$	**6** $k = 9$	**7** $d = 7$	**8** $c = 3$
9 $z = -1$	**10** $b = -4\frac{1}{2}$	**11** $p = -1\frac{2}{3}$	**12** $g = 8$

Exercise 11N

1 $h = 12$	**2** $t = -8$	**3** $d = -1$	**4** $f = -3$
5 $s = 7$	**6** $d = 6$	**7** $a = 4\frac{1}{2}$	**8** $q = 4$
9 $y = -\frac{2}{3}$	**10** $e = -1$	**11** $s = -1\frac{2}{3}$	**12** $u = -5\frac{1}{2}$
13 $t = -1\frac{1}{3}$	**14** $s = -1\frac{3}{4}$	**15** $q = 2\frac{3}{4}$	**16** $w = -1\frac{1}{5}$
17 $h = -1\frac{3}{5}$	**18** $s = -7$	**19** $r = -1$	**20** $a = 3\frac{2}{3}$

Exercise 11O

1 $p = \frac{2}{3}$	**2** $h = 66$	**3** $r = 3\frac{8}{9}$	**4** $t = 21$
5 $g = -3$	**6** $d = -7\frac{1}{2}$	**7** $k = 13$	**8** $m = 5\frac{1}{2}$
9 $d = -12\frac{1}{3}$	**10** $j = 23$	**11** $y = -1\frac{4}{5}$	**12** $t = -7$

Mixed exercise 11

1 $x = 5$	**2** $x = 6$	**3** $t = 1\frac{1}{2}$	**4** $g = 2$
5 $s = 4$	**6** $q = 6$	**7** $d = 3\frac{1}{3}$	**8** $k = 2\frac{1}{2}$
9 $a = \frac{1}{2}$	**10** $k = 3\frac{1}{2}$	**11** $d = -2\frac{1}{4}$	**12** $p = \frac{5}{7}$
13 $p = -11$	**14** $r = -4\frac{1}{3}$	**15** $t = 7\frac{1}{3}$	**16** $g = 6$
17 $a = -2\frac{3}{7}$	**18** $x = 20$		

Chapter 12 Sorting and presenting data

Exercise 12A

1

Hours	Tally	Frequency
0				2
1						4
2				2
3							5
4							5
5						4
6										8
7										8
8						4
9								6
10								6
11						4
12				2

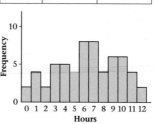

2

Force	Tally	Frequency
0	||	2
1	卌	5
2	卌卌	10
3	卌||||	9
4	卌卌|	11
5	卌||||	9
6	卌|	6
7	||||	4
8	||	2
9	|	1
10	|	1

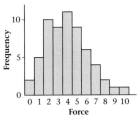

3

Temp °C	Tally	Frequency
16	|||	3
17	卌||	7
18	卌||||	9
19	卌卌||	12
20	卌	5
21	卌卌||||	14
22	卌||	7
23	|||	3

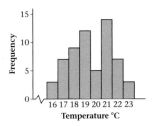

Exercise 12B

1 (a)

Marks	Tally	Frequency
0–4		0
5–9	卌|||	8
10–14	卌卌	10
15–19	卌卌|||	13
20–24	卌	5
25–29	||||	4

(b)

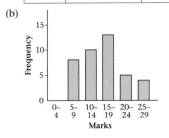

2 (a)

Marks	Tally	Frequency
0–5	||||	4
6–10	卌||||	9
11–15	卌卌卌	15
16–20	卌|||	8
21–25	卌||	7
26–30	||||	4
31–34	|	1

(b)   (c) 11-15

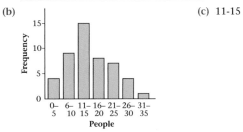

3 (a) For example: 1–2½ (6), 3–4½ (14), 5–6½ (18), 7–8½ (9), 9–10½ (3).
Other grouping of shoes into classes are possible.

Exercise 12C

1 (a)

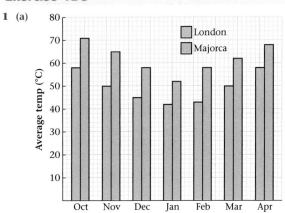

(b) Examples:
Majorca is warmest in October.
Majorca is always warmer than London.
January is the coldest month in both places.

2 (a)

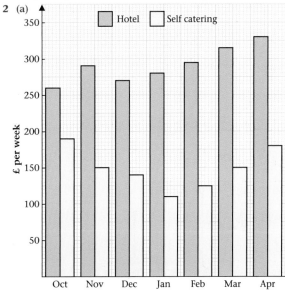

(b) Jan and Feb

(c) Examples:
Hotel prices are lowest in October.
Self catering prices are highest in October.
Self catering prices are lowest in January.
Difference in prices is lowest in October.

3 (a)

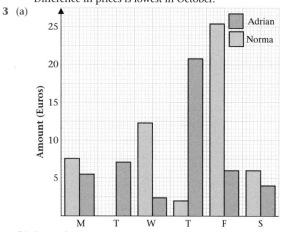

(b) Examples:
Norma's range €25.40. Adrian's range €18.40.
Norma spent most on Friday.
Adrian spent most on Thursday.

Exercise 12D

2 (a) (i) Tea   (ii) 30   (iii) 15   (c) 140   (d) 2.19

Exercise 12E

1 (a) discrete   (b) continuous   (c) continuous
(d) discrete   (e) discrete   (f) discrete
(g) continuous   (h) discrete   (i) discrete
(j) continuous

2 (a)

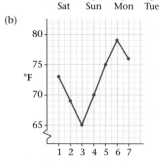

(b)

(c)

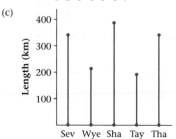

3 (a) (i) Cycleshop   (ii) Bikeshop
(b) 17
(c) (i) 110   (ii) 155
(d) April

4 (a)

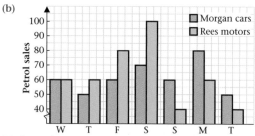

Petrol sales	Wed	Thur	Fri	Sat	Sun	Mon	Tue
Morgan Cars	60	50	60	70	60	80	50
Rees Motors	60	60	80	100	40	60	40

(b)

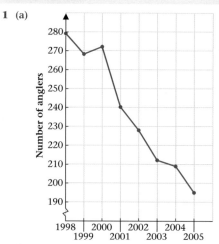

(c) Examples:
Range for Morgan Cars = 30
Range for Rees Motors = 60
The greatest difference in number of sales between the
two garages is on Saturday, and is a difference of 30 sales.

Exercise 12F

1 (a)

(b) For example:
Apart from a small rise in 2000, the numbers have fallen
steadily.
(c) 180

2 (a)

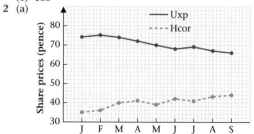

(b) Uxp: 64 or 65, steady decrease
Hcorp: 45 or 46, steady increase

3 (a)

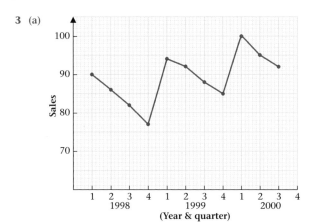

(Year & quarter)

(b) The sales decrease throughout each year but have risen over the last three years.

(c) 87–89. Steady decrease towards the end of each previous year.

Exercise 12G

1 (a)

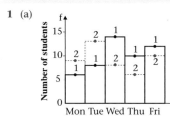

(b)

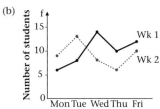

2 (a)

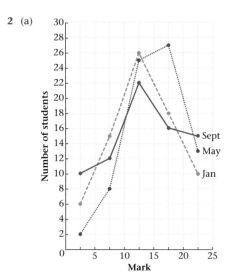

(b) The scores have gone up between September and May. There are more people with higher scores and fewer people with lower scores.

3

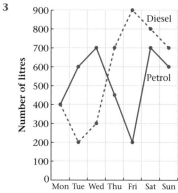

4

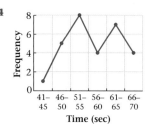

Mixed exercise 12

1 (a)

Length of leaf in cm	Tally	Frequency
2	I	1
3	II	2
4	IIII I	6
5	III	3
6	III	3
7	III	3
8	II	2

(b)

Frequency

Length of leaf (cm)

2 (a)

Weight of crisps (g)	Tally	Frequency
20–24	I	1
25–29	IIII	4
30–34	IIII	5
35–39	IIII II	7
40–44	III	3

(b) 35–39 g

(c)

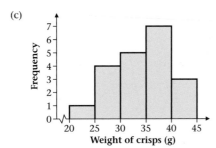

3 (a) July (b) January
(c)

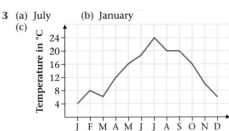

4 (a) (i) 24 (ii) 16 (iii) 20
(b)

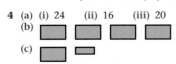

(c)

5 (a)

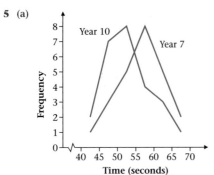

(b) Generally the students in Year 10 ran faster.

6 (a) 9:00 am
(b) Petrol put in the storage tank.
(c) Sales gradually increased.
(d) Line gets steeper.

7 (a)

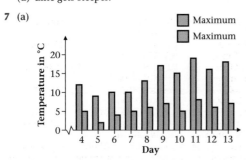

(b) Generally maximum and minimum temperatures are rising.

Chapter 13 3-D shapes

Exercise 13B

1

Shape	Number of faces	Number of vertices	Number of edges
A	6	8	12
B	6	8	12
C	5	5	8
D	5	6	9
E	6	8	12
F	8	6	12
G	4	4	6

2 Number of edges = number of faces + number of vertices − 2

Exercise 13C

1 For example:
Biscuit tin − cuboid   Flour container − cylinder
Kitchen bin − cylinder   Ice cream cone − cone
Biscuits − cylinder   Tennis balls − spheres
Various packets − cuboids   Choc box − cube
Food cover − square based pyramid
Cheese grater − triangular prism

Exercise 13D

1 (a) and (c)   **2** cylinder   **3** cube, cuboid

Exercise 13E

1 (a)   (b)   (c)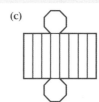

Other arrangements of the faces are possible.

2 (a)  (b)

3 (a) and (c)   **4** (b) and (c)

7

8 Sketches of solids and nets:
(a) 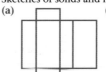 (b) 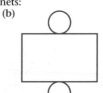 (c)

(d) 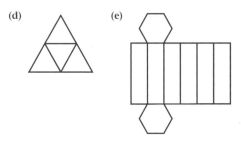 (e)

9 Sketches of:
  (a) square-based pyramid base edge 2 cm, slant height 4 cm
  (b) cuboid 2 cm by 4 cm by 9 cm

Exercise 13F

1 (a) (b) (c)

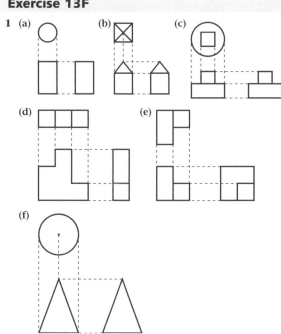

(d) (e)

(f)

2 (a) (b) (c)

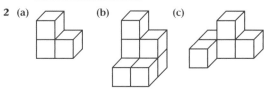

3 (a) cone   (b) triangular prism
4 (a) (b)

Side elevation

Exercise 13G

1 (a) 2   (b) 3   (c) 4
  (d) 1   (e) 5   (f) 5
2 (a) 2 planes   (b) 5 planes   (c) 9 planes
  (d) 6 planes   (e) 3 planes
3 (a) 2 planes   (b) 2 planes
  (c) 1 plane   (d) 4 planes
4 (a) isosceles triangular prism   (b) cone

Mixed exercise 13

1 (a) (i)   cube   (ii) 12 edges
    (iii) 6 faces   (iv) 8 vertices
  (b) (i)   triangular prism (ii) 9 edges
    (iii) 5 faces   (iv) 6 vertices
  (c) (i)   square based pyramid (ii) 8 edges
    (iii) 5 faces   (iv) 5 vertices
2 (i) (a) 8   (b) 6   (c) 4
  (ii) (a) 4   (b) 3   (c) 0
3 (a) yes   (b) no   (c) yes
4 (a) triangular pyramid (tetrahedron)
  (b) bottom right-hand vertex
5 (a) (i) 12 edges   (ii) 8 vertices   (iii) 6 faces
6 A and S, B and Q, C and R, D and T, E and P
7 (a) cuboid   (b) cylinder
8 (a) 3 cm by 4 cm
  (b) correct rectangle added to left or right of original
      diagram
9 (a)   (b)

10 (a)   (b)   (c)

  (d)   (e)

11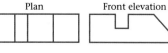

      Plan   Front elevation

      Side elevation

13 (a) rectangle 4 cm tall with 3 cm width

Chapter 14 Units of measure

Exercise 14A

1 (a) 300 cm   (b) 3 cm   (c) 600 cm
  (d) 1200 cm   (e) 10 cm
2 (a) 20 mm   (b) 50 mm   (c) 120 mm
  (d) 200 mm   (e) 1000 mm
3 (a) 5000 m   (b) 3 m   (c) 10 000 m
  (d) 20 m   (e) 60 000 m
4 (a) 5000 g   (b) 40 000 g   (c) 100 000 g
  (d) 250 000 g   (e) 1 000 000 g
5 (a) 3 l   (b) 8 l   (c) 50 l   (d) 75 l
6 (a) 6000 ml   (b) 40 000 ml   (c) 100 000 ml
  (d) 350 000 ml (e) 25 000 ml
7 (a) 3 km   (b) 7 km   (c) 40 km   (d) 45 km
8 (a) 4 tonnes (b) 7 tonnes (c) 30 tonnes (d) 55 tonnes
9 (a) 2 kg   (b) 3000 kg   (c) 50 kg
  (d) 12 000 kg   (e) 100 kg
10 1000   11 1 000 000   12 8 000 000
13 100 000   14 4000   15 1 000 000

Exercise 14B

1 250 kg, 3000 g, 2 kg, 250 g, 25 g
2 5 mm, 50 mm, 20 cm, 3 m, 3 km

3 4 cm, 75 cm, 2 m, 3000 mm, 4000 m
4 200 ml, 600 ml, 1 l, 2000 ml, 5 l

Exercise 14C

1 (a) 2.5 m   (b) 0.5 m   (c) 3600 m   (d) 0.75 m
   (e) 5 m   (f) 0.35 m   (g) 4.75 m   (h) 600 m
   (i) 40 m   (j) 0.005 m
2 (a) 4500 g   (b) 400 g   (c) 10 300 g
   (d) 30 g   (e) 5 g
3 (a) 35 cm   (b) 250 cm   (c) 540 cm   (d) 0.5 cm
   (e) 8 cm   (f) 80 cm   (g) 3.5 cm   (h) 5 cm
   (i) 8.5 cm   (j) 27.5 cm
4 (a) 3500 ml   (b) 500 ml   (c) 15 400 ml
   (d) 50 ml   (e) 3 ml
5 (a) 35 mm   (b) 7 mm   (c) 0.8 mm
   (d) 125 mm   (e) 5 mm
6 (a) 0.3 km   (b) 0.05 km   (c) 1.25 km
   (d) 0.075 km   (e) 0.375 km
7 (a) 0.25 l   (b) 0.1 l   (c) 0.05 l
   (d) 3.5 l   (e) 0.001 l
8 (a) 0.5 kg   (b) 300 kg   (c) 0.05 kg
   (d) 5500 kg   (e) 6 kg
9 (a) 3.5 tonnes   (b) 0.45 tonnes   (c) 0.05 tonnes
   (d) 0.003 tonnes   (e) 0.075 tonnes
10 20 glasses   **11** 60 pieces   **12** 8 batches

Exercise 14D

1 (a) 2.4 cm, 25 mm, 3 cm, 50 mm, 57 mm, 6 cm
   (b) 270 mm, 30 cm, 0.4 m, 45 cm, 500 mm, 1.2 m
   (c) 2 m, 340 cm, 3500 mm, 370 cm, 4 m = 4000 mm
   (d) 0.2 cm, 4 mm, 45 mm, 5 cm, 55 mm, 0.3 m, 36 cm
   (e) 34 cm, 0.4 m, 0.45 m, 50 cm, 560 mm
2 (a) 0.05 kg, 250 g, 0.3 kg, 500 g
   (b) 350 g, 0.4 kg, 500 g, 0.52 kg
   (c) 3000 g, 4 kg, 4.5 kg, 5000 g, 400 kg, 0.5 tonnes
3 (a) 250 ml, 0.3 l = 300 ml, 0.4 l, 500 ml
   (b) 45 ml, 0.05 l, 360 ml, 0.4 l, 450 ml, 500 ml

Exercise 14E

1 640 km   **2** $5\frac{1}{4}$ pints
3 67.5 litres   **4** 220 pounds
5 0.6 litres   **6** 6.7 gallons
7 0.875 pints   **8** 93.75 miles
9 1.76 pounds   **10** 2.625 pints

Exercise 14F

1 4.4 gallons
2 9.1 kg
3 15 cm
4 60 cm by 37.5 cm
5 They are the same.
6 11 pounds of bread and 1.1 pounds of spread
7 2.86 litres
8 600 g of fat, 1000 g of flour, 800 g of dried fruit
9 Hazel, her guess was about 5.06 pounds
10 7.7 pounds

Exercise 14G

1 (a) 120 minutes   (b) 300 minutes
   (c) 150 minutes   (d) 330 minutes
   (e) 375 minutes   (f) 315 minutes
2 (a) 3 hours
   (b) 4 hours
   (c) $1\frac{1}{4}$ hours or 1 hour 15 minutes
   (d) $4\frac{1}{3}$ hours or 4 hours 20 minutes
   (e) $5\frac{5}{12}$ hours or 5 hours 25 minutes

   (f) $1\frac{1}{2}$ hours or 1 hour 30 minutes
   (g) 72 hours
   (h) 132 hours
   (i) $8\frac{1}{3}$ hours or 8 hours 20 minutes
3 3600 seconds
4 1440 minutes
5 (a) 31 536 000 seconds   (b) 31 622 400 seconds
6 (a) 2 hours 30 minutes   (b) 3 hours 36 minutes
   (c) 5 hours 30 minutes   (d) 3 hours 45 minutes
   (e) 4 hours 6 minutes   (f) 3 hours 15 minutes
   (g) 1 hour $7\frac{1}{2}$ minutes   (h) 2 hours 42 minutes
7 (a) 2.5 hours   (b) 5.25 hours
   (c) 3.6 hours   (d) 4.2 hours
   (e) 6.3 hours   (f) 3.3 hours
   (g) 12.75 hours   (h) 8.05 hours
8 The journey took 2.25 hours which is 2 hours 15 minutes.

Exercise 14H

1 (a) 10:45   (b) 10:00   (c) 11:55   (d) 10:10
2 (a) 09:50   (b) 11:20   (c) 12:30   (d) 08:55
3 (a) 12:20   (b) 13:25   (c) 14:30   (d) 08:50
4 (a) 15:15   (b) 20:00   (c) 01:35   (d) 05:30
5 (a) 09:40   (b) 11:25   (c) 07:55   (d) 08:50
6 (a) 08:05   (b) 10:50   (c) 09:40   (d) 08:10
7 (a) 07:25   (b) 09:10   (c) 05:40   (d) 06:35
8 (a) 02:05   (b) 04:45   (c) 23:15   (d) 19:45
9 17:40

Exercise 14I

1 (a) 11th Jan   (b) 12th Mar   (c) 13th June
   (d) 15th July   (e) 20th Sept   (f) 30th May
   (g) 5th July   (h) 6th Sept
2 (a) 16th Feb   (b) 17th Mar   (c) 17th Apr
   (d) 21st Dec   (e) 29th Nov   (f) 2nd Oct
   (g) 6th Apr   (h) 9th Dec
3 (a) 5th May   (b) 6th July   (c) 16th June
   (d) 1st Oct   (e) 7th July   (f) 19th June
   (g) 30th Dec   (h) 4th Jan
4 Wed 10th April   **5** Thurs 2nd May
6 Mon 13th May   **7** Thurs 25th April
8 Fri 3rd May

Exercise 14J

1 07 55   **2** 08 35
3 07 25   **4** 07 40
5

Coate	08 35	09 05	09 35
Piper's Way	08 40	09 10	09 40
Old Town	08 50	09 20	09 50
Drove Rd.	08 55	09 25	09 55
New Town	09 00	09 30	10 00
Bus Station	09 05	09 35	10 05

6 07 45
7 08 35
8 (a)

Bristol	08 10	08 25	08 40
Bath	08 30	08 45	09 00
Swindon	08 45	09 00	09 15
Didcot	09 05	09 20	09 35
Reading	09 15	09 30	09 45
London	09 40	09 55	10 10

   (b) 09 15   (c) 08 10
9 30 mins   **10** 20 mins
11 $1\frac{1}{2}$ hours   **12** 30 mins
13 35 mins
14 (a) 07 10 and 07 45 or 08 00
   (b) 07 05 and 07 45 or 08 00
   (c) 07 50 and 08 15
   (d) 08 25 and 08 45 or 09 00
   (e) 08 20 and 08 45 or 09 00
   (f) 07 55 and 08 15

Mixed exercise 14

1 (a) 15 mm, 60 mm, 6.5 cm, 12 cm, 5 m
   (b) 1800 m, 2.5 km, 3000 m, 3.6 km
2 80 km   **3** 11 pounds   **4** 11 gallons   **5** 11:05
6 (a) 11 23   (b) 11 25
   (c) 43 minutes   (d) 24 minutes
7 (a) 316 km   (b) 85 miles
8 (a) 08 20   (b) 25 minutes
9 76 cm

Index to Books 1 and 2

You can find pages 277–557 in Book 2.

You can find pages 277–557 in Book 2.

You can find pages 277–557 in Book 2.

O

P

You can find pages 277–557 in Book 2.

You can find pages 277–557 in Book 2.

You can find pages 277–557 in Book 2.